MASTERCHEF

THE BEST OF BRITISH COOKING

MASTERCHEF

THE BEST OF
BRITISH COOKING

EBURY PRESS
LONDON

This edition published in 1999 by Dealerfield Ltd.
First published in 1999

1 2 3 4 5 6 7 8 9 10

First published in the United Kingdom in 1999 by Ebury Press
Random House, 20 Vauxhall Bridge Road, London SW1V 2SA

Random House Australia (Pty) Limited
20 Alfred Street, Milsons Point, Sydney,
New South Wales 2061, Australia

Random House New Zealand Limited
18 Poland Road, Glenfield, Auckland 10, New Zealand

Random House South Africa (Pty) Limited
Endulini, 5a Jubilee Road, Parktown 2193, South Africa

Random House UK Limited Reg. No. 954009

Papers used by Ebury Press are natural, recyclable products made from
wood grown in sustainable forests.

A CIP catalogue record for this book is available from the British Library.

Designed by Alison Shackleton
Photography by Philip Webb
Food styling by Janice Dalzell-Piper and Dagmar Vesely

Printed and bound in Italy by New Interlitho S.p.a.

CONTENTS

COOKERY NOTES

All recipes serve 4 unless otherwise indicated

Both metric and imperial measures are given for the recipes. Follow one set of measurements only, not a combination, because they are not interchangeable.

All spoon measures are level unless stated otherwise.

Ovens must be preheated to the specified temperature. Grills should also be preheated.

Size 2 eggs should be used except where otherwise specified. Free-range eggs are recommended.

Use fresh herbs unless otherwise suggested.

Stocks should be freshly made if possible. Alternatively buy good quality ready-made stock.

If you do not have an ice-cream maker, freeze ice-cream in a shallow container, whisking it several times during freezing to ensure an even-textured result.

INTRODUCTION

I am delighted that, for the first time, the recipes from the 1999 series of 'MasterChef' and 'Junior MasterChef' have been brought together in this one splendid volume, accompanied by mouth-watering photographs of many of the dishes. All the recipes have been grouped by courses, but those of you wishing to delve into them whilst watching the programme will find details of the complete menus at the end of the book.

The general trend of the past few years has continued in the 1999 series. Many of the recipes reflect a much simpler approach to cooking, resulting in dishes in which the flavours of the main constituents burst through. Many of our contestants have sourced their ingredients almost to the very farm on which they are grown or reared. Beef is making a more than welcome return, roe deer, rabbit and wild boar are all featured and Asian spices are being incorporated into an ever-increasing range of dishes.

For the majority of our contestants, the calm of the kitchen and the creativity of cooking is their ultimate relaxation. Although tension sometimes runs high on the big breadboard, by the time our cooks have started work in the red, yellow and blue kitchens, helped by our easy-going and food-loving studio crew who are never without a full set of cutlery in a handy back pocket, an atmosphere of calm extends over the studio for most of the two-and-a-half hours of cooking time. It is our hope that your time spent with this book will be equally relaxing and productive, and that the resulting dishes will give as much pleasure to your friends and family as our judges have enjoyed throughout the series.

And if, whilst watching or reading, you should feel tempted to join Loyd Grossman and his guests in a future series, a large stamped addressed envelope sent to:

MasterChef, PO Box 359, Kerdiston, Norwich NR10 4UU

will bring you an application form, together with all you need to know about the competition. We promise that you will enjoy it!

Richard Bryan
Producer of 'MasterChef' & 'Junior MasterChef'

SOUPS AND STARTERS

broccoli soup, goat's cheese and truffle oil tortellini

15 ml (3 tsp) sea salt
1.5 kg (3 lb 5 oz) broccoli florets, stalks trimmed
60 ml (4 tbsp) double cream
extra-virgin olive oil, to finish
few snipped chives, for garnish

TORTELLINI
1 egg plus 1 yolk
120 g (4 oz) pasta flour (00 grade)
10 ml (2 tsp) olive oil
salt and freshly ground black pepper
75 g (3 oz) soft goat's cheese, such as crottin
25 g (1 oz) mascarpone, beaten with 1 egg yolk
3–5 drops truffle oil
egg wash of 1 yolk plus a little salt plus 10 ml (2 tsp) water
10 g (¼ oz) butter

1 To make the tortellini, in a food processor, process the egg, egg yolk, flour, olive oil and salt until a dough forms. Knead briefly with your hands then wrap in cling film and refrigerate for an hour or so. Meanwhile, mix together the goat's cheese, mascarpone, truffle oil, salt and pepper for the filling.
2 Roll the pasta dough out and, using a pasta machine, roll out as thinly as possible. Stamp out 12 circles with a biscuit cutter and press a ball of filling onto 1 side of each of the circles. Brush the edges of each circle of pasta with egg wash, fold over to make a semi-circle, pressing the edges down well. Then curl the 2 tips of the straight edge round to touch and seal well. Repeat for each of the 12 discs until you have 12 tortellini. Blanch these for 2 minutes in boiling salted water, refresh in cold water and drain. Wrap in cling film and chill.
3 To make the soup, bring a saucepan of water to a rolling boil with the salt. Add the broccoli florets and cook for 10 minutes. Strain, but reserve the water. Return the florets to the saucepan and shake, over the heat, to dry out for 2 minutes. Blend in a food processor or with a blender, adding a ladleful of the reserved cooking liquid at a time, until you have a smooth, very bright green purée, with a glossy sheen to it. Thin with a little more of the reserved liquid. Return the broccoli purée to the saucepan, and bring to the boil, slowly stirring in most of the reserved liquid and the cream; check for seasoning.
4 Reheat the tortellini in the butter. To serve, ladle the soup into bowls and top with three tortellini per bowl. Drizzle with a touch of extra-virgin olive oil and garnish with the chives.

smoked haddock consommé

400 g (14 oz) carrots, sliced
2 sticks celery, sliced
150 g (5 oz) onion, sliced
butter, for frying
15 ml (1 tbsp) cardamom seeds
5 ml (1 tsp) coriander seeds
1.25 ml (¼ tsp) cumin seeds
200 g (7 oz) button mushrooms, halved
1.25 ml (¼ tsp) paprika
1.25 ml (¼ tsp) turmeric
500 ml (16 fl oz) good ale plus
300 ml (½ pint) water
3 finnan haddock
3 egg whites

1 In a large saucepan, cook the carrots, celery and onion gently in butter for 5 minutes without browning. Dry fry the spice seeds – the cardamom and coriander first and cumin last as it burns readily. Crush the spices in a mortar and pestle and add to the vegetables. Add the mushrooms, paprika, turmeric, ale and water, and simmer for 30 minutes.

2 Skin the haddock, reserving the best flesh, and add the remainder and the bones to the vegetables. Simmer for a further 20 minutes. Strain the soup and chill in the refrigerator. Skim any fat from the top and check the seasoning.

3 Whisk the egg whites to soft peak stage and add to the soup. Return the soup to the saucepan and bring to the boil, whisking constantly. Simmer for about 10 minutes by which time the soup should be clear and the egg white will have formed a crust on top.

4 Poach the pieces of reserved fish for 5 minutes. Strain the soup through muslin, tipping the egg white crust into the strainer and allowing the soup to strain through. If the soup has reduced too much, adjust the quantity with water and warm through. Place a piece of fish in each bowl and add the consommé.

soups and starters

cream of lettuce and spring onion soup with herby croûtons

25 g (1 oz) organic butter
1 large head of organic lettuce, torn into chunks
1 medium potato, diced
1 medium bunch of spring onions, chopped
1 plump clove garlic, crushed
750 ml (1½ pints) well-flavoured chicken or vegetable stock
1 tsp of salt
freshly ground black pepper
natural yogurt and single cream, to taste

HERBY CROÛTONS
25g (1 oz) organic butter
15 ml (1 tbsp) olive oil
2 thick slices of organic wholemeal bread, in small dice
15 ml (1 tbsp) fresh chopped herbs

1 Melt the butter in solid–based pan and add the lettuce, potato, spring onions and garlic. Sweat for up to 10 minutes on a low heat until the lettuce has wilted. Add the stock, salt and pepper, and bring to the boil and simmer for 20 minutes.

2 Meanwhile, make the croûtons. Melt the butter and oil in a heavy based frying pan. Add the diced bread and fry until starting to crisp. Throw in the fresh herbs, toss briefly and keep warm.

3 Liquidize the soup and and sieve if necessary. Add 10–15 ml (2–3 tsp) of natural yogurt and single cream, to taste. Check seasoning. Serve with herby croûtons.

tomato and freshwater crayfish soup

12 live freshwater crayfish, see note

15 ml (1 tbsp) dill seeds

4 sprigs of dill

butter, for baking

salt and freshly ground black pepper

chopped fresh dill, for sprinkling

900 g (2 lb) tomatoes

3 cloves garlic

2 spring onions

3 cloves

½ bay leaf

15 ml (1 tbsp) vermouth

3 drops of Tabasco

300 ml (½ pint) vegetable stock

300 ml (½ pint) crème fraîche

15 ml (1 tbsp) butter

1 To prepare the crayfish, bring a large pan of salted water with the dill seeds and sprigs of dill to the boil. Quickly drop the live crayfish into the boiling water and cook for 3 minutes. Remove the crayfish and drain. Reserve 4 whole crayfish for decoration. Twist off the tails from the remaining crayfish.

2 Carefully remove the meat from the tails by cutting with scissors along the side of the tail shell. Remove the black intestine by pinching the middle of the tail and gently pull the intestine. Cut the crayfish in half lengthways and place in an ovenproof dish, dot with butter, season and sprinkle with dill. Cover and set aside.

3 Reserve 2 whole tomatoes for garnish, and cut the remaining tomatoes in quarters. Place in a food processor or blender and process until smooth. Strain through a fine sieve into a saucepan.

4 Add the garlic, spring onions, cloves, bay leaf, vermouth ,Tabasco and salt and pepper. Boil for 10 minutes until the mixture is reduced by half. Remove from the heat and leave to infuse for 5 minutes. Remove the garlic, onions, cloves and bay leaf.

5 Add the vegetable stock and crème fraîche to the soup and mix well. Check the seasoning. Bring the soup to the boil, add the butter and whisk to emulsify.

6 Put the crayfish in a preheated 190°C (375°F) mark 5 oven for 3 minutes. Remove from the oven and cut into quarters if large. Warm the reserved whole crayfish through in the oven.

7 Divide the crayfish pieces between 4 soup bowls, and pour the soup over the crayfish and sprinkle with dill. Arrange the whole crayfish on the side; serve with finger bowls so that each person can break off the tail of the crayfish, remove the meat and dip it in the soup.

NOTE: When you buy freshwater crayfish, let them clean themselves for at least an hour before cooking. Put them in fresh water in a bucket and keep in a cool place – don't forget to put a lid on the bucket!

roast red pepper gazpacho with pesto croûtes

30 ml (2 tbsp) olive oil
1 red onion, chopped
10 ml (2 tsp) coriander seeds, crushed
2.5 ml (½ tsp) black peppercorns, crushed
4 large red peppers
900 g (2 lb) plum tomatoes, skinned, deseeded and chopped
3 cucumbers, skinned, deseeded and chopped
salt
1 head roast garlic, cloves removed from skin
15–30 ml (1–2 tbsp) tomato purée
50 g (2 oz) breadcrumbs (optional)
lemon juice

PESTO CROÛTES see note
120g (4 oz) pine nuts
50 g (2 oz) fresh basil leaves
25 g (1 oz) freshly grated Parmesan
120 ml (4 fl oz) olive oil
2 roasted garlic cloves (see above)
petit pain or French stick

1 Heat the olive oil in a frying pan and fry the onion with the coriander seeds and peppercorns for 2–3 minutes, then remove from the heat and allow to cool.

2 Roast the peppers in a preheated oven at 200°C (400°F) mark 4 for about 30 minutes, put into a plastic bag and allow to cool. When they are cool enough to handle, slip off their skins and deseed. Chop roughly and put in a large bowl, saving as much of the juices as possible. Add the tomatoes and onion mixture to the bowl. Add the chopped cucumbers and sprinkle with salt. Reserve 2 cloves garlic from the roast head of garlic, and add the remaining cloves and the tomato purée. Stir the mixture, and put in the refrigerator to allow the flavours to mingle.

3 Process with a hand–held blender; if the soup needs thickening add breadcrumbs and blend again. Taste for seasoning, and add lemon juice to taste. Keep chilled.

4 To make the croûtes, roast the pine nuts in a preheated oven for a few minutes. Put the basil, Parmesan, olive oil and garlic in a blender. Add the toasted pine nuts and blend; season lightly. Slice the petit pain on a diagonal and spread one side with the pesto. Place in the oven to crisp.

5 Serve the soup in chilled bowls and float the pesto croûtes on top at the last minute.

NOTE: This recipe will make more pesto than you need, but it will keep for 1 week in the refrigerator if covered with oil.

roasted red pepper gazpacho with herb soda bread

olive oil, for roasting
2 red peppers
450 g (1 lb) plum tomatoes, deseeded
½ cucumber, peeled
30 ml (2 tbsp) olive oil
5 ml (1 tsp) balsamic vinegar
½ glass sherry
salt and freshly ground black pepper
olive oil, for drizzling

HERB SODA BREAD
450 g (1 lb) plain flour
5 ml (1 tsp) bicarbonate of soda
5 ml (1 tsp) salt
15 ml (1 tbsp) chopped sage and thyme
125 ml (4 fl oz) natural yogurt
125 ml (4 fl oz) milk

1 Coat the peppers in olive oil and roast in a preheated oven at 200°C (400°F) mark 6 for 30 minutes until the skins are charred. Slip off the skins and roughly chop the peppers. Place the peppers, tomatoes, cucumber, olive oil, vinegar, sherry and salt and pepper in a food processor and process until smooth. Check for seasoning and strain if necessary; set aside in the refrigerator.

2 Sift the flour into a bowl with the bicarbonate of soda and salt. Add the chopped herbs; mix the yogurt and milk and add to the flour. Mix thoroughly. Make into a ball and place on a lightly floured baking sheet. Flatten slightly and make a deep cross with a knife. Sprinkle flour on top and bake for 45 minutes at 190°C (375°F) mark 5.

3 Spoon the gazpacho into bowls and drizzle a little olive oil onto the surface. Serve with a slice of herb soda bread.

clear gazpacho

150–200 g (5–7 oz) mixture of
some or all of the following:
cucumber, peeled, deseeded and
sliced
green courgette, diced and
blanched
yellow courgette, diced and
blanched
radish, diced
tomato concassée, diced
red pepper, cored, deseeded and
diced
avocado, cut into 1–cm (½–inch)
balls
red cherry tomatoes, halved
plum, peeled and diced
apple, peeled and diced
salt and freshly ground black
pepper
2 red chillies, cored, deseeded and
finely sliced
very finely chopped coriander,
basil and chervil

TOMATO WATER
800 g–1 kg (1 lb 12 oz–2 lb 4 oz)
very ripe tomatoes
10 ml (2 tsp) salt

1 To make the tomato water, lightly blend the tomatoes and salt in a blender. Line a colander with 2 layers of muslin. Pour the blended tomatoes into a colander. Position this over a bowl and leave in the refrigerator overnight.

2 Finely cut up the required selection of vegetables and fruit. Produce a variety of shapes – such as cube, diamond, match-stick etc. To stop the vegetables turning brown, keep in a little tomato water.

3 Scatter the vegetables, fruit and chillies in 4 serving bowls. Add about 100 ml of Tomato Water to each bowl. Season to taste and sprinkle the herbs on top.

red pepper and soft cheese flower on a yellow pepper coulis, served with green salad

400 g (14 oz) full–fat soft cheese
50 ml (2 fl oz) extra-virgin olive oil
3 spring onions, finely chopped
salt and freshly ground black pepper
4 small red peppers
4 large yellow peppers
150 g (5 oz) green salad leaves
balsamic vinegar, for sprinkling
finely chopped chives, to garnish

1 In a bowl, blend the soft cheese with 30 ml of the oil and the spring onions. Season with salt and pepper and set aside.

2 Cut the tops off the red peppers and remove the cores and seeds, being careful not to break the peppers. Fill them with a small ball of foil, to hold their shape during cooking. Place the whole yellow peppers and the red peppers in a preheated oven at 230°C (450°F) mark 8 and cook for 35 minutes. Remove the peppers from the oven; when cool enough to handle peel them, removing the cores and seeds from the yellow peppers.

3 Heat the remaining oil in a pan, add the yellow peppers and cook for 10 minutes, until very soft. Add some salt, remove from the heat, and allow to cool. Transfer the yellow peppers to a food processor and process to a purée. Cut the red peppers lengthwise into small petal–shaped strips.

4 To serve, spread the yellow pepper coulis in a circular shape on serving plates. Arrange a few red pepper strips on top, like the petals of a flower. Place a small ball of cheese mixture in the centre, and sprinkle some chives on the top. Arrange some green salad around it and sprinkle with a little balsamic vinegar.

bermuda salt cod fishcakes with banana relish

120 g (4oz) cooked mashed
potato
120 g (4oz) prepared dry salt cod
salt and freshly ground black
pepper
chopped parsley
chopped thyme
a little beaten egg to bind
flour, for dusting
oil, for frying

RELISH
knob of butter
1 thick slice of red onion, chopped
2 small bananas, sliced
15 ml (1 tbsp) brown sugar
15 ml (1 tbsp) redcurrant jelly
50 ml (2 fl oz) white wine

1 Mix the mashed potato and flaked fish together in a bowl, add seasoning and herbs to taste and, if necessary, add a little egg to bind. Take a small amount and shape into a ball then flatten and dust in flour. Repeat until all the mixture is used up. Place the fishcakes in the refrigerator to firm up.

2 To make relish, heat the butter in a frying pan and sauté the chopped onion; add the sliced bananas and the brown sugar. Add the jelly and wine, then reduce until it forms a marmalade. Taste and add salt if necessary.

3 Fry the fishcakes in a little oil and serve immediately, with the banana relish.

ravioli of rock lobster with sauce vierge on buttered cabbage

25 g (1 oz) butter
1 clove garlic, crushed
1 rock lobster
salt and freshly ground black pepper
7 g (¼ oz) black truffle, finely chopped
1 egg yolk

PASTA
120 g (4 oz) 00 grade flour
pinch of salt
1.25 ml (¼ tsp) olive oil
1 egg
2 egg yolks

SAUCE VIERGE
90 ml (3 fl oz) olive oil
25 ml (1 fl oz) lemon juice
5 ml (1 tsp) crushed coriander seeds
6 basil leaves, finely chopped
2 tomatoes skinned, deseeded and diced

BUTTERED CABBAGE
½ Savoy cabbage, finely shredded
2 cardamom seeds
50 g (2 oz) butter, melted

1 Make the pasta dough and process until quite fine. Set aside in refrigerator.

2 Melt the butter in a sauté pan and add the crushed garlic. Shell the lobster tail, add to the pan and sauté with salt and pepper to taste. Allow to cool.

3 Roll the pasta dough into 2 sheets. Slice the lobster into small pieces and place on one sheet of pasta, leaving enough space around each piece to make a ravioli. Sprinkle a little truffle onto each ravioli then brush the mixed egg yolk around each one. Lay the other sheet of pasta over the top, pressing out the air round each ravioli with your fingers. Seal carefully, cut around each ravioli and set aside.

4 To make the sauce vierge, heat the oil gently in a small pan then add the lemon juice. Remove from the heat and add the coriander and basil. Set aside to infuse for a few minutes.

5 Meanwhile, blanch the cabbage in boiling salted water with the cardamom seeds for 2 minutes, then drain. Heat the butter in a large pan, add the cabbage and toss for a further 2–3 minutes. Season and divide cabbage between serving plates; keep warm.

6 To cook the ravioli, bring a large pan of water to the boil and add the ravioli. Cook for 2–3 minutes, drain thoroughly. Add the diced tomato to the sauce vierge, stir, and pour over the buttered cabbage, then add the ravioli and serve immediately.

'railway breakfast'
hot crab soufflé on leaves with coriander relish

butter, for greasing
25 g (1 oz) clarified butter or ghee
15 ml (1 tbsp) groundnut oil
1 shallot, finely chopped
15 g (2 tbsp) plain flour
300 ml (½ pint) milk
pinch of ground fenugreek
2 Thai lemon grass stalks
salt and white pepper
4 medium eggs, separated
brown and white meat of 1 small or medium crab
fresh coriander leaves, to garnish

RELISH
bunch of coriander leaves
1 green chilli, cored and deseeded
1 onion, roughly chopped
lime juice
salt and freshly ground black pepper
1 tomato, skinned, deseeded and chopped
5 ml (1 tsp) dry fried coriander seeds

TO SERVE
rocket or radicchio leaves

1 Butter 4 ramekins and place in the refrigerator. Melt the clarified butter in a saucepan, add the oil, and fry the shallot, stirring, until softened but not coloured. Add the flour, creating a roux. Cook, stirring, for about 1 minute, then add the milk a little at a time. Add the fenugreek, lemon grass, salt and white pepper and gently simmer for 2–3 minutes. The mixture should resemble a white sauce. Allow to cool.

2 Place the egg yolks in a bowl and add the crab meat, mixing well. Remove the lemon grass from the white sauce, and add the sauce to crab meat mixture.

3 Beat the egg whites until soft peaks form. Using a metal knife or spatula, fold the whites into the crab mixture. Spoon the mixture into the prepared ramekins. Place on a baking tray and bake in a preheated oven at 200°C (400°F) mark 6 for 20 minutes.

4 Meanwhile, make the relish: put the coriander leaves, chilli, onion, lime juice to taste and seasoning in a liquidizer and process until smooth. Mix in the tomato and coriander seeds without blending.

5 To serve, place the leaves on serving plates. Carefully run a spatula round each soufflé, remove from the ramekins and place on the leaves. Place a quenelle of relish next to the soufflé and garnish with fresh coriander leaves. Serve hot.

crevettes in a roast pepper sauce

3 red peppers, cored, deseeded
and halved
400 g (14 oz) can plum tomatoes
about 30 ml (2 tbsp) extra-virgin
olive oil
knob of butter
12 uncooked crevettes (king
prawns)
2 cloves garlic, crushed

TO SERVE
fresh salad leaves (optional)

1 Place the pepper halves on a baking tray and fill with the tomatoes, using the juice to fill any spaces. Drizzle each pepper half generously with extra-virgin olive oil and place at the top of a preheated oven at 200°C (400°F) mark 6 and roast for 30 minutes.

2 Once the peppers have roasted, leave until cool enough to handle. Remove the stalks from the peppers and put all the peppers into a blender including any juices which are on the baking tray. Process the peppers until you get a smooth sauce, then pass the sauce through a sieve into a saucepan.

3 Heat some extra-virgin olive oil and butter in a frying pan. Fry the crevettes over a high heat with the garlic for 2–3 minutes until the crevettes turn a warm pink colour. Remove the crevettes, and carefully remove the body shell, leaving the head and tail on.

4 Reheat the pepper sauce and pour onto 4 serving plates, place a few salad leaves on the sauce, if you like, then place 3 crevettes on top of each serving in the pattern of your choice.

garlic tiger prawns with squid

20 ml (4 tsp) olive oil, plus extra
for oiling
3 cloves garlic, crushed
2 cm (¾ inch) cube fresh root
ginger, grated
400 g (14 oz) peeled uncooked
tiger prawns
4 small squid
mixed salad leaves

1 Mix the oil, garlic and ginger together and marinate the prawns and squid.

2 Heat a stove-top grill pan until hot. Remove the squid from the marinade and chargrill for 1 minute on each side.

3 Drizzle a little olive oil in a frying pan and heat until smoking. Carefully pour in the prawns and the oil mixture. Fry for 1–2 minutes until the prawns turn pink.

4 Arrange the prawns and squid on plates. Serve with mixed salad leaves and pour any remaining oil and ginger mixture over the top.

rosemary scented roast sea bass

¼ leek, white part only, finely julienned
vegetable oil, for deep frying
2 medium potatoes, thinly sliced
olive oil, for roasting
sea salt and freshly ground black pepper
unsalted butter
100 g (3½ oz) mange-tout, julienned
4 sea bass fillets
few sprigs of rosemary
juice of 2 lemons
olive oil, for glazing
fresh Parmesan shavings, to garnish

VINAIGRETTE
15 ml (1 tbsp) extra-virgin olive oil
15 ml (1 tbsp) white wine vinegar
juice of 2 limes
bunch of coriander leaves, finely chopped
2 tomatoes, deseeded and finely chopped
½ red onion, finely chopped
5 ml (1 tsp) capers
1.25 ml (¼ tsp) honey
good pinch sea salt
freshly ground black pepper

1 To make the vinaigrette, combine all the ingredients together in a blender or food processor and leave to infuse.

2 Deep fry the leek until golden brown and crisp, drain on paper towels and keep warm.

3 Arrange the potato slices in a well-oiled ovenproof dish, season and dot with butter and a sprinkling of olive oil. Bake in a preheated oven at 180°C (350°F) mark 4 for 45–55 minutes until tender and crispy on top.

4 Blanch the mange-tout in boiling water for 2 minutes until al dente, drain and keep warm.

5 Season the sea bass and place, skin-side down, in a well-oiled heavy based roasting tin. Scatter the sprigs of rosemary in the tin. Sprinkle the lemon juice over the fish. Place the tin over the heat and gently fry the fillets for 2 minutes.

6 Transfer the fish to a preheated oven at 200°C (400°F) mark 6 for 4 minutes until just done, taking care not to overcook.

7 To serve use a large biscuit cutter to cut rings out of the potato, and place one on each plate, keeping the cutter in place, put a quarter of the mange-tout on top and carefully remove the cutter taking care not to disturb the shape. Place a fillet of sea bass on top and glaze with olive oil, spoon some of the vinaigrette around the potato and fish and garnish with a few Parmesan shavings. Finally carefully place some of the leek 'straw' on top of the sea bass.

trout with bacon and mustard and dill sauce

4 fillets of trout, skinned
15–20 ml (3–4 tsp) Dijon mustard
salt and freshly ground black
pepper
4 rashers streaky dry–cure bacon
vegetable oil, for shallow frying

SAUCE
25 g (1 oz) unsalted butter
1 shallot, finely chopped
150 ml (¼ pint) dry white wine
200 ml (7 fl oz) well-flavoured fish
stock
15 ml (1 tbsp) white mustard
seeds
15 ml (1 tbsp) Dijon mustard
lemon juice
50 g (2 oz) unsalted butter, cubed
and chilled
30 ml (2 tbsp) chopped dill

WATERCRESS AND DRESSING
1 bunch watercress
4 chives
75 ml (5 tbsp) olive oil
15 ml (1 tbsp) red wine vinegar
pinch of dry mustard

1 Remove any bones from the trout fillets. Spread with a little mustard and season with salt and pepper. Roll up the fillets. Stretch the bacon slices and wrap around the trout. Chill.

2 To make the sauce, heat the butter in a saucepan, add the shallot and cook until soft. Add the wine and reduce by half. Add the fish stock and reduce by half again. Strain and return to the pan.

3 Dry roast the mustard seeds until they begin to pop, then crush lightly. Whisk the mustard seeds and Dijon mustard into the sauce. Season and add lemon juice to taste. Whisk the butter into the sauce and stir in the chopped dill. Keep warm.

4 Tie the watercress into individual bundles with a chive. Whisk together the olive oil, vinegar and mustard powder. Dip each watercress bundle into the dressing and shake off the excess.

5 Heat some oil in a frying pan and fry the trout pieces until the bacon is crisp. Serve the trout with the sauce, with the watercress bundles on the side.

thai spiced mussels

15 ml (1 tbsp) olive oil
1 onion, finely chopped
5–10 ml (1–2 tsp) green curry paste
5–10 ml (1–2 tsp) chilli relish
1.3 kg (3 lb) mussels, cleaned
50 g (2 oz) fresh root ginger, shredded
1 red pepper, julienned
1 green pepper, julienned
300 ml (½ pint) dry white wine
1 block creamed coconut
50 g (2 oz) coriander, finely chopped

1 Heat the olive oil in a large saucepan over a high heat. Add the onion and cook until translucent.

2 Add the curry paste, chilli relish, mussels, ginger and peppers. Pour in the wine and cover. Cook for about 2 minutes. Add the coconut and bring back to the boil. Stir and add the chopped coriander.

3 Discard any mussels that have not opened. Divide between serving bowls and serve.

salmon with pesto, tomato and pesto vinaigrette and parmesan crisps

4 pieces salmon fillet, about 7.5 x 5 cm (3 x 2 inches)
25 g (1 oz) basil
25 g (1 oz) pine nuts
125 g (4 oz) freshly grated Parmesan
1 clove garlic
salt and freshly ground black pepper
75 ml (5 tbsp) olive oil
15 ml (1 tbsp) red wine vinegar
1 tomato, skinned, deseeded and finely chopped
sprigs of basil, to garnish

1 Halve the salmon horizontally. Put the basil, pine nuts, 25 g (1 oz) of the Parmesan and the garlic into a food processor and process until smooth. Season to taste.

2 Spread 4 of the salmon pieces with a little of the pesto and top with the other 4 pieces. Sprinkle with salt. Wrap each piece loosely in foil and bake in a preheated oven at 190°C (375°F) mark 5 for 10 minutes. Allow to cool.

3 Whisk the olive oil and vinegar together. Stir in 5–10 ml (1–2 tsp) of the pesto. Stir in the finely chopped tomato.

4 Place teaspoonfuls of grated Parmesan well apart on a baking sheet. Cook at 190°C (375°) mark 5 for 6–8 minutes until the cheese is melted and golden. Leave to cool on the tray.

5 To serve, place a portion of salmon on each plate, drizzle some of the tomato and pesto vinaigrette around and place 3 Parmesan crisps on the side of each plate. Garnish the salmon with a sprig of basil.

THAI SPICED MUSSELS ILLUSTRATED OPPOSITE

salmon mousse with cucumber and dill sauce

175 g (6 oz) salmon, skinned and boned
1 egg white
½ lightly beaten egg
275 ml (9 fl oz) double cream
5 ml (1 tsp) chopped dill
5 ml (1 tsp) salt
butter, for greasing

CUCUMBER AND DILL SAUCE
175 g (6 oz) cucumber, peeled, deseeded and chopped (reserve some peel)
7 g (¼ oz) unsalted butter
60 ml (2 fl oz) crème fraîche
5 ml (1 tsp) chopped dill
10 ml (2 tsp) lemon juice
salt and freshly ground black pepper

1 Put the salmon, egg white and egg into the bowl of a food processor and process until it is a uniform colour. Chill for about 10 minutes. Add the cream, dill and salt and blend until thick and creamy. Grease 4 ramekins generously with butter and fill with the salmon mixture.

2 Place the ramekins in a baking dish with hot water approximately half way up the sides of the ramekins. Cook in a preheated oven at 180°C (350°F) mark 4 for about 30 minutes until just firm.

3 Meanwhile, make the sauce. Place the cucumber in a small pan with the butter. Heat over a gentle heat, stirring so that butter coats the cucumber. Cover and cook gently for 10–15 minutes. Remove the pan from heat, and process half the cucumber until smooth. Check the colour of the sauce – it should be a bright green. If necessary add some cucumber peel to the processor to improve the colour. Add the remaining cucumber with the crème fraîche, dill and lemon juice, and mix well. Check the seasoning and chill until ready to serve.

4 To serve, invert the ramekins over the serving plates and unmould. Decoratively spoon the sauce half over the mousse and half onto the plate.

spicy salmon on green leaves with sherry and walnut oil dressing

10 ml (2 tsp) plain flour
10 ml (2 tsp) Cajun seasoning
10 ml (2 tsp) Chinese five spice
1.25 ml (¼ tsp) milo chilli powder
1. 25 ml (¼ tsp) mixed peppercorns, crushed
2 middle cut salmon steaks, about 175 g (6 oz) each
5 ml (1 tsp) oil
knob of butter
150 g (5 oz) mixed green salad leaves

DRESSING
10 ml (2 tsp) sherry vinegar
25 ml (5 tsp) walnut oil
2.5 ml (½ tsp) sugar
salt and freshly ground black pepper

1 Mix together the flour, spices and peppercorns, and use to coat both sides of the salmon steaks.

2 Heat the oil and butter in a nonstick frying pan, and fry the salmon for 2–3 minutes each side over a medium heat.

3 Mix all the dressing ingredients until well blended.

4 Remove the salmon from heat. Remove the skin and bones and flake the fish.

5 Place the green leaves on serving plates, place the salmon on top and drizzle a little dressing over. Serve at once.

smoked salmon fillets, pear salsa and sweet chilli sauce

250 ml (8 fl oz) rice vinegar
200 g (7 oz) caster sugar
3 large red chillies, cored, deseeded and finely sliced
1 shallot, finely sliced
3 cloves garlic, chopped
15 ml (1 tbsp) sea salt
25 g (1 oz) butter
4 smoked salmon fillets

SALSA
4 dessert pears, peeled and chopped
juice of ½ lemon
15–30 ml (1–2 tbsp) mayonnaise
15 ml (1 tbsp) chives, chopped
15 ml (1 tbsp) coriander, chopped

TO GARNISH
sprigs of coriander
snipped chives

1 Place the rice vinegar and sugar in a pan over a low heat until the sugar has dissolved.

2 Coarsely crush the chillies, shallots, garlic and the sea salt with a mortar and pestle. Add to the pan of vinegar mixture. Bring to the boil and simmer gently for 20 minutes. Set aside and keep warm.

3 To make the salsa, combine the pears, lemon juice, mayonnaise, chives and coriander in a food processor or blender.

4 Heat the butter in a frying pan and cook the salmon fillets for 2 minutes on each side.

5 To serve, place the pear salsa on serving plates, place the salmon on the salsa and drizzle the chilli sauce around. Garnish with sprigs of coriander and chives.

asparagus and shiitake mushroom salad with walnut crostini

12–16 medium stalks asparagus
10 g (¼ oz) butter
300 g (10 oz) selection of fresh wild mushrooms
1 large bunch coriander

WALNUT CROSTINI
12 thin slices from a ciabatta loaf
1 clove garlic
80g walnuts, roughly chopped
20 ml (4 tsp) mascarpone
15 ml (1 tbsp) walnut oil
sea salt and freshly ground black pepper

LIME DRESSING
½ shallot, finely chopped
30–45 ml (2–3 tbsp) lime juice
10 ml (2 tsp) sherry vinegar
2.5 ml (½ tsp) Dijon mustard
2 pinches of sugar
30 ml (2 tbsp) sunflower oil
30 ml (2 tbsp) walnut oil
2 drops truffle oil (optional)

CHILLI DRESSING
1–2 red chillies, cored, deseeded and finely chopped
30 ml (2 tbsp) virgin olive oil

1 Prepare the crostini. Place the ciabatta slices on a baking tray and bake in a preheated oven at 110°C (225°F) mark ¼ for 30–40 minutes, or until dried out and crisp. Turn once during cooking.

2 Meanwhile, make the walnut paste. Place the garlic in a bowl and add 60 ml (4 tbsp) boiling water and leave to blanch for 5–10 minutes. Add to a blender with the walnuts, mascarpone, oil and seasoning and process until very smooth and slightly whipped.

3 For the lime dressing, place the shallot, 2 tbsp lime juice, vinegar, mustard and sugar in a bowl and whisk together. Whisk in the oils to emulsify and season to taste. Adjust the amount of lime juice; the dressing should be quite tart. Set aside.

4 For the chilli dressing, mix the chillies with the oil and season with sea salt. Set aside.

5 Blanch the asparagus in boiling salted water for 2 minutes or until just tender. Drain and refresh in cold water, then drain again.

6 Heat a frying pan until hot, add the butter, mushrooms and seasoning and sauté, stirring from time to time, for 5 minutes or until fragrant and browned.

7 Spread some walnut paste on each of the toasted ciabatta slices. Pick 12 even-sized small coriander leaves and place a leaf on each crostini.

8 Whisk the lime dressing again, and toss with the remaining coriander. Divide the coriander salad between 4 serving plates. Place the mushrooms on the salad, and arrange 3–4 stalks of asparagus on each plate. Drizzle the chilli dressing over the asparagus and mushrooms. Arrange 3 crostini on the edge of each plate and serve.

chicken livers in madeira sauce with balsamic vinaigrette salad

300 g (10 oz) chicken livers (trimmed weight)
salt and freshly ground black pepper
80 ml (3 fl oz) Madeira
50 g (2 oz) unsalted butter
30 ml (2 tbsp) groundnut oil
1 small clove garlic, crushed
2 small shallots, finely chopped
3 plum tomatoes, roughly diced
tomato purée (optional)
40 g (1½ oz) large raisins
about 100 ml (3½ fl oz) balsamic vinegar
20 g (¾ oz) pine nuts
30 ml (2 tbsp) groundnut oil
4 slices white bread, 2 shapes cut out of each slice
45 ml (3 tbsp) Cognac

BALSAMIC VINAIGRETTE SALAD
150 ml (¼ pint) balsamic vinegar
100 ml (3½ fl oz) olive oil
10 ml (2 tsp) lemon juice
1.25 ml (¼ tsp) sugar
200 g (7 oz) mixed salad leaves (lollo rosso, lambs' lettuce, radicchio, spinach etc.)

1 Trim the livers, removing all the discoloration and stringy bits. Wash and dry them and cut into bite–sized pieces. Put in a bowl and add a pinch of salt and pepper and the Madeira. Mix, cover and put aside.

2 Melt 25 g of the butter and 15 ml of the oil in a pan and add the garlic and then the shallots. Cook gently for about 10 minutes, stirring occasionally. Add the tomatoes and cook until thickened. Sieve the tomato mixture into a bowl and check the seasoning. If the tomatoes lack flavour add a little tomato purée. Put the mixture aside.

3 Put the raisins in a bowl and add boiling water. Leave them until they have plumped up. Then drain the raisins and put them in a small saucepan. Add 100 ml of balsamic vinegar (or until just covered) and simmer for 10 minutes. Then leave them in the hot vinegar until ready to serve.

4 Make the balsamic vinaigrette in a lidded container. Add 25 ml water, the balsamic vinegar, olive oil, lemon juice, sugar and salt and pepper to taste. Shake well and put aside.

5 Brown the pine nuts in a dry pan over a high heat (they burn easily so stir or shake the pan frequently) and put aside.

6 Heat the oil in a frying pan and fry the bread shapes until golden, keep warm.

7 Drain the livers, reserving the liquid. Heat the remaining butter and oil in a pan and fry the livers until brown on the outside but still pink inside. Remove from the pan. Add the marinade, the tomato mixture and the Cognac to the pan, season to taste and remove from the heat. Drain the raisins.

8 To serve, place the mixed salad leaves, dressed with balsamic vinaigrette, on the side of 4 serving plates. Arrange the chicken livers next to the salad with a little sauce spooned over them. Sprinkle with the browned pine nuts, put the croûtons on either side and place the raisins around the liver.

crispy chicken boudin on a bed of buttered leeks

15 ml (1 tbsp) olive oil, plus extra for roasting
squeeze of lemon juice
2 skinless boneless chicken breasts
salt and freshly ground black pepper
about 150 g (5 oz) unsalted butter, for frying
2 shallots, finely chopped
½ clove garlic, finely chopped
200 g (7 oz) ham, diced
75 ml (5 tbsp) double cream
5 ml (1 tsp) paprika
1 bunch flat–leaf parsley, finely chopped
2 leeks, julienned

1 Pour the olive oil and lemon juice over the chicken breasts and season. Place the chicken breasts in an oiled roasting tin and roast in a preheated oven at 200°C (400°F) mark 6 for about 30 minutes until cooked through and the juices run clear.

2 Heat a little of the butter in a frying pan and fry the shallots and garlic until soft, then set aside.

3 Roughly chop the cooked chicken and place in a liquidizer along with the ham, shallots, garlic, cream, paprika, half the parsley and seasoning to taste. Liquidize until combined and then scrape onto a board. Shape the mixture into four 'sausage' shapes, wrap in two layers of cling film and twist at the ends. Cook them in a saucepan of boiling salted water for 5 minutes.

4 Meanwhile, heat a little butter in a frying pan until almost smoking. Turn the sausages out of the cling film and pan fry until crisp.

5 Heat a little butter in a second frying pan and fry the leek until semi-soft.

6 To serve, place a bed of leeks on each plate with a sausage on each and garnish with chopped parsley.

asparagus risotto with shropshire blue cheese

300 g (10 oz) asparagus
25 g (1 oz) butter
1 medium onion, chopped
75 g (3 oz) risotto rice
1 litre (1¾ pints) hot vegetable stock
40 g (1½ oz) Shropshire blue cheese, diced

1 Cut the asparagus tips off and reserve. Roughly chop the asparagus stalks.

2 Melt the butter in heavy–based saucepan, add the onion and chopped asparagus stalks, and cook for 2 minutes. Add the rice and stir until all grains are coated.

3 Add the hot stock to the pan, cover and cook for 13–15 minutes.

4 Meanwhile, steam the asparagus tips for about 6 minutes.

5 Check the risotto for seasoning; pile onto warmed serving plates, scatter the asparagus tips on top and top with the cheese. Serve immediately.

tomato tartlet with an olive oil and parmesan crust served with crème fraîche and tapénade

15 ml (1 tbsp) olive oil
½ red onion, finely chopped
3 cloves garlic, crushed
700 g (1½ lb) plum tomatoes, skinned, deseeded and roughly chopped
10 ml (2 tsp) tomato purée
15 ml (1 tbsp) chopped basil
salt and freshly ground black pepper
5 ml (1 tsp) sugar
15 ml (1 tsp) balsamic vinegar

PASTRY
115 g (4 oz) plain flour
7.5 ml (½ tsp) salt
50 g (2 oz) freshly grated Parmesan
60 ml (2 fl oz) olive oil
2 cloves garlic, finely chopped

TAPÉNADE
115 g (4 oz) black olives, pitted
1 clove garlic
15 ml (1 tbsp) chopped parsley
30 ml (2 tbsp) olive oil

TO GARNISH
fresh basil leaves

TO SERVE
about 60 ml (4 tbsp) crème fraîche

1 To make the pastry, sift the flour and salt into a large bowl. Add the Parmesan. Gently warm the olive oil and garlic, then add 15 ml (1 tbsp) water. Combine the oil mixture with the flour to form a dough. Add more water if necessary. Roll out the pastry and line 4 individual tart cases; prick the bases with a fork. Leave to rest in the refrigerator for 20 minutes.

2 Bake the tart cases in a preheated oven at 200°C (400°F) mark 6 for 20–25 minutes or until the base is crisp.

3 Heat the olive oil in a saucepan and add the onion and garlic. Cook until soft but not coloured. Add the tomatoes, tomato purée, basil and salt and pepper. Cook on a very low heat for about 45–50 minutes, until reduced and thickened. Stir in the sugar and vinegar.

4 Spoon the tomato mixture into the tart cases and bake at 150°C (300°F) mark 2 for 15 minutes.

5 Meanwhile, make the tapénade. Put the olives, garlic and parsley in a food processor and process until finely chopped; add the olive oil and process again briefly to blend.

6 Serve the tarts garnished with basil, and with a spoonful of crème fraîche and tapénade.

olive oil poached tomatoes with peas and meat jus

8–12 vine-ripened plum tomatoes
about 500 ml (16 fl oz) olive oil
50 g (2 oz) shelled fresh peas, blanched

PEA SAUCE
20 g (¾ oz) chopped pea pods
125 ml (4 fl oz) chicken stock
80 g (3 oz) shelled fresh peas
60 ml (4 tbsp) olive oil
few leaves of basil
15 ml (1 tbsp) chopped parsley
freshly ground black pepper

MEAT JUS
450 g (1 lb) bones of chicken, veal, lamb etc.
30 ml (2 tbsp) olive oil
1 onion, roughly chopped
2 sticks celery, roughly chopped
2 carrots, roughly chopped
salt
1.5 litres (2¾ pints) well-flavoured brown chicken stock
100 ml (3½ fl oz) red wine
6 tomatoes, roughly chopped
sprig of thyme

1 Cut off the very top of the tomatoes and place in a small ovenproof dish. Pour in the olive oil just to cover, cover the dish and place in a preheated oven at 110°C (225°F) mark ¼ for 10–12 hours or overnight. Remove the tomatoes from the oven and allow to cool. Very carefully peel the tomatoes and, using a thin knife, remove as many of the seeds as possible.

2 To make the jus, roughly chop the bones and place in a roasting tin. Drizzle with a little olive oil. Roast at 200°C (400°F) mark 6 for about 15 minutes. Turn the bones frequently.

3 Add the onion, celery and carrots to the bones in the roasting tin with a little salt. Continue to roast for another 15 minutes until nicely brown. Drain off any oil and deglaze the pan with ½ cup chicken stock. Transfer the entire contents of the roasting tin to a large saucepan.

4 Add the rest of the stock, the wine, tomatoes and thyme and simmer for about 45 minutes. Strain through damp muslin into a clean saucepan. Reduce to the desired consistency.

5 To make the pea sauce, blanch the pea pods in boiling water for about 5 minutes and refresh in cold water. In a food process or blender, process the pods with about ½ of the chicken stock and pass through a fine strainer. 5

6 Blanch the peas in boiling salted water for about 1 minute and refresh in cold water. Purée with the remaining chicken stock. Add the strained pea–pod mixture, olive oil, basil and parsley. Purée until smooth and check seasoning.

7 To serve, place a small mound of the blanched peas in the centre of each serving plate. Pour some pea sauce over the peas. Place 2 or 3 tomatoes on the mound of peas. Spoon the jus around.

pea pots with herb and mint sauces

225 g (8 oz) fresh or frozen peas
knob of butter
freshly grated Parmesan, for dusting
150 ml (5 fl oz) double cream
2 eggs
2 egg yolks
sprig of mint
small pinch of freshly grated nutmeg

MINT SAUCE
45 ml (3 tbsp) mint
45 ml (3 tbsp) lemon juice
15 ml (1 tbsp) caster sugar

HERB SAUCE
300 ml (½ pint) natural yogurt
30 ml (2 tbsp) chives
30 ml (2 tbsp) parsley
salt and freshly ground black pepper

1 To make the mint sauce, put the mint, lemon juice and sugar in a bowl and pour 175 ml (6 fl oz) boiling water over. Allow to stand for 1 hour for the flavours to infuse.

2 To make the herb sauce, combine the yogurt with the chives, parsley and seasoning and chill in the refrigerator.

3 Cook the fresh or frozen peas in a pan of boiling salted water. Reserve 25 g (1 oz) of the cooked peas.

4 Grease 4 dariole moulds with butter and dust with the Parmesan cheese.

5 Place the cream, eggs, egg yolks, mint and nutmeg in a liquidizer and purée. Stir in half the reserved whole peas and pour the mixture into the prepared moulds.

6 Place the moulds in a baking pan and half fill the pan with boiling water. Bake the moulds in a preheated oven at 160°C (325°F) mark 3 for 30–35 minutes, until a skewer inserted in the mixture comes out clean. Remove from the oven and allow to cool.

7 To serve, turn the pea pots out of the moulds onto serving plates, and garnish with the remaining whole peas and the two sauces.

goats' cheese tower

1 clove garlic
1 bunch basil
25 g (1 oz) pine nuts
150 ml (5 fl oz) olive oil
25 g (1 oz) freshly grated Parmesan
2 medium aubergines
4 x 100 g (3½ oz) goats' cheeses, each cut in half
salt and freshly ground black pepper
20 cherry tomatoes
(½ tsp) sugar

1 In a blender or food processor, process the garlic and basil to a paste. Add the nuts then add 100 ml (3½ fl oz) of the olive oil slowly with the motor still running. Blend in the Parmesan quickly. Cover and set aside in a cool place.

2 Cut out 8 aubergine slices the same diameter as the cheese, brush with a little olive oil, season lightly then pan fry till tender.

3 Brush the tomatoes lightly with some olive oil. Season with salt, pepper and sugar then roast in a preheated oven at 200°C (400°F) mark 6 till the skins split.

4 Brush the goats' cheese slices with some olive oil and season with pepper only. Cook under a hot grill till slightly brown and the cheese is beginning to melt.

5 Decorate the plate with the pesto sauce and roast tomatoes. Then place alternate layers of aubergine and goats' cheese in the centre to form the tower.

pan-fried foie gras and leeks with orange muscat and shallots, and watercress salad with hazelnut oil dressing

50 g (2 oz) unsalted butter
50 g (2 oz) shallots, finely chopped
150 ml (5 fl oz) orange Muscat or other sweet wine
300 g (10 oz) leeks, thinly sliced
25 g (1 oz) watercress leaves
30 ml (2 tbsp) hazelnut oil
5 ml (1 tsp) Dijon mustard
4 slices fresh foie gras, about 25 g (1 oz) each

1 Melt half the butter in a small saucepan and add the shallots. Keep stirring over low heat until soft. Add the wine and cook over a high heat until almost all the wine is absorbed into the shallots. Set to one side until required.

2 Melt the remaining butter in a large frying pan and add the leeks. Cook over low heat until soft, then transfer into ovenproof dish, cover and keep warm.

3 Place the watercress leaves in a bowl. Mix together the hazelnut oil and mustard, pour over the watercress and toss the salad.

4 Heat a nonstick frying pan. When hot, quickly fry the foie gras for about 30 seconds on each side.

5 Place a portion of warm leeks in the centre of each serving plate. Put one slice of the hot foie gras on top of the leeks, and spoon the shallot sauce over. Arrange a little of the dressed watercress salad on the side, and serve immediately.

aubergine 'pitta' and rocket salad

4 small aubergines
about 30 ml (2 tbsp) olive oil
1 red pepper
2 red onions, thickly sliced horizontally
1 clove garlic, chopped
400 g (14 oz) can tomatoes
splash of balsamic vinegar
salt and freshly ground black pepper
15 ml (1 tbsp) chopped tarragon
175 g (6 oz) mozzarella, sliced
150 g (5 oz) rocket leaves

DRESSING
60 ml (4 tbsp) olive oil
60 ml (4 tbsp) walnut oil
30 ml (2 tbsp) lemon juice
30 ml (2 tbsp) balsamic vinegar

1 Create the 'pittas'. Trim the stalks of the aubergines and cut 1 slice, including the whole stalk, about 2.5 cm (1 inch) thick. Make a deep pocket in each, brush with olive oil and cook on a stove–top grill pan until just charred and softened.

2 Char the red pepper on a naked flame and place in a plastic bag. When cool, slip off the skin and cut into slices.

3 Brush the onion and pepper slices with oil and cook on the grill pan.

4 Meanwhile, heat 15 ml (1 tbsp) oil in a frying pan and fry the garlic until softened; add the can of tomatoes. Add the balsamic vinegar and season. Cook until the mixture is reduced by at least half. Add the tarragon.

5 Stuff each 'pitta' with the pepper, onion, mozzarella and tomato sauce (there may be a little tomato sauce over.) Place in a roasting tin, cover and cook in a preheated oven at 140°C (275°F) mark 1 for 45 minutes.

6 Whisk the dressing ingredients and season with salt and pepper. Toss the rocket in the dressing and divide the salad between 4 serving plates. Serve with the aubergine 'pitta'.

herbed savoury custards with a fresh tomato sauce and aubergine crisps

225 g (8 fl oz) milk
425 ml (¾ pint) double cream
30 ml (2 tbsp) minced rosemary leaves
3 fresh bay leaves
3 large eggs
2 egg yolks
25 g (1 oz) freshly grated Parmesan
1.25 ml (¼ tsp) freshly grated nutmeg
salt and freshly ground black pepper
butter, for greasing

TOMATO SAUCE
20 plum tomatoes, skinned and deseeded
45 ml (3 tbsp) olive oil
1 large clove garlic, crushed
handful of basil, chopped
pinch of caster sugar (optional)

AUBERGINE CRISPS
1 aubergine
olive oil, for frying
caster sugar, for sprinkling

1 In a medium saucepan combine the milk and cream and bring just to the boil. Add the rosemary and bay leaves, cover and set aside and infuse for 15 minutes. Strain through a fine sieve into a bowl and allow to cool.

2 In a small bowl, blend the eggs and egg yolks lightly with a fork but do not make it frothy.

3 When the milk mixture has cooled add the eggs, Parmesan, nutmeg, salt and pepper and stir to blend; taste for seasoning.

4 Butter 4 small ramekins and place in a large roasting tin on a sheet of greaseproof paper. Divide the custard evenly among the ramekins. Add enough hot water to the roasting tin to reach half way up the side of the ramekins. Place the tin in a preheated oven at 180°C (350°F) mark 4 for 50–55 minutes.

5 Meanwhile, make the tomato sauce. Reserve 2 tomatoes and dice the remainder. Heat the olive oil in a saucepan, add the garlic and cook until soft but not coloured and then add the diced tomatoes. Add the basil leaves and season to taste, adding a pinch of sugar if necessary.

6 Simmer for 30 minutes until a thick sauce is formed, then pass through a fine sieve, pressing with the back of a spoon. Return the sauce to a clean pan to warm through. Finely dice the remaining tomatoes and add to the sauce to warm through but not cook.

7 Make the aubergine crisps. Finely slice the aubergine and place in a colander. Sprinkle with salt and caster sugar and allow to drain for 15 minutes. Rinse and pat dry with paper towels. Heat the olive oil over a moderate heat and fry the aubergine, taking care not to over-brown. Remove and place on paper towels to drain.

8 Invert the ramekins onto warmed serving plates to unmould the custards and spoon the warm tomato sauce round. Place 3 or 4 aubergine crisps decoratively on top of the custards and serve at once.

savoury summer pudding with yellow pepper sauce

2 red peppers, cored, deseeded and quartered
2 yellow peppers, cored, deseeded and quartered
olive oil, for frying
1 red onion, finely chopped
400 g (14 oz) can chopped plum tomatoes
chopped fresh basil, to taste
salt and freshly ground black pepper
1 loaf sliced white bread, not too fresh
fresh basil leaves, to garnish

1 Place the peppers under the grill until the skins blacken. Place in a plastic box until cool and then rub off the skins under running water.

2 Heat the olive oil in pan and fry the onions gently until soft but not coloured. Chop the red peppers and add to pan; stir until coated with oil. Simmer gently for a few minutes and then add the tomatoes, chopped basil and salt and pepper to season. Bring to a gentle simmer. Allow to cool.

3 Line individual pudding moulds with cling film. Cut the crusts off the bread slices and cut to shape to line the moulds. Cut circles to place on top. Soak the bread in the juices from the pepper and tomato mixture and line the moulds. Spoon the pepper and tomato mixture into the lined moulds and place a round of bread on top. Place a board over the top of the moulds, weight down to press the contents and chill in the refrigerator.

4 Prepare the yellow pepper sauce: simmer the yellow peppers for 20 minutes in just enough water to cover then purée them in a food processor. Season with salt and pepper and thin, if necessary, with a little water.

5 Turn out the puddings into the centre of serving plates, surround with a pool of the yellow pepper sauce and garnish with whole fresh basil leaves.

bruschetta with spiced onion marmalade and toasted goats' cheese

50 ml (2 fl oz) olive oil
3 red onions, thinly sliced
2.5 ml (½ tsp) ground cinnamon
2. 5 ml (½ tsp) ground allspice
pinch of chilli powder
salt and freshly ground black pepper
45 ml (3 tbsp) red wine vinegar
75 g (3 oz) muscovado sugar
4 slices ciabatta, focaccia or French bread
1 clove garlic
4 slices goats' cheese
4 sage leaves

TO SERVE
dressed green salad

1 Heat 30 ml (2 tbsp) of the olive oil, add the onions and cook over a low heat for 1 hour.

2 Add the cinnamon, allspice, chilli, salt, pepper, wine vinegar and sugar. Bring to the boil and reduce the liquid until the consistency of syrup. Remove from the heat.

3 Toast the bread on one side. Rub the untoasted side with the garlic and drizzle with a little of the olive oil. Spread the untoasted side with the red onion marmalade and top with a slice of goats' cheese. Dip a sage leaf into olive oil and place on top. Grill until the cheese has slightly melted.

4 Serve with a green salad dressed with basic vinaigrette to which a pinch of sugar has been added.

roasted mediterranean vegetable tartlet

50 g (2 oz) yellow pepper, diced
50 g (2 oz) green pepper, diced
50 g (2 oz) courgette, diced
50 g (2 oz) red onion, diced
8 cloves garlic, finely chopped
60 ml (2 fl oz) olive oil
salt and freshly ground black
pepper
butter, for greasing
flour, for dusting
4 eggs, lightly beaten
175 ml (6 fl oz) double cream
pinch of cayenne pepper
mixed herb leaves, to garnish

FOR THE PASTRY
175 g (6 oz) plain flour
pinch of salt
75 g (3 oz) butter
25 g (1 oz) freshly grated
Parmesan
25 g (1 oz) ground hazelnuts
1 egg yolk

1 To make the pastry, place the flour, salt and butter in a large glass bowl and rub lightly until the consistency is that of fine breadcrumbs. Stir in the cheese and hazelnuts. Mix the egg yolk with 30 ml (2 tbsp) chilled water and add to the flour. Bring together into a dough and turn out onto a lightly floured board and knead until smooth. Wrap in cling film and refrigerate for 20–30 minutes.

2 Mix the peppers, courgette, onion and garlic in an ovenproof dish with the olive oil, salt and pepper. Bake in a preheated oven at 220°C (425°F) mark 7 for about 10–15 minutes, until the vegetables are charred but not fully cooked.

3 Grease 4 individual flan dishes, then dust with flour. Roll out the pastry and line the flan dishes. Bake in the oven at 220°C (425°F) mark 7 for about 10 minutes or until golden brown.

4 Mix the eggs and cream, add the cayenne pepper and season with salt and pepper. Arrange equal portions of the roasted vegetables in each flan case and cover with the egg and cream mixture. Return the flans to the oven for a further 20 minutes until the egg mixture has just set and is golden brown.

5 Serve the flans garnished with the mixed herb leaves.

Soups and starters

french brie in filo parcels with summer fruit coulis

200 g (7 oz) filo pastry
1 egg, lightly beaten
250 g (9 oz) French Brie, cut into
3 cm (1¼ inch) cubes
vegetable oil, for deep frying
100 g (3½ oz) strawberries
100 g (3½ oz) raspberries
20 g (¾ oz) caster sugar
mixed salad leaves, to serve

1 Cut the filo pastry into 12 cm (4½ inch) squares. Brush a little egg around the edges of the pastry, and place a cube of Brie in the centre of each square. Make parcels by wrapping the pastry around the cheese.

2 Heat the oil in a deep fat fryer and fry the parcels for about 1 minute or until crisp.

3 In a blender, purée the strawberries and raspberries with the sugar, then press through a fine sieve.

4 Arrange a spoonful of the fruit coulis on each serving plate, and place the parcels on the coulis. Serve with mixed salad leaves.

grilled irish goats' cheese with red pepper sauce

4 x 3 cm (1¼ inch) thick slices
from a crusty loaf
1 clove garlic
olive oil, for brushing
2 red peppers, cored and
deseeded
1 red chilli, cored, deseeded and
roughly chopped
15 ml (1 tbsp) olive oil
1 goats' cheese log, cut into 3 cm
(1¼ inch) thick slices
mixed salad leaves, to garnish

1 Lightly grill the slices of bread, rub with the garlic and brush with olive oil.

2 Grill the red peppers for about 20 minutes, until soft. Process in a blender or food processor with the chilli, then sieve the mixture into a bowl. Stir in the olive oil to mix.

3 Brush the goat's cheese slices with olive oil. Place them on the toasted bread and grill for 1–2 minutes until golden on top.

4 To serve, place grilled goats' cheese toasts in the centre of serving plates, garnish with the salad leaves, and drizzle with the red pepper sauce.

wild mushroom risotto with parmesan tuiles

15 g (½ oz) dried wild mushrooms (trompette de mort/horn of plenty, cep etc.)
40 g (1½ oz) unsalted butter
175 g (6 oz) fresh wild mushrooms (chantrelle, shiitake etc.), sliced
about 300 ml (½ pint) chicken or vegetable stock
2 shallots, finely chopped
150 g (5 oz) Arborio or carnaroli rice
75 ml (2½ fl oz) white wine
truffle oil, for greasing
25 g (1 oz) freshly grated Parmesan
salt and freshly ground white pepper
thinly sliced black truffle, to garnish (optional)

PARMESAN TUILES
50 g (2 oz) coarsely grated Parmesan

1 Make the Parmesan tuiles. Line a baking sheet with nonstick baking parchment. Spoon the grated Parmesan in oval shapes onto the paper. Cook in a preheated oven at 180°C (350°F) mark 4 for about 5 minutes until the cheese is melted and golden. Carefully remove with a palette knife, bend the tuiles over a rolling pin and allow to cool.

2 Cover the dried wild mushrooms with boiling water and leave to soak for 15 minutes.

3 Melt 15 g (½ oz) of the butter in a large frying pan or wok and cook the fresh mushrooms for 3 minutes. Remove and reserve.

4 Remove the dried mushrooms from the soaking liquid and strain the liquid. Pour the strained liquid and stock into a saucepan and bring to a simmer. Coarsely chop the dried mushrooms and add to the fresh mushrooms.

5 Heat 15 g (½ oz) of the butter in a large saucepan. Add the shallots and sweat for 3 minutes until soft and translucent. Add the rice and cook for 1–2 minutes. Add the wine and when it has been absorbed, add the mushrooms. Gradually add ladlefuls of the simmering stock, stirring constantly at first, and continuing to add stock as each addition is absorbed. The risotto will take about 20 minutes to cook.

6 Meanwhile lightly grease 4 small dariole moulds with truffle oil.

7 Stir the remaining butter, grated Parmesan and seasoning. Lightly press the risotto into the dariole moulds and invert onto serving plates. Garnish with black truffle slices, if you like, and serve with the Parmesan tuiles.

gorgonzola and mascarpone cheesecake served with onion compôte

115 g (4 oz) breadcrumbs
50 g (2 oz) freshly grated
Parmesan
25 g (1 oz) unsalted butter, melted
freshly ground white pepper
4 medium eggs
450 g (1 lb) mascarpone
225 g (8 oz) Gorgonzola
150 ml (¼ pint) olive oil
450 g (1 lb) red onions, finely
sliced
30 ml (2 tbsp) soft brown sugar
5 ml (1 tsp) white wine vinegar

1 Mix together the breadcrumbs, Parmesan, butter and one grind of white pepper. Pat the mixture firmly into the base of a loose–bottomed 23 cm (9 inch) cake tin.

2 Bake in a preheated oven at 190°C (375°F) mark 5 for 10–15 minutes until the base is golden and crisp. Remove from the oven and reduce the temperature to 180°C (350°F) mark 4.

3 Beat together the eggs, mascarpone and Gorgonzola until smooth. Season to taste. Pour the mixture onto the cooked crumb base and return to the oven for 30 minutes, until the top is golden brown and the edges are set. Remove from the oven and allow to cool.

4 Meanwhile, make the onion compôte. Heat the olive oil in a frying pan and gently sauté the onions until tender. Add the sugar, increase the heat and allow to caramelize slightly. Stir in the vinegar and bring to the boil. Remove from the heat and allow to cool slightly.

5 Slice the cheesecake and serve with a spoonful of the onion compôte on the side.

roasted beetroot with goats' cheese fondant and potato wafers

3 medium beetroot, scrubbed
olive oil, for roasting
freshly ground rock salt
15 ml (1 tbsp) walnut oil
30 ml (2 tbsp) balsamic vinegar
12 walnut halves, lightly roasted
45 ml (3 tbsp) basil oil (see below)

GOATS' CHEESE FONDANT
125 g (4 oz) goats' cheese
100 ml (3½ fl oz) whipping cream, at room temperature
salt and freshly ground white pepper

POTATO WAFERS
1 large baking potato, baked and peeled
30 ml (2 tbsp) butter
3 egg whites
30 ml (2 tbsp) finely chopped fresh herbs

1 Coat the beetroot in olive oil, add a grind of rock salt and bake, covered, in a preheated oven at 190°C (375°F) mark 5 for about 1½ hours until tender.

2 For the fondant, place the goats' cheese in a small pan and beat over a low heat until very smooth. Whip the cream to firm peaks and fold into the cheese. Season with salt and pepper. Place in the refrigerator to set.

3 For the potato wafers, place the potato in a bowl with the butter and egg whites. Beat with an electric mixer for 3–4 minutes or until smooth. Pass through a fine sieve and fold in the herbs. Season to taste.

4 Make a cardboard template with a 6 cm (2½ inch) square hole. Using the template, spread a thin layer of the potato mixture onto a nonstick baking sheet until you have 16 squares.

5 Remove the beetroot from the oven and reduce the temperature to 150°C (300°F) mark 2. Bake the potato wafers for 7–10 minutes until golden brown, watching carefully as they burn easily. Remove the squares from the baking sheet and allow to cool.

6 When the beetroot is cool, peel and slice. Dress with the walnut oil, a little of the balsamic vinegar and salt and pepper to taste. Allow to stand for about 30 minutes to absorb the flavours.

7 To serve, place a slice of beetroot in the centre of each plate. Top with some goats' cheese fondant and then a potato wafer. Repeat until you have 4 layers. Arrange 3 walnut halves on each plate. Drizzle the basil oil and remaining balsamic vinegar around.

BASIL OIL: Blanch 1 cup fresh basil leaves in boiling salted water for about 10 seconds. Immediately refresh in very cold water and drain. Squeeze out the excess water and coarsely chop. Blend with 150 ml (5 fl oz) light olive oil for 3–4 minutes. Pour into a container and refrigerate for a day. Strain though some muslin before using and store in the refrigerator.

MAIN COURSES: POULTRY AND GAME

fricassée of chicken with morels and vin jaune d'arbois

about 25 g (1 oz) butter
¼ fennel bulb, finely chopped
2 shallots, finely chopped
1.3 kg (3 lb) free–range chicken, jointed (see note)
salt and freshly ground black pepper
15 ml (1 tbsp) olive oil
30 ml (2 tbsp) marc or white wine (Chablis or Arbois), see note
300 ml (½ pint) vin jaune d'Arbois or dry sherry
175 g (6 oz) bottled morels or 40 g (1½ oz) dried and soaked or 115 g (4 oz) fresh morels
350 ml (12 fl oz) crème fraîche
chopped parsley, to garnish

1 Melt the butter in a casserole. Sweat the fennel and shallots until soft and translucent. Remove and place in a bowl.

2 Season the chicken portions with salt and pepper. In the same pan, add a little more butter if needed and the olive oil, and cook the chicken for 5 minutes each side. Remove the chicken and place in an ovenproof dish. Cover and cook in a preheated oven at 190°C (375°F) mark 5 for 10–15 minutes, watching them carefully and checking for doneness after 10 minutes. Remove from the oven and keep warm.

3 Meanwhile, return the vegetables to the casserole and add the marc and vin jaune. Deglaze the pan and reduce the liquid by half.

4 Add the morels and crème fraîche. Taste and adjust seasoning. Bring to the boil and simmer. Add the chicken pieces and simmer for 5 minutes.

5 Serve garnished with chopped parsley.

NOTES: Ask your butcher to joint your chicken for you. Ask him to cut it into 6 pieces, making sure that the breast is boneless and has the wing bone still attached.

Marc is also called Eau-de-vie de Marc and is a spirit distilled from the residue of grapes; it is available in specialist shops.

chicken fajitas

SERVES 2
½ large red pepper, cored, deseeded and quartered
½ large green pepper, cored, deseeded and quartered
½ large yellow pepper, cored, deseeded and quartered
2 skinless, boneless chicken breasts, sliced in 1 cm (½ inch) strips
¾ onion, thinly sliced
2 large cloves garlic, peeled and thinly sliced
25 g (1 oz) coriander leaves
juice of 2 limes
salt and freshly ground black pepper

1 Place the peppers under a hot grill until the skin is black and blistered, then place in a plastic bag and seal. When cool enough to handle, peel the peppers and cut the flesh into 2 cm (¾ inch) wide strips.

2 Place the pepper strips, chicken, onion, garlic, coriander leaves and lime juice in a large bowl with plenty of black pepper and leave to marinate for at least 1 hour.

3 Meanwhile, make the salsa. Mix all the salsa ingredients, season to taste, and chill until ready to serve.

4 To make the guacamole, liquidize the tomatoes, onion, lemon juice, olive oil and chilli powder until smooth. Peel the avocado and mash or liquidize into the tomato mixture. Cover with cling film and chill until ready to serve.

5 Make the tortillas. Blend the flour, fat and salt in a food processor. With the motor running, gradually add about 300 ml (½ pint) water until a soft dough is formed. Place the dough on a lightly floured surface and knead briefly. Divide the dough into 6 pieces and keep damp. Roll out each piece into a 18–20 cm (7–8 inch) circle. Heat an ungreased frying pan and cook each tortilla for about 1 minute on each side until slightly browned but still

15–30 ml (1–2 tbsp) olive oil, for frying

SALSA
½ red onion, finely chopped
1 green chilli, cored, deseeded and finely chopped
25 g (1 oz) coriander leaves, chopped
300 g (10 oz) canned chopped tomatoes
5 ml (1 tsp) sugar

GUACAMOLE
100 g (3½ oz) canned chopped tomatoes
¼ onion, quartered
juice of ½ lemon
10 ml (2 tsp) olive oil
pinch of chilli powder
1 large ripe avocado

FLOUR TORTILLAS
125 g (4 oz) strong plain white flour
25 g (1 oz) white vegetable fat
1.25 ml (¼ tsp) salt

TO GARNISH
lime quarters
fresh coriander
soured cream

soft. Keep the tortillas warm, wrapped in a clean tea towel.

6 Heat the oil in a large frying pan or wok until hot. Stir fry the chicken mixture, including marinade for about 8 minutes, until the chicken is cooked and the onions slightly browned.

7 Serve the chicken fajitas in warmed bowls, garnished with quarters of lime, and the guacamole garnished with fresh coriander. Serve with soured cream, salsa and flour tortillas.

grilled chicken breast and king prawns

2 bunches spring onions
20 ml (4 tsp) white wine vinegar
30 g (1 oz) fresh root ginger, peeled and finely sliced
2.5 ml (½ tsp) sugar
salt and freshly ground black pepper
4 skinless chicken breasts
15 ml (1 tbsp) peanut oil
15 ml (1 tbsp) lime juice
100 g (3½ oz) shallots, finely diced
6 cardamom pods
1.25 ml (¼ tsp) ground turmeric
60 ml (4 tbsp) Noilly Prat
300 ml (½ pint) well-flavoured chicken stock
60 ml (4 tbsp) whipping cream
200g (7 oz) butter, diced
12 king prawns, peeled with tails left on

TO SERVE
Garam Masala Pommes
Parisiennes (see page 154)

1 Slice the spring onions diagonally into 3 cm (1 1/4 inch) lengths and marinate with the vinegar, ginger, sugar and a large pinch of salt; cover and leave for at least 1 hour.

2 Brush the chicken breasts with oil then place on a very hot stove top grill pan, turning once through 90° degrees after about 30 seconds to give a criss-cross effect on one side. Season with salt and pepper then roast in a preheated oven at 200°C (400°F) mark 6 for about 10 minutes until tender. Remove from the oven, adjust the seasoning with salt, pepper and lime juice and keep warm.

3 Sweat the shallots in the remaining oil with the cardamoms and turmeric until tender. Add the Noilly Prat and reduce to a syrup. Add the chicken stock, bring to boil then gradually whisk in the cream; take the pan off the heat and whisk in the butter a little at a time. Pass through a fine sieve, adjust the seasoning if necessary then set aside and keep warm.

4 In a wok or sauté pan, stir fry the spring onions with their marinade, together with the prawns, and season with pepper.

5 Place a chicken breast at the top of each serving plate, arrange three nests of spring onions and place a king prawn on top of each. Pour the sauce around and between the nests and serve with spicy pommes Parisiennes.

WELSH ORGANIC CHICKEN BREAST, STUFFED AND WRAPPED IN BACON ILLUSTRATED OVERLEAF

welsh organic chicken breast, stuffed and wrapped in bacon

100 g (3½ oz) unsalted butter
¼ small red pepper, cored, deseeded and chopped
¼ stick celery, green part, finely chopped
1 bird's eye chilli, cored, deseeded and finely chopped
6–8 rashers back bacon
1 garlic flavoured boursin, diced
250 g (9 oz) young leaf spinach
1 large organic chicken breast
olive oil, for roasting
1 litre (1¾ pints) well-flavoured chicken stock
125 g (4 oz) Puy lentils
freshly grated nutmeg
tandoori spices
4 organic carrots, peeled and chopped
sea salt and freshly ground black pepper
100 ml (3½ fl oz) double cream
small pinch of saffron
1 sprig of tarragon

TO GARNISH (OPTIONAL)
¾ small red pepper, cored and deseeded

1 Make the stuffing. Melt 25 g (1 oz) of the butter in a large pan and sauté the chopped red pepper, celery and chilli over a low heat for 2 minutes just to soften. Allow to cool and coagulate, this aids the stuffing process.

2 Trim the fat from the bacon and on a flat surface stretch with the back of a knife to prevent shrinkage when cooking, slightly overlap each rasher lengthways to form a wrap.

3 Dot the boursin on the bacon, and press some of the spinach leaves onto the cheese in a single layer.

4 Score and butterfly the chicken breast lengthways to form a cavity, stuff with the red pepper and celery mixture and place on the spinach and bacon and carefully wrap, overlapping the ends of the bacon where necessary to hold firmly together.

5 Drizzle some olive oil into a heavy–based roasting tin, and carefully turn the chicken breast, seam–side down, and place in the tin. Roast in a preheated oven at 200°C (400°F) mark 6 for about 30 minutes or until the bacon is nicely browned and the chicken is cooked. Keep warm.

6 Meanwhile, place 500 ml (16 fl oz) of the chicken stock in a pan, add the lentils, a pinch of nutmeg and tandoori spices and simmer for about 40 minutes until the liquid has been absorbed, keep warm.

7 Boil the carrots until tender, drain and toss in the remaining butter to coat well. Season with a little salt and plenty of black pepper.

8 Finely chop the remaining spinach and sweat with a little water and a very small pinch of nutmeg and tandoori spices for about 4 minutes until just tender. Drain and keep warm.

9 Place the remaining chicken stock in a saucepan and reduce to a quarter, then add the cream, saffron and sprig of tarragon. Simmer the sauce for 5 minutes, remove the tarragon if you like, and season to taste. Simmer for a further 2 minutes until thick and creamy.

10 Make the red pepper garnish, if using. Cut the pepper into long wide strips and place under a very hot grill until well charred, place in a plastic bag until cool enough to handle and peel. Julienne the pepper and keep warm.

11 To serve, slice the chicken into slices. Spoon the lentils into a small round mould, and turn out onto each serving plate and arrange the chicken slices on top. Sprinkle the red pepper julienne garnish on the chicken, if using. Fill a small round mould, ¾ full of carrot and then top up with the spinach. Remove the mould to make a timbale on each plate. Carefully spoon the sauce around the chicken and vegetable timbale.

grilled lemon chicken

SERVES 2

25 g (1 oz) spring onions, finely
chopped
5 ml (1 tsp) grated fresh root
ginger
5 ml (1 tsp) finely chopped garlic
finely grated zest of ½ lemon
2 chicken breasts

SAUCE

finely grated zest of ½ lemon
1 chicken stock cube, crumbled
120 g (4 oz) crème fraîche
25 g (1 oz) spring onions, finely
chopped
5 ml (1 tsp) cornflour

TO SERVE

Herbed Duchess Potatoes (see
page 154)
broccoli florets and honey glazed
carrots

1 Mash the spring onions, ginger, garlic and lemon zest together with a fork and spread the paste on the chicken breasts. Marinate the chicken overnight in the refrigerator. When ready to cook, scrape the paste from chicken breasts and reserve; grill the chicken for 20 minutes under a pre-heated grill, turning occasionally.

2 To make the sauce: pour 500 ml (16 fl oz) of water into a pan, add the lemon zest, and bring to the boil; boil for 3 minutes. Add the marinade paste and chicken stock cube and boil for 20 minutes until reduced by half.

3 Place the crème fraîche in a bowl and add the spring onions. Slowly add a little of the hot marinade mixture, stirring constantly to avoid it curdling. Return the crème fraîche mixture to the pan, add the cornflour, and cook over a very low heat, stirring constantly, until the sauce is thickened.

4 Serve the chicken breasts with the sauce, accompanied by the duchess potatoes, broccoli florets and honey glazed carrots.

punjabi tikka with bhindi masala and pilau rice

SERVES 2

NOTE: This recipe contains
ingredients which should be
available in specialist Asian food
shops.

PUNJABI TIKKA

45 ml (3 tbsp) sunflower oil
1 large onion, finely chopped
15 ml (1 tbsp) tomato purée
5 ml (1 tsp) finely chopped fresh
root ginger
5 ml (1 tsp) salt
3.75 ml (¾ tsp) garam masala
2.5 ml ½ tsp) crushed fresh garlic
2.5 ml (½ tsp) chilli powder

1 To make the Punjabi tikka, heat the oil in a pan and add the onion; cook until it is golden brown. Add the tomato purée and mix well. Then add the ginger, salt, garam masala, garlic, chilli powder, jeera and tandoori masala and stir to mix. Add the yogurt, stirring, and cook until the sauce starts to give off some oil. Add the chicken pieces and cook for 30 minutes or until the chicken is tender, stirring occasionally.

2 While the chicken is cooking, prepare the batter for the dhai balas; mix the dhai bala mix with 120 ml (4 fl oz) of water, whisking well until smooth. The batter should be quite thin. Let the batter stand for 20 to 30 minutes, until it has thickened.

3 Meanwhile, make the bhindi masala, heat the oil in a pan and add the onion. Cook until golden brown, stirring occasionally. Add the tomato purée. Mix the ginger, salt, garam masala, garlic, chilli powder and jeera in a small bowl. Make a slit along the side of each bhindi and fill with the mixed spices. Carefully add the bhindi to the onion and tomato purée mixture together with any remaining spice filling. Cook over a moderate heat for 15

2.5 ml (½ tsp) jeera
2.5 ml (½ tsp) tandoori masala
60 ml (4 tbsp) yogurt
350 g (12 oz) boneless chicken,
in bite-sized pieces

BHINDI MASALA
45 ml (3 tbsp) sunflower oil
1 large onion, finely chopped
15 ml (1 tbsp) tomato purée
5 ml (1 tsp) finely chopped fresh
root ginger
5 ml (1 tsp) salt
3.75 ml (¾ tsp) garam masala
2.5 ml (½ tsp) crushed fresh garlic
2.5 ml (½ tsp) chilli powder
2.5 ml (½ tsp) jeera
225 g (8 oz) bhindi (okra),
trimmed

DHAI BALA
75g (3 oz) dhai bala mix
200 ml (7 fl oz) water
500 ml (16 fl oz) sunflower oil
175 ml (6 fl oz) yogurt
50 ml (2 fl oz) milk

PILAU RICE
22.5 ml (1½ tbsp) sunflower oil
½ onion, finely chopped
50 g (2 oz) frozen peas
225 g (8 oz) long-grain rice
5 ml (1 tsp) salt

TO GARNISH
freshly chopped coriander
chilli powder
garam masala powder

TO SERVE (OPTIONAL)
poppadoms
green salad

to 20 minutes or until the bhindi are tender.

4 When the batter has finished standing, heat the oil in a large saucepan until very hot. Add enough of the remaining water to the dhai bala batter to make the consistency of a thick pancake batter and whisk to mix thoroughly. Drop spoonfuls of the dhai bala batter into the hot oil so it forms balls. Deep fry the dhai balas until they are light golden outside. With a slotted spoon, transfer the dhai balas from the saucepan to a bowl of lukewarm water for 2 minutes. Remove and gently squeeze out the water, taking care not to lose the shape of the balas.

5 Mix the yogurt and milk together in a bowl, add the balas and leave for 10 minutes; garnish with chopped coriander and a sprinkling of chilli powder and garam masala.

6 Prepare the rice; wash and soak the rice in cold water for 5 to 10 minutes.

Meanwhile, heat 1 tbsp of the oil in a large saucepan, add the onion and cook until golden brown. Add the peas and cook for a few minutes. Drain the rice thoroughly and add to the pan with 500 ml (16 fl oz) of boiling water. Add the salt, cover the pan and simmer until the rice has soaked up the water. Take off the heat and let the rice cook in its own steam, covered, for 5 to 10 minutes.

7 Serve the Punjabi tikka on the rice, accompanied by the bhindi masala and dhai bala, with poppadoms and green salad, if you like.

PUNJABI TIKKA WITH BHINDI MASALA AND PILAU RICE ILLUSTRATED OVERLEAF

tarragon chicken in a lime and crème fraîche sauce

SERVES 2

30 g (1 oz) butter softened

finely grated zest and juice of 1 lime

2 skinless, boneless chicken breasts

7.5 ml (1½ tsp) chopped fresh tarragon

salt and freshly ground black pepper

75 ml (5 tbsp) crème fraîche

lime slices, to garnish

TO SERVE

Butternut Squash (see page 165)

Parmesan Mashed Potatoes (see page 160)

1 Combine the butter and lime zest in a small bowl. Make 3 or 4 deep diagonal cuts across each chicken breast and fill the cuts with the lime butter.

2 Place the chicken breasts in a roasting tin and sprinkle with the lime juice, tarragon and salt and pepper. Bake in a preheated oven at 200°C (400°F) mark 6 for 20 minutes or until chicken is cooked through.

3 Transfer the chicken breasts to a warmed plate and keep warm.

4 Make the sauce: place the roasting tin over a medium heat, add 7.5 ml (½ tbsp) water to the cooking juices, stirring to dissolve the sediments. Bring to the boil and cook, stirring, for 1 to 2 minutes. Stir in the crème fraîche and heat through.

5 To serve: slice the chicken into strips, drizzle the sauce over the top and garnish with a lime slice. Serve with the Parmesan mashed potatoes and butternut squash.

roast herb–stuffed chicken with pomme fondant and confit of garlic

SERVES 2
100 g (3½ oz) unsalted butter
80 g (3 oz) breadcrumbs
40 g (1½ oz) mixed herbs,
chopped (parsley, tarragon, chives
and chervil)
1 small chicken, legs and wings
removed
50 ml (2 fl oz) extra-virgin olive oil

CONFIT OF GARLIC
6 cloves garlic
1 bay leaf, torn
1 sprig of thyme
duck fat

POMME FONDANT
2 large potatoes
50 g (2 oz) slightly salted butter,
plus extra for frying
salt and freshly ground black
pepper

TO GARNISH
30 g (1 oz) mixed herbs, chopped
(parsley, tarragon, chives and
chervil)

TO SERVE
Jus Rôti (see note)
blanched vegetable bundles

1 To make the confit of garlic, put the cloves of garlic in a saucepan with the bay leaf, thyme and duck fat. Put it on the lowest heat possible and cook for 20–30 minutes until the garlic is soft. When cool, place in the refrigerator and leave for as long as possible (preferably overnight).

2 Melt the butter in a saucepan, and then add the breadcrumbs and herbs and mix together thoroughly. Stuff this mixture evenly under the skin of the chicken breast on both sides, about 5 cm (2 inches) thick. Heat the olive oil in a roasting tin and seal the chicken on all sides. Place the chicken in a preheated oven at 220°C (425°F) mark 7 for about 30 minutes.

3 Meanwhile, make the pomme fondant. Cut the potatoes into quarters and then shape them like small bananas. Spread the butter on the bottom of a roasting tin, add the potatoes and sprinkle with salt and pepper; add enough water just to cover. Place in the preheated oven at 220°C (425°F) mark 7 for 10–20 minutes until soft and slightly golden brown. Remove and place the tin on the hob with a little butter and fry until golden brown.

4 Remove the cloves of garlic from the fat and place them on a tray in the preheated oven at 220°C (425°F) mark 7 for about 5 minutes until crisp on the outside.

5 To serve, cut away the chicken breast and place on separate plates. Pour some Jus Rôti on top of each chicken breast and place the potatoes and cloves around the plate in separate fans, along with the vegetable bundles. Use the remaining herbs for garnish.

NOTE: The Jus Rôti can be prepared in advance: place 6 chicken legs in a roasting tin with a little extra–virgin olive oil. Roast in a preheated oven at 140°C (275°) mark 1 for about 1 ½ hours. Remove the chicken legs and add 200 ml (7 fl oz) water and 400 ml (14 fl oz) chicken stock to the juices in the pan. Place a rack over the liquid, and squeeze the juices out of the chicken legs so that they drip into the liquid. Discard the chicken legs, place the roasting tin over a high heat and boil to reduce and concentrate the flavour.

main courses: poultry & game

sesame glazed duck breast with plum and yellow pepper confit

SERVES 2

2 duck breasts, 200–225 g
(7–8 oz) each
15 ml (1 tbsp) honey
7 g (¼ oz) sesame seeds

PLUM AND YELLOW PEPPER
CONFIT

25 g (1 oz) butter
1 large yellow pepper, cored,
deseeded and finely sliced
½ onion, finely sliced
3 firm plums, pitted and finely
sliced
30 ml (2 tbsp) brandy
30 ml (2 tbsp) red wine vinegar
1 star anise
15 ml (1 tbsp) redcurrant jelly
5 ml (1 tsp) brown sugar
150 ml (¼ pint) concentrated
consommé
orange juice to taste

TO SERVE

small new potatoes, baby
sweetcorn, young runner beans,
baby carrots

1 To make the confit. Heat the butter in a saucepan and add the pepper, onion and plums; fry over a moderate heat for 10–15 minutes until they are soft.

2 Add the brandy, vinegar, anise, redcurrant jelly and brown sugar to the mixture; stir and add the consommé. Cook over a moderate heat for 15–20 minutes until the mixture is reduced by half. Add orange juice to taste.

3 Trim any sinews from the duck breasts and score the skin with a sharp knife. Heat a frying pan, and place the duck, skin–side down, until brown and crispy.

4 Place the duck breasts on a rack over a roasting tin, skin–side up. Drizzle honey over the duck then sprinkle with sesame seeds.

5 Cook the duck in a preheated oven at 220°C (425°F) mark 7 for about 15 minutes. Slice the duck and serve with the confit and baby vegetables.

duck stuffed with langoustines and parma ham

SERVES 2

2 medium duck breasts, trimmed

salt and freshly ground black pepper

15 ml (1 tbsp) olive oil

4 langoustines, shells removed

2 cloves garlic

10 large leaves of spinach, stalks removed

4 slices Parma ham

2 pig's cauls (optional)

FONDANT POTATO AND SPINACH

2 large potatoes

120 g (4 oz) unsalted butter

2.5 ml (½ tsp) salt

15 ml (1 tbsp) olive oil

2 large handfuls spinach

TO SERVE

a reduction of well-flavoured duck stock

1 Season the duck breasts and place them on a board, skin–side down. Make a lengthways cut down the centre of each breast, making sure not to cut all the way through. Then, holding the knife almost parallel to the work surface, make a cut from the middle cut outwards, though not all the way to the edge. Do this on both sides of the original cut, creating two pockets. Refrigerate.

2 Meanwhile, prepare the potatoes. Cut off both ends from the potatoes, and stand them on a board; then cut vertically downwards to form a hexagonal shape. Rinse the potatoes and place in an ovenproof casserole of water, just to cover. Add the butter and salt and bring to the boil. Simmer until the liquid is reduced by two-thirds. Set aside.

3 Heat the olive oil in a frying pan and flash fry the langoustines and garlic for 45 seconds. Take the pan off the heat and allow to cool.

4 Cook the spinach in a little boiling salted water for about 30 seconds until softened. Refresh in cold water. Remove and pat dry.

5 Lay a piece of cling film on the work surface. Arrange half the spinach leaves in a rectangle about 10 cm (4 inches) by 15 cm (5 inches), with the widest side nearest to you and season with pepper. Place half the Parma ham to cover the spinach. Place 2 langoustines at the edge nearest you, lift the cling film and roll the spinach and ham over the langoustines, as tightly as possible, Swiss roll fashion. Make a second roll in the same way.

6 Season the pockets inside the duck breasts, open one pocket and place one roll inside, trimming the ends of the roll if necessary. Then roll the stuffed half of the breast over and push it as far as possible into the opposite pocket so that you have a tightly rolled duck breast. Set aside. Repeat for the second duck breast.

7 Lay the pig's cauls on the board, if using, and roll the duck breasts in them. Tie 4 strings around the length of the rolled duck breast. Heat a dry saucepan, season the rolls and place the breast rolls in the pan, skin–side down. When the skin is golden, transfer the duck breasts to a roasting tin and cook in a preheated oven at 220–230°C (425–450°F) mark 7–8 for 15–20 minutes, turning once during cooking.

8 Add the potatoes to the oven for 10 minutes until the top is brown. Heat the olive oil in a pan, and add the spinach and seasoning. Sauté it for 1–2 minutes, then arrange on serving plates. Carve the duck into 15 mm (½ inch) thick slices and place on the bed of spinach, with the potatoes. Drizzle with the stock reduction and serve.

pan-fried breast of duck in honey and balsamic vinegar

SERVES 2

2 duck breasts
sesame oil and butter, for pan-frying
5 ml (1 tsp) cornflour

MARINADE

30 ml (2 tbsp) balsamic vinegar
30 ml (2 tbsp) honey
15 ml (1 tbsp) Worcestershire sauce
15 ml (1 tbsp) dark soy sauce
2 cloves garlic, finely chopped
finely grated zest and juice of ½ lemon
salt and freshly ground black pepper

TO SERVE

Stir-fried Summer Vegetables (see page 153)
Puréed Parmesan Potatoes with Nutmeg (see page 160)

1 Mix together all the ingredients for the marinade in a shallow dish, and marinate the duck breasts for at least 2 hours in the refrigerator.

2 Remove the duck from the marinade, reserving the marinade. Heat a little sesame oil and butter together in a pan, and gently fry the duck for 15–20 minutes, turning once. Remove the duck breasts from the pan and keep warm.

3 Add the marinade to the pan, stir in the cornflour and bring to the boil, stirring, until reduced. Taste for seasoning. Serve the duck with the sauce poured over, and with the stir-fried vegetables and Parmesan potatoes.

crispy duck confit with honey and hoisin, served with cucumber ribbons and puy lentil dhal

100 ml (3½ fl oz) peanut oil
2 cm (¾ inch) cube fresh root ginger, finely grated
3 whole star anise, finely chopped
20 ml (4 tsp) honey
1 clove garlic, crushed
20 ml (4 tsp) soy sauce
4 duck legs
400 ml (14 fl oz) rendered duck fat (see note)
knob of butter
1 onion, finely diced
350 ml (12 fl oz) stock
40 ml (2½ tbsp) sherry vinegar
50 g (2 oz) Puy lentils, rinsed
2 carrots, finely diced
1 large potato, finely diced
1 leek, finely chopped
1 stick celery, finely diced
½ cucumber
salt
20 ml (4 tsp) hoisin
½ chilli pepper, cored, deseeded and finely chopped
1 spring onion, finely chopped, to garnish

1 Mix the oil, ginger, star anise, honey, garlic and soy sauce in a shallow dish and marinate the duck legs for 24 hours in the refrigerator.

2 Remove the duck from the marinade, reserving the marinade. Rinse the excess marinade from the legs, and pat dry. Boil the duck for 30 minutes in the rendered duck fat, then simmer for a further hour. Remove from the fat and set aside.

3 In a large pan, melt a little butter and soften the onion for 1–2 minutes; add the stock, vinegar and lentils and bring to the boil. Add the carrots, potato, leek and celery and simmer for 30 minutes until all the liquid is absorbed.

4 With a vegetable peeler, shave the cucumber into long ribbons, sprinkle with salt and allow to stand for about 20 minutes.

5 In a small pan, heat the remaining marinade with the hoisin and chilli to make a sauce.

6 Crisp the skin of the duck under a preheated grill for 5 minutes before serving. To serve, place the cucumber ribbons on serving plates, and arrange the crispy duck on top; surround with the lentil dhal and drizzle with the sauce. Sprinkle with the chopped spring onion.

NOTE: This recipe calls for rendered duck fat which may be difficult to obtain. A good alternative would be ⅓ lard, melted with ⅓ vegetable oil and ⅓ stock.

grilled duck breast on red wine onions

SERVES 2

25 g (1 oz) unsalted butter
25 g (1 oz) demerara sugar
3–4 large red onions, finely sliced
85 ml (5½ tbsp) red wine vinegar
salt and freshly ground black
pepper
½ bottle red wine
5 ml (1 tsp) crème de cassis
15 ml (1 tbsp) sunflower oil
2 duck breasts

TO SERVE

Layered Stilton Potatoes and Leeks
(see page 155)

1 Heat the butter and sugar in a saucepan, add the onions and cook until softened but not brown. Add the red wine vinegar, and reduce until almost dry. Season with salt and pepper and add the red wine. Reduce again until almost dry. Check the seasoning. Stir in the crème de cassis and keep the onions warm.

2 Heat the oil in a nonstick frying pan and fry the duck skin-side down for 7–8 minutes. Turn over and fry for 3–4 minutes. Transfer the duck breasts to a preheated grill, and grill, skin–side up, for 5–7 minutes until cooked with just a trace of pink. Transfer to a cutting board, cover with foil, and let stand for 3 minutes.

3 To serve, spoon the onions onto two warmed plates; carve the duck into slices and arrange on top of the onions. Serve with layered Stilton potatoes and leeks.

duck breasts stuffed with figs, wrapped in speck, with a cider and honey sauce

4 duck breasts
40 g (1½ oz) unsalted butter
4 ready to eat figs, finely chopped
8 slices Speck (smoked air-cured
ham)
300 ml (½ pint) medium cider
5 ml (1 tsp) honey
salt and freshly ground black
pepper

TO SERVE

Carrot and Fennel Purée (see
page 157)
Dauphinoise Potatoes (see page
154)

1 Skin the duck breasts and trim fat, and reserve the fat. Cover the duck breasts with cling film and gently flatten with a rolling pin until they are 5–10 mm (¼–½ inch) thick.

2 Combine 15 g (½ oz) of the butter with the figs and place thin rolls of the mixture down the centre of the duck breasts. Roll up and wrap in slices of the Speck, securing with cocktail sticks.

3 In a frying pan over a moderate heat, melt down a small piece of the duck fat, then pan–fry the rolled duck breasts for 4 minutes on each side. Set aside and keep warm for about 10 minutes.

4 Meanwhile, deglaze the pan with the cider, scraping all the crusty bits into the sauce. Boil for 5 minutes to reduce, then pass through a sieve lined with muslin and return the sauce to the pan. Stir in the honey and the remaining butter. Season to taste.

5 Slice the duck rolls and place on warmed plates with the cider and honey sauce.

rabbit marinated in cider, pan–fried with lemon grass

NOTE: The most important step in this recipe is to make friendly contact with a butcher, you do not, under any circumstances, want to bone a rabbit.

4 boned rabbits
500 ml (16 fl oz) strong dry cider
15 ml (1 tbsp) extra–virgin olive oil
knob of butter
75 g (3 oz) lemon grass, crushed
100 ml (3½ fl oz) single cream
salt and freshly ground black pepper
freshly chopped coriander, to garnish (optional)

TO SERVE
Baby Roast Vegetables (see page 152)
Parsnip Purée (see page 162)

1 Trim the rabbit meat, discarding any fat or sinew. Cut the meat into bite–size pieces and marinate in the cider in a cool place for at least 1 hour. After marinating, remove and pat dry on paper towels. Reserve the cider.

2 Heat the olive oil and butter in a large frying pan. Add the lemon grass and rabbit pieces and fry for 10–15 minutes over a medium heat. With a slotted spoon, transfer the rabbit meat to well–warmed plates.

3 Add about half the cider to the pan with the lemon grass and reduce over a high heat. Once reduced, remove the lemon grass and add the single cream to make a thick sauce seasoning well with salt and a touch of pepper.

4 Pour the sauce over the rabbit portions. Garnish with coriander, if you like. Serve with baby roast vegetables and parsnip purée.

smoked loin of venison with liquorice and game jus, grilled polenta, morel mushrooms, runner beans and pears

NOTE: The saddle of venison will yield 2 striploins and 2 fillets. This recipe requires about 600 g (1 lb 5 oz) of meat which would be the loins of a small saddle; use the fillets for another meal.

1 small boned saddle of venison, bones reserved (see note)
olive oil, for marinating
finely sliced cloves garlic, to taste

LIQUORICE AND GAME JUS
12 morel mushrooms, dried
bones and trimmings from the saddle of venison, roughly chopped, about 450 g (1 lb)
30 ml (2 tbsp) olive oil
2 sticks celery, roughly chopped
2 carrots, roughly chopped
1 onion, roughly chopped
salt and freshly ground black pepper
1.4 litres (2½ pints) well-flavoured chicken stock
6 tomatoes, roughly chopped
30 ml (2 tbsp) tomato paste
1 sprig of thyme
10 ml (2 tsp) liquorice extract

GRILLED POLENTA
100 g (3½ oz) polenta
knob of butter
fresh herbs, finely chopped
oil, for greasing

TO SERVE
1 pear, sliced
50 g (2 oz) runner beans, sliced diagonally and blanched

1 Marinate the venison in olive oil and garlic overnight, or for up to 7 days.
2 Cook the polenta according to the instructions on the packet. Fold in the butter and herbs. Pour the polenta into an oiled dish and leave to cool for about 30 minutes.
3 Make the liquorice and game jus. Soak the morel mushrooms in warm water for 30 minutes. Place the bones and trimmings from the venison in a roasting tin, and drizzle with olive oil. Roast in a preheated oven at 200°C (400°F) mark 6 for about 15 minutes, turning frequently. Add the celery, carrots and onion to the roasting tin with a little salt; continue to roast for another 15 minutes until browned. Drain off any oil and deglaze the pan with 125 ml (4 fl oz) of the chicken stock. Remove the mushrooms from the soaking liquid and set aside, reserving the liquid.
4 Transfer the contents of the roasting tin to a large saucepan. Add the remaining chicken stock, the tomatoes, tomato paste, thyme and mushroom soaking liquid. Simmer for about 45 minutes, then strain a damp muslin cloth into a clean saucepan. Add the morel mushrooms and liquorice extract and cook for about 30 minutes until reduced to the desired consistency.
5 Meanwhile, cook the venison in a smoker for 15 minutes then turn off the heat and leave to rest for about 15 minutes. The venison should still be red in the middle. Slice the venison.
6 Remove the mushrooms from the jus with a slotted spoon; reserve 4 for garnish and roughly chop the remainder.
7 Cut the polenta into 4 circles using a 7.5 cm (3 inch) cutter. Grill the polenta under a preheated grill until lightly browned.
8 To serve, place a circle of grilled polenta in the centre of each plate. Top with a few slices of pear. Arrange the sliced venison on top of the pears in a fan. Place a morel mushroom on top. Spoon the jus around the plate and add the beans and remaining morel mushrooms.

marinated wild boar in a rich port wine sauce
with poached pears and onion spätzle

500 g (1 lb 2 oz) wild boar
tenderloin
90 ml (6 tbsp) akvavit/schnapps
1 large bay leaf
1 large sprig of thyme
4 whole allspice
4 mixed peppercorns
4 juniper berries
4 cloves
4 pine shoots (the new buds of a
pine tree)
50 g (2 oz) unsalted butter
30 ml (2 tbsp) light oil

POACHED PEARS AND PORT
SAUCE
2 firm pears
400 ml (14 fl oz) full-bodied red
wine
120 ml (4 fl oz) port
juice of 1 orange
juice of ¼ lemon
1 sprig of thyme
1 clove garlic, crushed
50 g (2 oz) each of roughly
chopped carrots, celery, leek and
fennel
50 g (2 oz) white onion
1 stalk lemon grass, crushed
4 leaves of lemon verbena
(optional)
1 star anise
20 ml (4 tsp) red wine vinegar
2 thin slivers of fresh root ginger
300 ml (½ pint) beef glacé
(thickened beef stock)
salt and freshly ground black
pepper

1 Wash and trim the boar tenderloin and place in a bowl. Add the akvavit, bay leaf and sprig of thyme. Crush the allspice, peppercorns, juniper berries, cloves and pine shoots in a mortar and pestle and add to the bowl. Stir the marinade, cover and allow to marinate in a cool place for about 1 hour, turning occasionally.

2 Peel the pears, cut lengthways into quarters and core. Reserve all the trimmings. Cut each quarter into 3 slices.

3 Put the wine, port, orange juice and lemon juice in a shallow pan and heat. Add the pear slices and simmer for 2–4 minutes until coloured but still firm. Take out the pears with a slotted spoon and set aside.

4 Boil the wine mixture until it is reduced by half. Add the thyme, garlic, chopped carrots, celery, leek, fennel, onion, lemon grass, lemon verbena (if using), star anise, red wine vinegar, pear trimmings, ginger and beef glacé. Reduce again by half until the sauce is thick and coats the back of a spoon. Strain, return to the pan and season; keep the sauce warm and covered.

5 To make the spätzle: Heat a knob of the butter in a frying pan and cook the onion until soft. Set aside to cool. Put the pasta flour in a bowl, add the eggs, salt and 150 ml (¼ pint) cold water. Mix for at least 1 minute until smooth. Add the cooled onion to the dough and mix well. In a large pan bring salted water and the oil to the boil. Push the spätzle mixture through the press and into the water as quickly as possible. When the spätzle rise to the surface, after about 30 seconds, drain immediately and refresh in cold water. Set aside.

6 Cook the tenderloin. Melt the butter and oil in a frying pan and quickly seal the tenderloin on all sides. Turn the heat down and gently fry for 10–15 minutes, turning occasionally, ensuring that the meat is still pink inside.

7 Meanwhile, melt the remaining spätzle butter in a pan and gently warm the spätzle constantly tossing them. Just before serving, add the chopped parsley and plenty of freshly ground black pepper. Gently reheat the port sauce, check the seasoning and warm the pear slices in the microwave oven for 20 seconds.

8 Take the boar out of the pan and cut it into 1 cm thick slices.

9 Place a portion of spätzle in the centre of each plate. Arrange 3 slices of boar in a circle on top of the spätzle and fan the pear slices out between the slices of meat. Pour the sauce around the spätzle, taking care not to pour it on them.

INGREDIENTS CONTINUED ON
FACING PAGE

SPÄTZLE

100 g (3½ oz) unsalted butter
150 g (5 oz) very finely chopped
white onion
200 g (7 oz) pasta flour
2 large free-range eggs
2.5 ml (½ tsp) salt
30 ml (2 tbsp) groundnut oil
50 g (2 oz) finely chopped parsley

NOTES: If you have trouble finding akvavit, use vodka and add a couple of caraway seeds for flavour. Using a spätzle press is preferable to achieve well-formed spätzle.

venison steaks in a red wine sauce

SERVES 2

15 ml (1 tbsp) vegetable oil
2 steaks of venison, weighing
175 g (6 oz) each

SAUCE

250 ml (8 fl oz) red wine
1 small onion, finely chopped
1 small carrot, finely chopped
1 celery stick, chopped
1 bouquet garni
1 clove
2 juniper berries
15 ml (1 tbsp) redcurrant jelly
5 ml (1 tsp) cornflour
salt and freshly ground black
pepper
chopped fresh parsley, to garnish

TO SERVE

game chips
baby carrots
button Brussels sprouts

1 Make the sauce. Combine the wine, onion, carrot, celery and bouquet garni in a saucepan. Bring to the boil and then simmer for 25 minutes.

2 Heat the oil in a frying pan and fry the steaks for 3 to 4 minutes each side.

3 Strain the sauce and wipe out the pan with paper towels. Replace the sauce in the pan and boil rapidly for 5 minutes with the clove, juniper berries and redcurrant jelly until reduced.

4 Blend the cornflour with a little water to make a thick paste, and add to the sauce, stirring. When the sauce has thickened, remove the pan from the heat. Taste for seasoning.

5 Transfer the cooked venison to warmed serving plates and pour the sauce over. Garnish with freshly chopped parsley. Serve with game chips, baby carrots and button Brussels sprouts.

roast loin of roe deer wrapped in prosciutto on a bed of leek julienne with a fennel mash

½ saddle of roe deer, trimmed
1 sprig of rosemary, torn into small sprigs
2 cloves garlic, thinly sliced
25 g (1 oz) bacon fat, slivered
salt and freshly ground black pepper
6 slices prosciutto
50 g (2 oz) unsalted butter
30 ml (2 tbsp) olive oil
240 ml (8 fl oz) red wine

LEEK JULIENNE
25 g (1 oz) butter
2 leeks, finely sliced lengthwise

FENNEL MASH
450 g (1 lb) potatoes, quartered
15 ml (1 tbsp) olive oil
1 fennel bulb, finely sliced lengthwise
50 g (2 oz) butter

1 Place the venison on a board, and make small incisions along the grain of the meat; insert the rosemary, garlic and bacon fat. Season with salt and pepper.

2 Spread a sheet of nonstick baking parchment on the work surface, and arrange half the prosciutto slices on it, overlapping. Place the loin on the prosciutto, then arrange the remaining prosciutto slices on top to cover the venison completely. Secure with string if necessary.

3 Heat the butter and oil in a heavy–based roasting tin and seal the wrapped venison on all sides. Add half the red wine and roast in a pre-heated oven at 220°C (425°F) mark 7 for 20 minutes. Turn the meat over and roast for a further 15 minutes.

4 Prepare the leeks: melt the butter in a gratin dish and place the leeks in the dish, gently tossing to coat. Season well, cover with foil, and cook in the oven for 20 minutes with the venison. Remove the foil and cook for a further 10 minutes until just soft.

5 Meanwhile, prepare the fennel mash: boil the potatoes until tender in a large pan of salted water. Heat the olive oil in a frying pan and fry the fennel gently until golden and soft. Drain the potatoes and mash with the cooked fennel, butter and seasoning.

6 Test the venison for rare by pressing in the middle of the loin. It should feel soft and giving. For medium to well done cook for a further 5–10 minutes. Remove from the pan and let stand for at least 5 minutes. Deglaze the tin with the remainder of the red wine. Slice the meat and arrange on warmed plates, on a bed of leeks; serve with the jus and fennel mash.

MAIN COURSES:
MEAT

roast striploin of lincoln red beef with mustard and basil gravy

900 g (2 lb) striploin of Lincoln red beef

flour for dusting

1.25 ml (¼ tsp) dry English mustard, plus extra for dusting

salt and freshly ground black pepper

300 ml (½ pint) well-flavoured beef stock

15 ml (1 tbsp) cornflour

2.5 ml (½ tsp) freeze dried basil

2.5 ml (½ tsp) smooth Dijon mustard

5 ml (1 tsp) wholegrain Dijon mustard

small handful of chopped fresh basil

TO SERVE

broad beans with herb butter

spinach

Horseradish Mashed Potatoes (see page 156)

1 Score the fat on the meat. Dust the lean surfaces of the meat with a mixture of flour, English mustard and pepper.

2 Heat a frying pan until hot and seal all the sides of the meat. Place the meat in a roasting tin with the fat uppermost and roast in a preheated oven at 245°C (475°F) mark 9 for 15 minutes.

3 Lower the oven temperature to 190°C (375°F) mark 5 for 45 minutes. Check the meat and if too rare cook for a further 15 minutes. Allow to rest before carving.

4 To prepare the gravy, whisk the stock, cornflour, English mustard, dried basil and two Dijon mustards together. Bring slowly to the boil and allow to thicken. Check the seasoning.

5 Just before serving. add the chopped basil to the sauce and allow to heat through.

6 Serve the meat with broad beans with herb butter, spinach and horseradish mashed potatoes.

fillet of beef wrapped in parma ham served on a bed of creamed spinach with a red wine sauce

whole fillet of beef, weighing
900 g (2 lb)
50 g (2 oz) prosciutto fat
2 cloves garlic, finely sliced
fresh rosemary leaves
6 slices Parma ham
about 25 ml (1 fl oz) olive oil
about 25 g (1 oz) butter
100 g (3½ oz) young spinach
leaves
a little cream

RED WINE SAUCE
15 ml (1 tbsp) olive oil
4 shallots, finely chopped
1 clove garlic, finely chopped
splash of red wine vinegar
splash of cognac
50 ml (2 fl oz) port
600 ml (1 pint) veal stock
1 bottle of red wine
15 ml (1 tbsp) of fresh tomato
purée
salt and freshly ground black
pepper
25 g (1 oz) unsalted butter, chilled

TO SERVE
Mustard Soufflé Jackets (see
page 155)
Glazed Baby Onions (see
page 148)
Mirepoix of Carrot and Celeriac

1 Make the red wine marinade. Heat the oil in a frying pan and cook the shallots and garlic until softened. Add the vinegar and reduce until virtually disappeared; add the cognac and port and reduce again. Add the veal stock, red wine, and tomato purée and simmer, skimming any scum from the surface from time to time, until reduced to 600 ml (1 pint).

2 Marinate the beef for 24 hours in the red wine stock.

3 Remove the beef from the marinade and stud all over with prosciutto fat, garlic and rosemary. Wrap the beef in Parma ham slices and tie with string. Heat the olive oil and butter in a heavy-based casserole and brown the beef on all sides.

4 Add the marinade to the casserole and bring to the boil, place the beef in the casserole, cover and simmer for 35 minutes until rare; it will give gently to the touch. Remove the beef and keep warm.

5 Boil the marinade to reduce by three quarters, taste for seasoning, then whisk in cubes of chilled butter to make a smooth sauce.

6 Blanch the spinach leaves for 1 minute in boiling water, then squeeze dry in a clean tea towel. Reheat in a small pan with cream and seasoning.

7 Place the creamed spinach in the centre of warmed serving plates, slice the beef into 2.5 cm (1 inch) slices and place on the spinach. Pour the sauce over and serve with mustard jacket soufflé potatoes, glazed baby onions and carrot and celeriac.

sirloin of highland beef with pepper cheese and pastry

120 g (4 oz) plain flour
40 g (1½ oz) unsalted butter
15 g (½ oz) lard
pinch of salt
25 g (1 oz) grated smoked cheese
1 egg
flour, for dusting
milk, for brushing
knob of butter, plus extra for greasing
700 g (1½ lb) boned sirloin Highland beef, cut into 4 round steaks
175 g (6 oz) creamed pepper cheese, cut into 4 slices

MERLOT AND BLACKBERRY JELLY SAUCE
300 ml (½ pint) Merlot wine
300 ml (½ pint) veal stock
10 ml (2 tsp) blackberry jelly
salt and freshly ground black pepper

TO SERVE
Creamed Celeriac (see page 157)
Blackberry Glazed Shallots (see page 148)

1 Place the flour, butter, lard and salt into a food processor and process to fine breadcrumb stage. Place the mixture in a bowl and stir in the grated cheese. Bind together with the egg, mixed with 30 ml (2 tbsp) cold water. Turn the dough out onto a floured board and knead lightly. Wrap in cling film and chill for 1 hour.

2 Roll out the pastry and cut into four 7.5 cm (3 inch) rounds; decorate with pastry leaf shapes, and brush with milk. Place the pastry on a greased baking tin and prick the rounds once or twice with a fork.

3 Heat a little butter in a frying pan and fry the steaks on both sides and edges, for no more than 1 minute. Place in an ovenproof dish.

4 Make the sauce: pour the wine into the frying pan used for the steak, add the stock and reduce slowly. Add the blackberry jelly and season to taste.

5 Place the pastry on the top shelf in a preheated oven at 220°C (425°F) mark 7 and cook for 8–10 minutes until light brown. Place the steaks on the bottom shelf of the oven and cook for about 8 minutes.

6 To serve, place the steaks on warmed serving plates, place a round of pepper cheese on each steak, and top with a pastry round. Serve at once with the wine and blackberry jelly sauce and the creamed celeriac and blackberry glazed shallots.

fillet of beef with sherry sauce

1 whole beef fillet, preferably
organic, about 400–450 g
(14 oz–1 lb)
15–30 ml (1–2 tbsp) olive oil, for
pan frying

CREAMED PARSLEY QUENELLES
1 large bunch curly leaf parsley,
stalks removed
1 bunch (same volume as parsley)
spinach, stalks removed
75 ml (5 tbsp) double cream
sea salt and freshly ground black
pepper
squeeze lemon juice (optional)

SAUCE
400 ml (14 fl oz) sherry (medium
dry e.g. Amontillado)
15 ml (1 tbsp) olive oil
2–3 shallots
2 bay leaves
6 peppercorns
sprig of oregano
5 ml (1 tsp) sherry vinegar
400 ml (14 fl oz) well-flavoured
brown chicken stock

DEEP–FRIED GARLIC CLOVES
24 cloves garlic
250 ml (9 fl oz) chicken stock
seasoned flour, for coating
1 egg, beaten
breadcrumbs, for coating
500 ml (16 fl oz) sunflower oil

CARROT CAKES
25 g (1 oz) butter
1 medium parsnip, coarsely grated
500 g (1 lb 2 oz) carrots, coarsely
grated
30 g (1 oz) white breadcrumbs
15 ml (1 tbsp) cornflour
2.5 ml (½ tsp) chopped mint

1 Trim the beef to make a nice even piece, reserving the trimmings. Wrap the beef in cling film in a neat cylinder shape and put in refrigerator to firm up for 2 hours.

2 Make the parsley quenelles. Bring a pan of water to the boil and blanch the parsley for 4 minutes, adding the spinach after 1 minute. Drain well, but do not refresh in cold water. Cool, and dry thoroughly by wrapping in a tea towel or muslin and squeezing. The parsley-water can be reserved to use in green mash (see below). Meanwhile, boil the cream down until reduced by half.

3 Process the spinach and parsley to a purée, add the cream, seasoning and lemon juice if you like and process again, then chill until needed. To make quenelles, form the creamed parsley between 2 teaspoons.

4 To make the sauce, put the sherry in a saucepan and reduce to a syrup. In another saucepan, heat the olive oil. Add the shallots, beef trimmings, bay leaves, peppercorns and oregano and fry until the shallots are well caramelized. Deglaze with the sherry syrup and sherry vinegar, then add the chicken stock and reduce until a rich brown jus has formed. Strain through muslin, taste to check seasoning, and set aside.

5 Make the deep–fried garlic cloves. Place the garlic in a saucepan. Cover with cold water, bring gently to the boil, drain, cover with fresh water and repeat. Then return them to the pan, cover with chicken stock, bring to the boil and simmer gently for about 10 minutes until soft but not collapsed. Drain, reserving the stock for the green mash (see below). Roll them in seasoned flour, then egg, then breadcrumbs. When you are ready to serve them, heat the sunflower oil in a deep saucepan until a cube of bread dropped in sizzles and carefully fry the cloves in batches, draining on paper towels.

6 Make the carrot cakes. Heat the butter in a pan and cook the parsnip and carrots for a couple of minutes until softened. Tip them into a bowl and mix in the breadcrumbs, cornflour, mint, oregano and seasoning. Shape the mixture into 4 patties. Heat the olive oil in a frying pan and fry the patties over a low heat, until a crust has formed on both sides. Drain on paper towels and keep warm until needed.

7 Make the green mash. Rinse the potato chunks under cold water. Place in a large saucepan, cover with the reserved cooking liquids and water and bring to the boil. Simmer for 12–15 minutes until tender, then add the spinach and cook for 30 seconds. Drain well, reserving a little of the liquid. Return to the pan and shake to dry slightly. Mash the potatoes and spinach with the butter, nutmeg, lemon juice and seasoning to taste. If it is too dry, add a little of the cooking liquid. Keep warm.

8 Cut the beef into 4 even-sized slices and season with salt and pepper. Heat a little olive oil in a frying pan and sear the beef all over, then cook until done to your preference. Test by pressing with a finger; the meat should spring back slightly.

2.5 ml (½ tsp) chopped oregano
15 ml (1 tbsp) olive oil

GREEN MASH
3 large potatoes, peeled and cut into chunks
80 g (3 oz) spinach, stalks removed
80 g (3 oz) butter, chopped
freshly grated nutmeg
squeeze lemon juice

9 Remove the meat and wrap in greaseproof paper. Allow to rest for 5–10 minutes. Reheat the sherry sauce and pour the juices from the beef into the sauce.

10 To serve, place a dollop of green mash on each plate, top with a carrot cake, followed by the beef. Trickle a little sauce over the top. Place a parsley quenelle on each of the steaks, surround with deep-fried garlic and finally drizzle a little sauce around each plate.

saturday beef

SAUCE
25 g (1 oz) butter
4 shallots, chopped
300 ml (½ pint) chicken stock
300 ml (½ pint) beef stock
150 ml (¼ pint) red wine
50 ml (2 fl oz) port
50 ml (2 fl oz) red wine vinegar
sprig of thyme
1 bay leaf, torn
salt and freshly ground black pepper
50 g (2 oz) clarified butter
700 g (1½ lb) sirloin or rib eye of Aberdeen Angus

TO SERVE
Fricassée of Mushrooms (see page 166)
Pommes Savoyarde (see page 156)

1 Heat half the butter in a large pan and sauté the shallots until soft. Add the chicken and beef stocks, the wine, port, vinegar, thyme and bay leaf to the pan, bring to the boil and reduce to thicken. Stir in the remaining butter and taste for seasoning. Remove and discard the thyme and bay leaf and keep the sauce warm.

2 Melt the clarified butter in a large pan; season the beef well and add to the pan. Seal the beef over a high heat to brown on all sides. Place the beef in a preheated oven at 200°C (400°F) mark 6 for about 40 minutes or until done to preference.

3 Let the beef rest for 5 minutes and carve into thick slices. Fan the meat slices on 4 warmed plates and serve with the fricassée of mushrooms and Pommes Savoyarde. Pour the sauce over the meat.

fillet steak with elderberry sauce

20 ml (4 tsp) olive oil
30 ml (2 tbsp) elderberry wine
freshly chopped thyme
freshly chopped parsley
4 fillet steaks from the tail end,
weighing about 150 g (5 oz) each
clarified butter (ghee)

ELDERBERRY SAUCE
1 shallot, finely chopped
100 ml (3½ fl oz) elderberry wine
30 ml (2 tbsp) preserved
elderberries
150 ml (¼ pint) well-flavoured
beef stock
salt and freshly ground black
pepper

TO SERVE
Spinach Creams (see page 163)

1 Mix the oil and the elderberry wine with thyme and parsley to taste in a shallow dish and marinate the steaks, turning occasionally, for 2 hours.

2 Heat a little clarified butter in a frying pan until very hot and fry the steaks for about 5 minutes on each side, or until done to your liking.

3 Allow the steaks to rest in a warm oven for at least 10 minutes.

4 Add the shallot to the pan, and fry for about 1 minute. Add the wine to deglaze, then the elderberries and stock. Cook for 5 minutes, and check the seasoning. Serve the venison steaks with spinach creams, and the elderberry sauce.

calves livers with cassis sauce, savoy cabbage parcels and garlic mashed potato

12 leaves Savoy cabbage, 4
whole, 8 finely sliced
2 rashers streaky bacon, finely
chopped
about 50 g (2 oz) butter
175 g (6 oz) shallots, chopped
15–20 juniper berries, crushed
15 ml (1 tbsp) chicken stock
450 g (1 lb) floury potatoes
1 clove garlic
30 ml (2 tbsp) cream
salt and freshly ground black
pepper
1 glass red wine
4 calves liver slices, about 175 g
(6 oz) each
15 ml (1 tbsp) crème de cassis
blackcurrants to garnish

1 To make the cabbage parcels, butter 4 ramekins. Blanch the whole cabbage leaves in boiling water until soft. Fry the bacon until crispy. Heat a knob of butter in a separate pan, and fry ⅔ of the shallots until soft. Add the bacon, the sliced cabbage and juniper berries. Add the stock and cook for 1–2 minutes until the stock has almost evaporated.

2 Line the ramekins with the blanched cabbage leaves, and fill will the cabbage mixture. Fold the leaves over the top of the ramekins and steam for 20 minutes.

3 Put the potatoes and garlic in a large pan of salted water and boil until tender. Drain and mash the potatoes and garlic with a little butter, the cream and seasoning.

4 Heat a little butter and fry the remaining shallots until soft; add the wine and reduce to one third the quantity.

5 Heat a separate pan with a little butter and sear the calves' liver for about 2 minutes each side, until pink in the middle. Remove and keep warm.

6 Add the wine reduction to the liver juices with the crème de cassis; warm through and strain onto 4 warmed serving plates. Arrange the liver, cabbage parcels and mash on the sauce. Garnish with blackcurrants, if available.

loin of lamb on fragrant fruity couscous, spicy apricot sauce and balsamic reduction

5 ml (1 tsp) Malden salt
2 garlic cloves, crushed
2 sprigs rosemary, finely chopped
30 ml (2 tbsp) olive oil
900 g (2 lb) loin of lamb
250 ml (8 fl oz) balsamic vinegar

APRICOT SAUCE
25 g (1 oz) unsalted butter
75 g (3 oz) shallots, sliced
1 garlic clove, crushed
5 ml (1 tsp) turmeric
2.5 ml (½ tsp) ground cumin
2.5 ml (½ tsp) ground coriander
120 g (4 oz) ready to eat apricots, diced
5 ml (1 tsp) soft brown sugar
150 ml (¼ pint) chicken stock

COUSCOUS
25 g (1 oz) unsalted butter
5 ml (1 tsp) soft brown sugar
2.5 ml (½ tsp) ground cinnamon
5 ml (1 tsp) ground cumin
5 ml (1 tsp) ground coriander
425 ml (¾ pint) chicken stock
25 g (1 oz) couscous
50 g (2 oz) toasted pine nuts
25 g (1 oz) raisins
1 apple, peeled and chopped
15 ml (1 tbsp) lemon juice
45 ml (3 tbsp) olive oil
1 bunch coriander, chopped
salt and freshly ground black pepper

1 Mix the Malden salt and garlic together to a paste, add the rosemary and the olive oil. Pour the marinade over the lamb, and rub in with your fingers. Cover and set aside until ready to cook.

2 To make the sauce, melt the butter in a saucepan, add the shallots and garlic and allow to soften without colouring. Stir in the turmeric, cumin and ground coriander, then the apricots and sugar. Cook for 2 minutes.

3 Add the chicken stock, bring to the boil and simmer for 20 minutes until the apricots are tender. If the sauce looks too thick, dilute with boiled water to the desired consistency. Place the apricot mixture in a food processor and process until smooth, then pass through a fine sieve. Set aside and keep warm.

4 Meanwhile, boil the vinegar in a saucepan until it has reduced by half. Set aside and keep warm.

5 To cook the lamb, heat a large frying pan and add the lamb, cooking for 4 minutes on each side. Remove from the heat and leave to rest in a warm place for 10 minutes.

6 Meanwhile, make the couscous. Melt the butter in a large saucepan add the sugar, cinnamon, cumin and ground coriander and cook for 20 minutes, taking care not to burn the butter. Add the chicken stock and bring to the boil. Stir in the couscous, pine nuts and raisins. Remove from the heat and place the chopped apple on top. Cover with a tea towel and the saucepan lid. After 5 minutes, add the lemon juice, olive oil and coriander, check the seasoning and place on warmed serving plates.

7 To serve, slice the lamb and place on the bed of couscous surrounded by apricot sauce drizzled with the balsamic reduction.

braised lamb shank

15–30 ml (1–2 tbsp) olive oil
1 onion, quartered
sprigs of rosemary
4 lamb shanks
300 ml (½ pint) lamb stock or water
5 heads of garlic
8–10 cardamom pods, lightly crushed
450 g (1 lb) dried butter, haricot and/or cannellini beans, soaked and drained
16–20 small potatoes
75 g (3 oz) butter, softened
salt and freshly ground black pepper
oil, for deep frying
1 small beetroot, finely julienned
1 carrot, finely julienned
40 g (1½ oz) chilled butter, diced

1 Heat the oil in a frying pan, add the onion and some sprigs of rosemary. Sauté to flavour the oil. Remove the onion and rosemary with a slotted spoon and transfer to a roasting tin, large enough for the lamb shanks.

2 Fry the lamb shanks in the flavoured oil until browned on all sides. Transfer them to the roasting tin and add the stock and 1 head of garlic, some sprigs of rosemary and the cardamom. Cover the tin with foil and cook in a preheated oven at 200°C (400°F) mark 6 for 2 hours, basting regularly.

3 Put the beans in a saucepan and cook in salted water for about 45 minutes until tender; drain and purée.

4 With a knife, shape the potatoes into 2.5 cm (1 inch) cylinders. Place in a casserole with the softened butter. Add enough water to half cover the potatoes and season. Cover the casserole and cook for 10–15 minutes. Turn the potatoes, and add the remainder of the garlic, in the skin but broken into segments. Place in the oven and cook for a further 25–30 minutes.

5 Deep fry the beetroot and carrot in small batches for 1–2 minutes and drain on paper towels. Set aside.

6 Transfer the lamb shanks to a plate and keep warm. Strain the juices from the roasting tin into a saucepan and reduce. Add the chilled butter and whisk well.

7 Place the bean purée in the centre of warmed serving plates, put a lamb shank on top and arrange the potatoes and garlic around. Spoon the lamb jus over the potato and garlic, and top the lamb with the beetroot and carrot.

pan–fried lambs' liver with creamed potatoes and caramelized aubergine

SERVES 2
450 g (1 lb) lambs' liver
about 125 ml (4 fl oz) virgin olive oil

CREAMED POTATOES
2 large potatoes
salt and freshly ground black pepper
40 ml (1½ fl oz) double cream
25 g (1 oz) fresh chives, chopped

AUBERGINE
1 aubergine, sliced diagonally

1 Cook the potatoes in a pan of boiling salted water for about 20 minutes until soft.

2 Cover the aubergine slices in sea salt and the thyme and leave to stand for about 20 minutes.

3 Meanwhile, make the sauce; heat 30 ml (2 tbsp) of the olive oil in a large pan and cook the shallots until soft. Add the peppercorns, garlic powder, coriander seeds and stir for a minute or two, until aromatic. Add the chunks of lambs' liver, the lamb stock, wine, both vinegars, Worcestershire sauce, sugar, honey, brandy, port, soya sauce, walnut oil, mustard, bay leaf and saffron. Add the salt, pepper and thyme and simmer gently for about 30 minutes.

4 Make the shallot confit; heat the butter with a little olive oil and fry the shallots until soft and golden. Add the honey and balsamic vinegar and cook over a low heat, stirring frequently, until mixture reaches a

25 g (1 oz) sea salt

sprig of thyme, leaves chopped

SAUCE

6 shallots, sliced

5 ml (1 tsp) pink peppercorns

5 ml (1 tsp) garlic powder

2.5 ml (½ tsp) coriander seeds

175 g (6 oz) trimmed lambs' liver, cut into chunks

200 ml (⅓ pint) lamb stock

150 ml (¼ pint) good red cooking wine

45 ml (3 tbsp) balsamic vinegar

25 ml (1½ tbsp) red wine vinegar

25 ml (1½ tbsp) Worcestershire sauce

15 g (½ oz) demerara sugar

15 ml (1 tbsp) honey

10 ml (½ tbsp) brandy

10 ml (½ tbsp) port

10 ml (½ tbsp) soya sauce

5 ml (1 tsp) walnut oil

2.5 ml (½ tsp) coarse–grain mustard

1 bay leaf

pinch of saffron

10 ml (2 tsp) cooking salt

7.5 ml (1½ tsp) freshly ground black pepper

2 sprigs of thyme

25 g (1 oz) fresh chives, chopped

SHALLOT CONFIT

15 g (½ oz) unsalted butter

8 shallots, sliced

15 ml (1 tbsp) honey

45 ml (3 tbsp) balsamic vinegar

CABBAGE AND PEAS

15 g (½ oz) unsalted butter

100 g (3½ oz) unsmoked ham, very finely sliced

150 g (5 oz) cabbage, very finely sliced

120 g (4 oz) fresh peas

syrupy consistency.

5 To cook the cabbage, heat the butter with a little olive oil in a large saucepan and cook the ham for about a minute, stirring, until beginning to brown. Add the cabbage and peas and cook over a moderate heat for 2–3 minutes until the cabbage and peas are tender but not soft.

6 Drain the potatoes and mash with a little seasoning. Add the cream and chives and mash until blended.

7 Scrape the salt off the aubergine slices and pat dry with a paper towel. Heat a little of the olive oil in a frying pan and fry the aubergine slices for about 2 minutes each side. Place the aubergine in a preheated oven at 180°C (350°F) mark 4 for a few minutes before serving.

8 Heat a little of the oil in a frying pan and fry the lambs' liver for 3 minutes on each side, remove from the pan and drain over a rack. Place the lamb in the preheated oven at 180°C (350°F) mark 4 for a few minutes before serving.

9 Remove the sauce from the heat and carefully purée with a hand–held blender, then pass through a fine sieve into a clean pan. Reheat the sauce, and add the chives just before serving.

10 Serve the liver and aubergines on warmed serving plates, with the cabbage and creamed potatoes. Pour the sauce over, as desired, and drizzle the shallot confit around.

fillet of lamb with a mushroom and olive stuffing

SERVES 2

1 whole lamb fillet
15 ml (1 tbsp) olive oil
285 ml (9½ fl oz) beef or lamb
stock
95 ml (3 fl oz) red wine
7.5 ml (½ tbsp) pitted black olives,
cut into slices
7.5 ml (½ tbsp) butter
flat–leaf parsley to garnish

STUFFING

15 ml (1 tbsp) light olive oil
½ onion, finely chopped
15 ml (1 tbsp) finely chopped
garlic
55 g (2 oz) button mushrooms,
finely sliced
salt and ground black pepper
15 ml (1 tbsp) pitted black olives,
chopped
15 ml (1 tbsp) chopped flat–leaf
parsley
7.5 ml (½ tbsp) chopped rosemary

TO SERVE

Goats' Cheese Mash (see page
157)
Chargrilled Mediterranean
Vegetables (see page 150)

1 To make the stuffing, heat the oil in a saucepan over a moderate heat. Add the onion and garlic and gently cook for 5 minutes, then add the mushroom and a little salt. Cook for a further 5 minutes until the mushrooms are soft and the juices have evaporated.

2 Place the mixture in a sieve so that any excess liquid drains out. Place in a food processor and add the olives, parsley and rosemary, and process to a rough purée. Season to taste and set aside.

3 Cut a pocket in the lamb fillet, season lightly, and spread the stuffing in the centre, reserving 15 ml (1 tbsp) of the mixture. Fold the meat closed and tie with kitchen string.

4 Heat the oil in a frying pan and brown the lamb on all sides. Transfer to a roasting tin and place in a preheated oven at 200°C (400°F) mark 6 for 15 minutes for medium rare, 25 minutes for well done.

5 Meanwhile, boil the stock over a high heat until reduced by half, adding the reserved stuffing mixture.

6 Transfer the lamb to a warm plate, cover with foil, and let it rest in a warm place.

7 Stir the wine into the roasting tin to deglaze and boil over a high heat until the mixture reaches a syrupy consistency. Add the reduced stock, bring to the boil, and stir until it coats the back of a spoon. Strain into a clean pan, add the olives and stir in the butter. Keep warm.

8 Cut the lamb into slices and arrange on warmed serving plates. Garnish with parsley, and serve with the sauce, accompanied by the goats' cheese mash and chargrilled Mediterranean vegetables.

FILLET OF LAMB WITH A MUSHROOM AND OLIVE STUFFING ILLUSTRATED ON PREVIOUS PAGES

fillet of aberdeenshire lamb with red wine and port gravy, anchovy sauce and rosemary

1 tin of anchovies in oil
2 cloves garlic, crushed
50 ml (2 fl oz) olive oil
150 ml (5 fl oz) double cream
handful of chopped parsley
30 ml (2 tbsp) oil, for sealing
3 fillets of lamb
30 ml (2 tbsp) red wine vinegar
sprig of rosemary
salt and freshly ground black pepper
1 glass red wine
½ glass port
15 ml (1 tbsp) butter
sprigs of thyme and parsley, to garnish

TO SERVE
Red Onions and Potato (see page 149)

1 Place the anchovies with their oil, the garlic and olive oil in a saucepan and simmer over a very low heat for 15 minutes, stirring constantly. Add the cream and parsley, whisk in well and allow to thicken over a low heat. Remove the pan from the heat and set aside. Reheat the anchovy sauce just before serving.

2 Heat the oil in a frying pan, and sear the lamb fillets on all sides; add the vinegar, rosemary and seasoning. Cook the lamb for about 4 minutes on each side.

3 Transfer the lamb and juices to a roasting tin and cook in a preheated oven at 200°C (400°F) mark 6 for 10–15 minutes according to taste. Remove and allow to stand for 10 minutes.

4 Deglaze the pan with the wine and port and stir over a high heat until reduced by half. Beat in the butter and then strain.

5 Slice the lamb into thick slices, garnish with thyme and parsley, and serve with the red onions and potato, the anchovy sauce and the red wine gravy.

fillet of lamb with port and redcurrant sauce

SERVES 2
1 fillet of lamb
oil, for brushing and pan frying
salt and freshly ground black pepper
300 ml (½ pint) well-flavoured lamb stock
50 ml (2 fl oz) port
5 ml (1 tsp) redcurrant jelly
few sprigs redcurrants plus extra redcurrants without stalks
sprigs of rosemary, to garnish

TO SERVE
Camargue Rice (see page 152)
Seasonal Green Vegetables (see page 166)

1 Brush the lamb fillet with oil and season. Heat a drizzle of oil in a frying pan and fry the lamb for 7 minutes, turning in order to brown all sides. Remove the fillet, cover with foil, and keep warm.

2 Add the stock to the pan with the port and redcurrant jelly. Reduce to a syrup over a high heat and add the redcurrants.

3 Slice the lamb, adding any meat juices to the sauce, and serve on warmed serving plates garnished with sprigs of redcurrants and rosemary.

roast rack of lamb with thyme and a red wine sauce

30 ml (2 tbsp) olive oil
salt and freshly ground black pepper
2 racks of lamb (total of 12 bones), French trimmed
1 shallot, chopped
1 clove garlic, chopped
bunch of thyme
100 ml (3½ fl oz) full–bodied red wine
200 ml (7 fl oz) brown chicken stock
50 g (2 oz) butter, chilled and cut into cubes

TO SERVE
Mediterranean Vegetable Gâteau (see page 148)
Griddled Potatoes (see page 154)

1 Heat the oil in an ovenproof frying pan or heavy–based roasting tin; season the lamb and sear on all sides in the hot oil. Remove the lamb from the pan and reduce the heat.
2 Cook the shallot and garlic in the same pan until soft and golden.
3 Reserve a few sprigs of thyme for the garnish, put the rest on top of the shallot and garlic. Place the lamb on top and roast in a preheated oven at 230°C (450°F) mark 8 for 20 minutes. Remove the lamb and cover loosely with foil.
4 To make the sauce, remove most of the thyme from the pan, then add the wine to deglaze. Boil over a high heat to reduce by half. Add the stock, bring back to the boil and reduce to a sauce consistency. Season to taste, then strain. Reheat and whisk in the butter.
5 To serve, carve the lamb and place 3 cutlets on each plate. Pour the sauce over and garnish with the reserved thyme; serve with Mediterranean vegetable gâteau and griddled potatoes.

pan-fried herbed welsh lamb

SERVES 2
225g (8 oz) fillet of lamb
salt and freshly ground black pepper
about 50 g (2 oz) unsalted butter
pinch of herbes de Provence
sprig of fresh rosemary, leaves finely chopped
50 ml (2 fl oz) lamb stock
50 ml (2 fl oz) dry Madeira

TO SERVE
Mushroom, Bacon and Spinach Rösti (see page 161)
Caramelized Shallots (see page 162)

1 Trim the lamb fillet of excess fat and sinew (talk nicely to your butcher and he will do this for you). Heat the frying pan over a high heat and sprinkle salt on the pan; add a knob of butter. Heat the butter until sizzling and place the lamb fillet in the pan; turn to seal both sides. Remove the lamb to a plate.
2 Wipe out the frying pan with paper towels and return to the heat. Add another knob of butter. Return the fillet to the pan and cook over a low heat for 3–4 minutes or according to taste. Remove the fillet from the pan, place on a plate to rest and cover with foil.
3 Add the herbes de Provence and the rosemary to the juices in the pan, then the stock and Madeira; bring to the boil and reduce by two thirds. Lower the heat under the pan and whisk in 25 g (1 oz) butter until it is incorporated and the sauce is thickened and glossy. Season to taste.
4 Carve the lamb into slices, divide between two plates and drizzle the sauce over. Serve with the rösti and caramelized onions.

ROAST RACK OF LAMB WITH THYME AND A RED WINE SAUCE ILLUSTRATED OPPOSITE

eastern spiced lamb with spiced apricot and nut pilau and cucumber raita

SERVES 2
30 ml (2 tbsp) sunflower oil
15 ml (1 tbsp) soft brown sugar
1 clove garlic, finely chopped
10 ml (2 tsp) paprika
10 ml (2 tsp) ground cumin
10 ml (2 tsp) ground coriander
1 fillet of lamb
salt and freshly ground black
pepper

SPICED APRICOT AND NUT
PILAU
425 ml (15 fl oz) vegetable stock
1.25 ml (¼ tsp) turmeric
55 g (2 oz) dried apricots
15 ml (1 tbsp) sunflower oil
1 onion, finely chopped
115 g (4 oz) basmati rice
4 green cardamom pods
1 cinnamon stick
4 whole cloves
60 g (1½ oz) pistachio nuts
5 ml (1 tsp) clear honey
salt and freshly ground black
pepper

CUCUMBER RAITA
¼ cucumber, diced
200 ml (7 fl oz) natural yogurt
10 ml (2 tsp) mint jelly

TO SERVE
Roasted Vegetables (see page
149)

1 In a shallow dish, mix the oil, sugar, garlic, paprika, cumin and ground coriander to a paste. Place the lamb in the marinade and turn to coat on all sides. Allow to marinate for 1 hour in the refrigerator.

2 Meanwhile, make the pilau. Pour the stock into a saucepan and heat over a moderate heat. Stir in the turmeric and apricots. Heat the oil in a large frying pan and fry the onion for 10 minutes over a moderate heat. Add the rice, cardamom pods, cinnamon stick, cloves and nuts. Fry for a few seconds, then stir in the stock with the apricots, and the honey. Season to taste, cover and simmer for 10–12 minutes until all the liquid is absorbed.

3 Remove the lamb from the marinade, season and cook on a preheated stove–top grill pan for 6–8 minutes. Allow to stand for a few minutes before slicing.

4 Meanwhile, combine all the cucumber raita ingredients.

5 Remove the cloves, cardamom pods and cinnamon stick from the pilau and serve with the sliced lamb, accompanied by the cucumber raita and roasted vegetables.

herb lamb cutlets with speck and saffron gnocchi

70 ml (2½ fl oz) extra virgin olive oil

15 g (½ oz) herbs (rosemary, thyme, sage), finely chopped

8 lamb cutlets

40 g (1½ oz) butter

50 ml (2 fl oz) double cream

SPINACH CAKES

800 g (1 lb 12 oz) spinach

40 ml (3 tbsp) extra virgin olive oil

4 cloves garlic, crushed

4 eggs, beaten

salt and freshly ground black pepper

30 ml (2 tbsp) double cream

30 g (1 oz) butter

SPECK AND SAFFRON GNOCCHI

60 g (2½ oz) butter

60 g (2½ oz) Speck (smoked air–cured ham), thinly sliced and cut into small strips

300 ml (½ pint) whipping cream

a few saffron threads

800 g (1 lb 12 oz) gnocchi

40 g (1½ oz) grated Parmesan

20 g (¾ oz) parsley, finely chopped

1 Mix the oil and herbs, brush onto the lamb cutlets and leave to marinate for about 1 hour.

2 Meanwhile, prepare the spinach cakes. Cook the spinach in boiling water until soft, then drain well. In a nonstick pan, heat the olive oil and fry the garlic. Add the spinach and stir fry for about 10 minutes, until the spinach does not release any liquid when squeezed. Remove from the hob and add the eggs, stirring continuously. Season with salt and pepper and stir in the cream.

3 In a large nonstick pan, melt the butter and put in four 10 cm (4 inch) pastry cutters or poached egg rings. Fill the rings with the spinach mixture and cook on a medium heat for 10 minutes each side, until golden brown. Remove the cakes from the rings and keep warm.

4 Prepare the gnocchi. Heat the butter in a small pan, add the Speck and cook for 1 minute. Add the cream and a few saffron threads and cook until the sauce turns yellow. Cook the gnocchi in boiling water for about 2 minutes, until they float. Drain well and toss in the cream sauce, with the Parmesan and chopped parsley.

5 Remove the cutlets from the oil marinade. Heat the marinade in a large pan with the butter and cook the cutlets for 4–5 minutes each side. Remove the cutlets from the pan and keep warm. Stir the cream into the pan juices and keep warm.

6 Arrange 2 cutlets on each warmed serving plate, with a spinach cake and a serving of gnocchi. Drizzle the lamb pan juices over the cutlets and the spinach cake.

lamb with mint pesto

4 noisettes of lamb

MARINADE
350 ml (12 fl oz) tamari or soya
sauce
175 ml (6 fl oz) cider vinegar
1 red chilli, deseeded
6 cloves garlic
10 ml (2 tsp) whole grain mustard
2.5 ml (½ tsp) salt and freshly
ground black pepper
10 ml (2 tsp) dark molasses
olive oil, for roasting

PESTO
3 cloves garlic
175 g (6 oz) basil
175 g (6 oz) mint
50 g (2 oz) flat–leaf parsley
120 g (4 oz) pine nuts, toasted
40 g (1½ oz) grated Parmesan
240 ml (8 fl oz) olive oil

TO SERVE
new potatoes
Summer Vegetables (see page 164)

1 Make the marinade. Put the tamari, vinegar, chilli and garlic into a blender and purée. Add the mustard, salt and pepper and molasses. Pour the marinade over the lamb, ensuring it is well covered. Cover and refrigerate for at least 2 days, turning every 12 hours.

2 Make the pesto. Put the garlic, basil, mint, parsley and pine nuts into a food processor and blend. Add the Parmesan and olive oil and blend very briefly.

3 Take the lamb out of the marinade and dry with a cloth. Place in a roasting dish with a drizzle of olive oil and cook at 200°C (400°F) mark 6 for about 10 minutes until pink. Leave to stand for 15 minutes.

4 Slice the lamb noisettes thinly and serve with the pesto, accompanied by new potatoes and summer vegetables.

chargrilled lamb tossed in a warm basil and pepper salad, served on crispy buttered potatoes with plum and ginger sauce

1 yellow pepper, cored and
deseeded
4 baking potatoes
200 g (7 oz) plum compote
1 clove garlic, crushed
10 ml (2 tsp) honey
2 cm (¾ inch) cube fresh root
ginger, finely chopped
small bunch fresh basil, finely
chopped

1 Roast the yellow pepper in a preheated oven at 200°C (400°F) mark 6 for 15 minutes until soft. Remove and allow to cool slightly and slice.

2 Meanwhile, cook the potatoes in a microwave at a high setting for 4–5 minutes; allow to cool slightly.

3 In a small pan, heat the plum compote together with the garlic, honey, ginger and half the basil to make a sauce.

4 Slice the potatoes into 1 cm (½ inch) thick slices, brush with melted butter and place in the preheated oven at 200°C (400°F) mark 6 for about 5 minutes.

5 Place the lamb on a hot stove top grill pan and seal all over, 2–3 minutes. Roast the lamb in the preheated oven at 200°C (400°F) mark 6

20 g (¾ oz) butter
1 whole lamb fillet
mixed salad leaves

for 5–8 minutes. Meanwhile, crisp the potato slices under a preheated grill.
6 Slice the lamb fillet and toss into the mixed salad leaves with the yellow pepper and remaining basil. Place the crispy potatoes on serving plates, add a serving of lamb with warm salad, and drizzle with the plum compote.

pan-fried fillet of lamb, aubergine and tomato salad, potato and carrot dauphinoise

juice of ½ lemon
large sprig of rosemary
30 ml (2 tbsp) olive oil plus extra
for pan frying
30 ml (2 tbsp) honey
2 cloves garlic, crushed
salt and freshly ground black
pepper
4 lamb fillets, about 175 g (6 oz)
each
300 ml (½ pint) beef stock

POTATO AND CARROT
DAUPHINOISE
125 ml (4 fl oz) milk
125 ml (4 fl oz) cream
50 g (2 oz) grated Gruyère cheese
butter, for greasing
1 clove garlic, halved
350 g (12 oz) potatoes, peeled
and sliced
1 carrot, peeled and sliced
15 ml (1 tbsp) chopped coriander
melted butter, for brushing

AUBERGINE AND TOMATO SALAD
1 large aubergine, sliced
olive oil, for brushing
2 plum tomatoes, skinned,
deseeded and finely chopped
10 ml (2 tsp) chopped tarragon

TO GARNISH
roasted cherry tomatoes
sprig of rosemary

1 Mix the lemon juice, rosemary, olive oil, honey, garlic and a little salt in a shallow dish and marinate the lamb fillets for 1 hour in a cool place.
2 Prepare the Dauphinoise: place the milk and cream in a small pan over a low heat and warm through, taking care not to boil. Stir in the Gruyère until melted.
3 Rub an ovenproof dish with butter and garlic, then layer half the potatoes, the carrot, coriander and seasoning in the dish. Pour the milk mixture into the dish, then finish with a layer of the remaining potatoes. Brush with melted butter, cover, and bake in a preheated oven at 140°C (275°F) mark 1 for 1½ hours.
4 Prepare the aubergine salad: brush the aubergine slices with olive oil and cook on a stove–top grill pan until soft and browned. Allow to cool. Arrange the tomatoes around the aubergine and sprinkle with tarragon and salt.
5 Remove the lamb from the marinade, and strain the marinade into the stock. Place in a pan over a high heat and reduce to about 60 ml (2 fl oz) for a sauce.
6 Heat a little olive oil and a pan and fry the lamb fillets for about 15 minutes so that the honey in the marinade caramelizes, but the lamb remains pink inside.
7 Place the Dauphinoise under a preheated grill for 10 minutes to brown and crisp the top.
8 Slice the lamb and garnish with roasted cherry tomatoes and rosemary; serve the lamb with the aubergine and tomato salad, and potato and carrot Dauphinoise, drizzled with the sauce.

mozzarella and sun-dried tomatoes wrapped in bacon

SERVES 2

60–75 ml (4–5 tbsp) extra-virgin olive oil, or to taste
4 slices mozzarella, about 1 cm (½ inch) thick
4 sun-dried tomatoes, finely sliced
4 slices prosciutto

OLIVE OIL AND GARLIC MASH

2–4 garlic cloves, or to taste
2 King Edward or Desirée potatoes, peeled and cut into quarters
salt and freshly ground black pepper

STIR-FRIED YELLOW PEPPER AND PAK CHOI

30 ml (2 tbsp) sunflower oil
yellow pepper, cored, deseeded and finely sliced
1 pak choi, finely sliced

1 Heat about 30 ml (2 tbsp) of the olive oil in a frying pan and cook the garlic cloves over a very gentle heat for 1 hour, making sure that the garlic does not burn.

2 Take a slice of mozzarella and arrange half the sun-dried tomato slices on top. Put another slice of mozzarella on top to create a sandwich. Wrap the prosciutto around, one slice lengthways and the other widthways, and tie with string to create a parcel. Repeat with the remaining mozzarella and tomatoes. Wrap them in foil and allow to set in the refrigerator for about 30 minutes.

3 Cook the potatoes in boiling salted water for 15 minutes or until tender. Drain. Using a hand–held blender, break up the potatoes using half the remaining olive oil. Then add the garlic with the oil from the frying pan, and blend until smooth. Adjust the consistency and taste by adding a little more olive oil if necessary. Season to taste.

4 Heat a wok or frying pan until smoking, add the sunflower oil and stir-fry the pepper for 30 seconds, then add the pak choi and stir-fry for 1 minute.

5 Heat a little olive oil in a frying pan and cook the mozzarella sandwiches on both sides until brown on the outside. Serve immediately with the olive oil and garlic mash, and stir-fried yellow pepper and pak choi.

air-dried ham and chicken rolls with a pork stuffing and a cider sauce

SERVES 2
4 boneless skinless chicken thighs
4 slices air-dried ham
olive oil, for roasting
250 ml (9 fl oz) dry cider

PORK STUFFING
15g (½ oz) unsalted butter
1 small diced shallot
100g (3½ oz) minced pork
10 ml (2 tsp) chopped parsley
5 ml (1 tsp) lemon juice
freshly ground black pepper

TO SERVE
new potatoes
Carrot Gratin (see page 165)
Rocket and Apple Salad (see page 163)

1 Make the stuffing: heat the butter in a frying pan and cook the shallot until soft. Allow to cool. Mix the pork, parsley, lemon juice and seasoning into the shallots.

2 Insert about 10 ml (2 tsp) of the stuffing mixture into each chicken thigh, and wrap each thigh in a slice of air-dried ham.

3 Place the chicken rolls in a roasting tin and drizzle olive oil over them. Cook in a preheated oven at 190°C (375°F) mark 5 for 30 minutes, basting twice during cooking. Remove the chicken rolls from the oven and leave to rest in a warming oven at 100°C (225°F) mark ¼.

4 Drain the fat from the meat juices in the roasting tin, place over a moderate heat and deglaze the tin with the cider. Pour into a saucepan and boil to reduce to a quarter of the quantity.

5 Slice each chicken roll into three, using a sharp knife or the ham will tear. Arrange on warmed serving plates and pour the cider sauce over the meat. Serve with new potatoes, carrot gratin and rocket and apple salad.

fillet of pork with lemon and parsley with white wine and cream sauce

1 fillet of pork
salt and freshly ground black pepper
30 ml (2 tbsp) chopped parsley
grated zest of ½ lemon
25 g (1 oz) unsalted butter
¼ bottle white wine
150 ml (¼ pint) well-flavoured chicken stock
150 ml (¼ pint) double cream

TO SERVE
seasonal vegetables
Himmel und Erde with Sage (see page 158)

1 Trim the pork and slice lengthways almost in half. Season, open out and season inside. Sprinkle the parsley and lemon zest inside, fold back into shape and tie with string.

2 Heat the butter in a heavy–based roasting tin and fry the pork until golden brown on all sides.

3 Add the wine to the pan and place in a preheated oven at 200°C (400°F) mark 6 for 20 minutes. Remove the pork from the pan and leave to rest.

4 Add the stock to the juices in the pan and bring to the boil and reduce by half. Add the cream and reduce by half again. Season to taste.

5 Remove the string from the pork and slice. Serve with the sauce accompanied by seasonal vegetables and Himmel und Erde with Sage.

fillet of pork in an apricot and madeira glaze

SERVES 2

75 g (3 oz) dried apricots, finely chopped
120 ml (4 fl oz) Madeira or sweet sherry
300 g (10 oz) pork fillet
salt and freshly ground black pepper
vegetable oil, for pan-frying
5 ml (1 tsp) wholegrain mustard
squeeze of lemon juice

TO SERVE

Parmesan Potato Croquettes (see page 161)
Stir-fried Vegetables (see page 153)

1 Place half the dried apricots in a small bowl and add the Madeira or sweet sherry. Leave to soak, preferably overnight.

2 Trim the pork fillet and make a lengthways cut down the fillet, three quarters through the meat. Open out as flat as possible. Spread the remaining chopped apricots along the open fillet, season with salt and pepper, and roll up, securing the roll with cocktail sticks.

3 Heat the oil in a sauté pan over a high heat. Add the pork fillet and turn to seal on all sides. Remove the meat from the pan and set aside.

4 Add about 150 ml (¼ pint) of water to the pan to deglaze, together with the mustard, lemon juice and the apricots in Madeira. Stir thoroughly to scrape up the brown bits in the pan. Replace the meat in the pan, cover and simmer gently for 6–7 minutes over a low heat.

5 Transfer the meat to a cutting board and cover with foil. Boil the glaze, stirring occasionally, until reduced to about one third. Slice the fillet and serve with the glaze poured over, accompanied by the potato croquettes and stir–fried vegetables.

madurai pork

1 lb (450 g) fillet of pork trimmed, trimmings reserved
125 ml (4 fl oz) Harvey's Bristol Cream sherry
15 ml (1 tbsp) ghee (clarified butter)
1 shallot, finely chopped
2 black cardamom pods
1.25 ml (¼ tsp) roasted cumin seeds ground

CHARRED PEPPERS

3–4 large peppers, different colours, cored, deseeded and halved
15 ml (1 tbsp) groundnut oil
1 shallot, chopped
1 clove garlic crushed and chopped
½ chilli, cored, deseeded and chopped

1 Cut the pork fillet into 'leaves' or fine slices. Marinate in the sherry until ready to cook.

2 Prepare the charred peppers. Put the peppers, skin–side up, on a baking tray and roast in a preheated oven at 200°C (400°F) mark 6 until the skins are charred. When cool enough to handle, peel the peppers and slice. Heat the oil in a frying pan and add the shallot, garlic and chilli. Cook until the shallots are light brown then add the mustard seeds. When they are cooked they will pop. Add brown sugar to taste, the peppers, and salt. Stir in the turmeric. Keep warm.

3 Prepare the spiced lentil rice. Place the rice and lentils in a pan with a well–fitting lid. Add the bay leaves, cumin seeds, Ghee and turmeric, with salt to taste. Add 800 ml (28 fl oz) water, bring to the boil and cook, covered, on a very low heat for 20 minutes. Keep covered until ready to serve.

4 Make the sauce. Heat the ghee in a large frying pan or saucepan. Add the cinnamon stick and bay leaf and fry for about 30 seconds. Add the pork trimmings and fry for 2–3 minutes. Add the shallots and fry for about 10 minutes until browned. Add the chilli, ginger, turmeric and coriander and the salt and pepper, mix well and add the game stock. Simmer for 10 minutes. Add the honey, then pass through a muslin sieve, pressing with the back of a wooden spoon. Return the liquid to a pan and boil to reduce by

2.5 ml (½ tsp) of brown mustard
seeds
brown sugar, to taste
1. 25 ml (¼ tsp) turmeric

SAUCE
15 ml (1 tbsp) ghee (clarified
butter)
1 cinnamon stick
1 bay leaf
3 shallots, finely chopped
1 red chilli, cored, deseeded and
chopped
1 cm (½ inch) cube fresh root
ginger, very finely chopped
2.5 ml (½ tsp) turmeric
15 ml (1 tbsp) ground coriander
salt to taste
5 ml (1 tsp) black pepper
600 ml (1 pint) game stock
30 ml (2 tbsp) honey
juice of 2 oranges

SPICED LENTIL RICE
250 g (9 oz) rice, rinsed and
drained
3 oz (85g) lentils, rinsed and
drained
2 bay leaves
2. 5 ml (½ tsp) cumin seeds
30 ml (2 tbsp) Ghee
1. 25 ml (¼ tsp) turmeric

TO GARNISH
orange zest

a third. Strain again, and add the orange juice. Set aside.
5 Cook the pork; heat the ghee in a frying pan and fry the shallot, black cardamom pods and cumin seeds for a few minutes until the onions brown.
6 Remove the pork from the marinade and add to the pan with the onions; turn to brown both sides. Add the sherry marinade and let it steam off the alcohol.
7 Make a bed of spiced lentil rice on warmed serving plates, and layer the pork on top. Garnish with orange zest. Reheat the sauce and pour around the rice and over the meat through a sieve.

main courses: meat

roasted rosemary pork with red wine sauce and orange vegetables

SERVES 2

350 g (12 oz) pork fillet
30 ml (2 tbsp) chopped rosemary
30 ml (2 tbsp) sunflower oil
100 g (3½ oz) green beans
40 g (1½ oz) butter
finely grated zest and juice of 1
orange, plus extra zest strips for
sprinkling
100 g (3½ oz) button mushrooms,
halved or quartered

SAUCE

150 ml (¼ pint) red wine
50 g (2 oz) stoned prunes
3 shallots, chopped
1 chicken stock cube, crumbled
30 ml (2 tbsp) double cream

TO SERVE
creamed potatoes

1 Roll the pork fillet in the rosemary until well coated.

2 Heat the oil in a large frying pan until very hot and beginning to brown. Add the pork fillet and seal on all sides. Transfer the pork to a roasting tin and cook in a preheated oven at 220°C (425°F) mark 7 for about 20 minutes.

3 Make the sauce; pour the wine into a small saucepan, add the prunes, shallots and stock cube and bring to the boil. Lower the heat and simmer for 10 minutes.

4 Meanwhile, bring a saucepan of water to the boil, and cook the green beans for 2–3 minutes until tender but still firm. Drain and refresh the beans.

5 Melt the butter in another pan, add the orange zest and juice and the mushrooms and cook for 5 minutes. Add the drained green beans and toss to mix. Sprinkle with a few strips of orange zest.

6 Stir the cream into the wine and prune sauce. Slice the pork fillet and arrange on warmed plates; pour the sauce over the pork and serve with the orange vegetables, and creamed potatoes.

fillet of pork with fennel & apple salad, fennel purée, apple chips and mustard seed vinaigrette

olive oil, for sealing
4 centre cut fillets of pork, about 150 g (5 oz) each

APPLE CHIPS
12 paper thin slices of Granny Smith apple

FENNEL PURÉE AND GREEN FENNEL SAUCE
30 ml (2 tbsp) butter
3 small onions, chopped
1 Granny Smith apple, peeled, cored and chopped
2 fennel bulbs, finely chopped
15 ml (1 tbsp) Pernod (optional)
salt and freshly ground black pepper
fronds from 2 fennel bulbs, blanched and refreshed

MUSTARD SEED VINAIGRETTE
15 ml (1 tbsp) cider vinegar
70 ml (2½ fl oz) olive oil
10 ml (2 tsp) Dijon mustard
10 ml (2 tsp) water
15 ml (1 tbsp) mustard seeds

FENNEL AND APPLE SALAD
225 g (8 oz) fennel, finely julienned
225 g (8 oz) unpeeled Granny Smith apple, finely julienned

1 The apple chips can be made in advance. Lay the apple slices on a non-stick baking sheet and place in a preheated oven at 100°C (225°F) mark ¼ for about 1 hour or until lightly golden and crisp. Allow to cool and store in an airtight container.

2 Make the fennel purée and green sauce. Heat the butter in a frying pan and sweat the onions until soft. Add the apple and fennel and continue to sauté for about 5 minutes until the fennel starts to soften. Add about 500 ml (16 fl oz) water and simmer for 20–25 minutes until the fennel is very soft. Drain off the liquid and reserve. Purée the fennel and apple in a blender until smooth, or pass through a food mill.

3 Transfer ¾ of the fennel and apple mixture to a bowl. Stir in the Pernod, if you like, check the seasoning and set aside.

4 Allow the remainder of the purée to cool, then blend in the blanched fennel fronds and enough of the reserved cooking liquid to make a sauce. Check the seasoning.

5 Make the mustard vinaigrette: whisk all the vinaigrette ingredients together and season to taste.

6 Make the fennel and apple salad. Toss the fennel and apple together in a medium–sized bowl.

7 Heat a little oil in a heavy–based roasting tin or ovenproof frying pan and seal the fillets of pork all over. Place the pan in a preheated oven at 220°C (425°F) mark 7 and cook for 5–6 minutes. Remove from the oven and allow to rest.

8 Form the fennel purée into 12 quenelles using two spoons. Pour some green fennel sauce in the centre of each warmed serving plate. Arrange 3 quenelles of fennel purée around the plate. Place a mound of fennel and apple salad in the centre of the plate. Slice the pork fillet and arrange around the salad. Stand an apple crisp upright in each quenelle and spoon the vinaigrette around.

pork and herefordshire cider sauce and cidered apple sauce

150 ml (¼ pint) quality Herefordshire cider
15 ml (1 tbsp) juniper berries lightly crushed
6 sage leaves
good sprig of rosemary
6 black peppercorns
2 x 450 g (1 lb) pieces of filleted loin of pork (Gloucestershire Old Spot)
8 rashers of dry cured smoked bacon
oil, for greasing
5–10 ml (1–2 tsp) cornflour
salt and freshly ground black pepper
45 ml (3 tbsp) double cream

CIDERED APPLE SAUCE
1 large Bramley apple, peeled, cored and roughly chopped (some peel reserved)
1 large Cox's Orange Pippin, peeled, cored and diced
150 ml (¼ pint) cider

1 Mix the cider, juniper berries, sage, rosemary and peppercorns in a shallow dish and marinate the pork for at least 1 hour or overnight if possible.

2 Remove the pork from the marinade, reserving the marinade. Wrap the pork in the bacon and secure with cocktail sticks.

3 Place the fillets in a greased roasting tin and cook in a preheated oven at 200°C (400°F) mark 6 for 10 minutes, then lower the temperature to 160°C (325°F) gas 3 and cook for about 1 hour.

4 Meanwhile, make the apple sauce; place the apples in a pan with half the cider and cook, gently adding a little more cider from time to time if needed. Neatly dice up the reserved peel and add just before serving.

5 Strain the reserved marinade, mix with the cornflour, and heat gently. Check the seasoning. Put the mixture into a blender until airy and a little frothy. Add the cream.

6 Slice the pork and serve with the cider sauce and cidered apple sauce.

roasted fillet of organic pork, served on a bed of dijon mashed potato, with braised red cabbage

2 fillets of organic pork, trimmed of fat
30 ml (2 tbsp) Somerset cider brandy
sea salt and freshly ground black pepper
pork rind with plenty of fat for crackling

BRAISED RED CABBAGE
½ large red cabbage, finely sliced
4 ready to eat apricots, chopped
½ apple, peeled and chopped
10 ml (2 tsp) Normandy cider vinegar
knob of butter, plus extra for glazing
freshly grated nutmeg, to taste

DIJON MASHED POTATO
5 medium–sized potatoes, peeled and cubed
25 g (1 oz) organic butter
60 ml (4 tbsp) single cream
10 ml (2 tsp) Dijon mustard

APPLE SAUCE
2 baking apples, peeled, cored and diced
10 ml (2 tsp) cider brandy

GRAVY
15 g (½ oz) plain flour
300 ml (½ pint) well-flavoured stock
1 glass red wine
few drops of gravy browning
knob of butter

TO SERVE
Timbale of Summer Vegetables
(see page 165)

1 Place the pork in a dish and rub in the cider brandy and a grinding of black pepper. Place in the refrigerator and allow to marinate for 1 hour.

2 For the crackling, wash and dry the rind. Place fillet on a wire rack in a grill pan and leave to dry at room temperature. Score the skin with a very sharp knife every 5 mm (¼ inch) across the rind. Only cut through the skin and halfway through the fat, do not separate the strips. Sprinkle the skin with freshly ground salt, place in a roasting tin, and cook in a preheated oven at 220°C (425°F) mark 7 for 20 minutes.

3 Reduce the oven temperature to 180°C (350°F) mark 4 and move the cracking to the sides of the pan. Place the pork fillets in the roasting tin between the crackling and cook for a further 30–50 minutes depending on the thickness of the rind and the size of the fillets.

4 Meanwhile, prepare the cabbage. Put the cabbage, apricots, apple, vinegar and a little butter, with nutmeg and seasoning to taste, in a heavy–based pan and add 175 ml (6 fl oz) water. Cook over a moderate heat for 30–40 minutes until the cabbage is just cooked. Turn up the heat to reduce any remaining liquid and add a final knob of butter for glazing.

5 Prepare the Dijon mashed potatoes: boil the potatoes for 15–20 minutes until tender. Mash with the butter, cream, mustard and seasoning. Return to a low heat to warm through.

6 Make the apple sauce: place the apples in a pan over a low heat with the cider brandy and enough water to prevent drying out. Cook until tender but not mushy.

7 Remove the meat and crackling from the oven. Wrap the pork loosely in foil and leave to stand in a warm place for at least 10 minutes before serving. Break the pork crackling into individual sticks and drain on paper towels until ready to serve.

8 Pour off most of the fat and juices from the roasting tin and set over a low heat. Sprinkle in the flour to make a roux. Slowly add the stock, red wine and gravy browning and boil to reduce by half. If you like, strain the gravy before serving. A final knob of butter will give gloss to the finished gravy.

9 Using a ring, fill with mashed potato on each warmed serving plate and level off with a palate knife. Slice each fillet at an angle into 8–10 medallions and arrange 4 or 5 medallions on the potato. Serve a heaped spoonful of cabbage in the middle of the pork medallions. Drizzle the gravy around the mashed potato. Arrange dollops of apple sauce around the plate and top each with a stick of crackling. Serve with a timbale of summer vegetables.

MAIN COURSES:
FISH & SHELLFISH

crab cakes with sweet potato and celeriac purée

SERVES 2

150 g (5 oz) waxy potatoes
250 g (9 oz) crab meat
2 spring onions, finely chopped
15 ml (1 tbsp) grated lime zest
15 ml (1 tbsp) freshly squeezed lime juice
15 ml (1 tbsp) beaten egg
2.5 ml (½ tsp) grated fresh root ginger
pinch of cumin
salt and freshly ground black pepper
vegetable oil, for frying
sesame seeds, for coating

SWEET POTATO AND CELERIAC PURÉE

200 g (7 oz) sweet potato, peeled and quartered
200 g (7 oz) celeriac, peeled and quartered
50 g (2 oz) butter
30 ml (2 tbsp) double cream
pinch of freshly grated nutmeg

TOMATO AND MANGO SALSA

50 g (2 oz) red onion, chopped
¼ green chilli, cored, deseeded and chopped
¼ red chilli, cored, deseeded and chopped
4 sprigs fresh coriander, chopped
6 tomatoes, skinned and deseeded
½ mango, peeled and roughly chopped
½ cooked beetroot, peeled and roughly chopped
15 ml (1 tbsp) lime juice

1 Bring a large saucepan of water to the boil and cook the potatoes for 10 minutes. Remove from the heat and drain; when cool enough to handle, remove the skins. Grate the potatoes coarsely into long strips.

2 For for the sweet potato and celeriac purée, bring a saucepan of water to the boil, and boil the sweet potato and celeriac for 15 minutes.

3 Meanwhile, in a large bowl, combine the crab meat, spring onions, lime zest and juice, beaten egg, grated ginger, cumin, and salt and pepper. Carefully mix in the grated potato, taking care to keep the potato strips intact for a rösti look.

4 Make 6 round cakes of the crab and potato mixture and refrigerate for 20 minutes.

5 Meanwhile, make the salsa: process the red onion, green and red chillies and coriander in a blender for 20 minutes. Add the tomatoes, mango and beetroot to the blender, with the lime juice and salt and pepper. Process again, transfer to a serving bowl and refrigerate.

6 Drain the celeriac and sweet potato and separate the vegetables into separate small saucepans. Add half the butter and cream to each pan. Mash each vegetable until smooth. Season with salt, pepper and nutmeg. Using 6 cm (2½ inch) ramekins, fill one side of each with mashed sweet potato and the other side with mashed celeriac. Keep the ramekins warm.

7 Heat some vegetable oil in a frying pan. Dip the crab cakes in sesame seeds to coat and fry briefly on both sides until cooked through.

8 To serve, turn out the ramekins onto warmed plates, arrange the crab cakes on the plates, and serve with the salsa.

leek risotto served with tiger prawns, monkfish and scallops and a tarragon vinaigrette

SERVES 2

75 g (3 oz) unsalted butter
1 onion, finely chopped
small clove garlic, finely chopped
600 ml (1 pint) well-flavoured
chicken stock
175 g (6 oz) leeks, chopped
120 g (4oz) risotto rice
35 ml (2½ tbsp) freshly grated
Parmesan

PARMA HAM

olive oil, for deep frying
2 slices Parma ham

VINAIGRETTE

35 ml (2½ tbsp) olive oil
15 ml (1 tbsp) tarragon vinegar
15 ml (1 tbsp) grated lemon zest
0.5 ml (⅛ tsp) Dijon mustard
few sprigs tarragon, finely chopped
salt and freshly ground black
pepper

TIGER PRAWNS, MONKFISH AND
SCALLOPS

4 pieces of monkfish, about
40–50 g (1½–2 oz) each
4 scallops
4 peeled uncooked tiger prawns

1 First fry the ham. Heat the olive oil and fry the Parma ham until slightly crisp. Reserve the oil and set aside the ham.

2 To make the vinaigrette, place all the ingredients in a screw–topped jar and shake to blend thoroughly.

3 Melt the butter in a large heavy–bottomed pan and cook the onion and garlic for a few minutes until soft but not coloured. Heat the stock until boiling, add the leeks and boil for about 2 minutes. Drain the leeks and reserve the stock.

4 Add the rice to the pan with the onion and cook for 1 minute, stirring to coat. Gradually add the stock, allowing each quantity to be absorbed before adding more. When the rice is cooked through but still al dente, remove the pan from the heat. Stir in the leeks and Parmesan, and season.

5 Prepare the fish: steam the monkfish and scallops for 2 minutes. Remove and place on paper towels. Heat a little of the ham-flavoured oil in a frying pan and fry the monkfish and scallops for 1–1½ minutes. Add the tiger prawns and fry until the colour changes to pink.

6 Serve the risotto topped with the deep fried Parma ham. Arrange the fish around the edge and drizzle with the tarragon vinaigrette.

posh fish and chips

SERVES 2

2 large potatoes for chips, peeled
2 sweet potatoes, peeled
vegetable oil, for deep frying
6 slices sliced white bread
2 large eggs
20 ml (1 heaped tbsp) wholegrain mustard
20 ml (1 heaped tbsp) chopped parsley
20 ml (1 heaped tbsp) chopped dill
2 fillets cod

TOMATO SAUCE

50 g (2 oz) butter
50 ml (2 fl oz) extra-virgin olive oil
1 large onion, chopped
2 cloves garlic, crushed
6 plum tomatoes, roughly chopped
15 ml (1 tbsp) tomato purée
salt and freshly ground black pepper
300 ml (½ pint) vegetable stock
10 fresh basil leaves, chopped
dash of Tabasco sauce

TO SERVE

sea salt
white wine vinegar
lemon wedges

1 Cut the potatoes into even lengths with a crinkle cutter, and the sweet potatoes into very thin straight chips to resemble American fries. Soak the chips in fresh water to remove the excess starch for about 10 minutes.

2 Make the tomato sauce: in a heavy–based saucepan, melt the butter in the oil. Add the onion and garlic and cook until softened but not brown. Add the tomatoes, tomato purée and seasoning to taste and simmer for 5 minutes. Add the stock and simmer for a further 20 minutes. Remove from the heat and allow to cool. Pass the sauce through a sieve into a clean pan, pressing with the back of a wooden spoon. Stir in the basil and Tabasco, and keep the sauce warm.

3 Drain the cut potatoes, rinse, and dry on a clean tea towel. Place the chips in a preheated deep fat fryer at 170°C (325°F) to blanch to a pale colour and then remove the chips with a slotted spoon and cover.

4 Place the slices of bread in a preheated oven at 180°C (350°F) mark 4 until toasted and golden brown. Process the bread in a food processor for 1 minute to make fine breadcrumbs. Spread the breadcrumbs in a shallow plate.

5 Whisk the eggs with mustard, salt, pepper and chopped herbs in a shallow bowl. Dip the cod fillets in the egg mixture to coat. Remove the cod fillets from the egg mixture and dip in the breadcrumbs to coat both sides. Deep fry the cod fillets at 190°C (375°F) for about 4 minutes, and keep warm.

6 Re-fry the chips until crisp and golden brown. Dust the chips with sea salt and sprinkle with white wine vinegar; serve with the cod garnished with the lemon wedges.

seared tuna on celeriac mash and spinach with coriander and lime salsa

1 celeriac, chopped

juice of 1 lime, peel reserved (see note)

4 red-skinned or Maris Piper potatoes, peeled and chopped

30 ml (2 tbsp) double cream

a little butter

700–900 g (1½–2 lb) tuna loin

about 45 ml (3 tbsp) olive oil

salt and freshly ground black pepper

450 g (1 lb) spinach

white pepper

4 tomatoes, skinned, deseeded and chopped

bunch of coriander leaves, chopped

¼ red onion, finely chopped

¼ bird's eye chilli, cored, deseeded and chopped (optional)

RED WINE REDUCTION

1 stick celery, chopped

1 small red pepper, cored, deseeded and chopped

3 shallots, chopped

6 cloves garlic, chopped

1 slice pancetta or bacon, or olive oil

4 tomatoes, chopped

10 ml (2 tsp) balsamic vinegar

1 bottle red wine

1 Cook the celeriac in a pan of boiling salted water with the lime peel for 10–15 minutes until tender. Drain and set aside. Cook the potatoes in a pan of boiling salted water for 20 minutes until tender. Drain and combine with the celeriac. Add the cream and a knob of butter; mash and set aside.

2 Next, make the red wine reduction. In a large pan fry the celery, red pepper, shallots and garlic with the pancetta or bacon (or a little olive oil) for a few minutes or until softened. Add the tomatoes and balsamic vinegar. Reduce until the mixture is sticky. Add the red wine and reduce slowly to half the volume. Sieve the reduction and continue to reduce to around 200 ml (⅓ pint).

3 Cut the tuna loin lengthways through the centre, and then into quarters. Dress the tuna pieces in the olive oil, salt and pepper, and roll each piece tightly in cling film. Chill in the refrigerator.

4 Microwave the spinach, or cook over a low heat until just wilted. Season with salt, white pepper and a knob of butter. Set aside.

5 Place the tomatoes in a bowl and add the lime juice, coriander leaves and red onion. Add the chilli, if using, and 15–30 ml (1–2 tbsp) olive oil. Mix well and set aside.

6 Sear the tuna in a smoking hot pan until browned on the outside and rare in the centre. Reheat the celeriac mash and spinach.

7 Place the spinach on serving plates, then the mash, shaping with a scone cutter. Place a spoonful of the salsa mix on top and then slice the tuna and arrange on top of the salsa. Pour the red wine reduction around the fish and spinach and serve immediately.

NOTE: If you put the the lime into a microwave for 30 seconds it helps to maximize the amount of juice extracted.

seared tuna steak with a lemon grass, lime and coriander marinade

SERVES 2

2 x 140 g (5 oz) pieces blue–fin tuna

olive oil, for frying

FOR THE MARINADE

2 lemon grass stalks

1 bunch coriander stalks

finely grated zest and juice of 2 limes

60 ml (4 tbsp) olive oil

FOR THE SAUCES

50 ml (2 fl oz) soy sauce

50 ml (2 fl oz) honey

25 g (1 oz) sesame seeds, toasted

50 g (2 oz) butter

20 g (¾ oz) sugar

TO SERVE

Shiitake Risotto (see page 164)

Mixed Vegetable Stir-fry (see page 153)

1 To prepare the marinade: purée the lemon grass, coriander and lime zest with the olive oil in a small food processor or blender.

2 Place the tuna on a sheet of cling film, smother with the marinade, roll and up and refrigerate for 1 hour.

3 Remove the tuna from the marinade and reserve the marinade. Heat some olive oil in a frying pan, and sear the tuna portions on both sides; reduce the heat slightly and cook until opaque throughout.

4 Meanwhile, put the soy sauce and honey in a small pan, cook for a minute and then add the sesame seeds; keep warm.

5 Melt the butter in another small pan and add the marinade; whisk thoroughly. When ready to serve, remove the sauce from the heat and whisk in the lime juice and the sugar.

6 Serve the tuna with the two sauces, accompanied by the shiitake risotto and mixed vegetable stir-fry.

marinated tuna steaks with avocado cream and parmesan potato cakes

SERVES 2

15 ml (1 tbsp) olive oil, plus extra
for frying
15 ml (1 tbsp) light soy sauce
10 ml (2 tsp) lemon juice
1.15 ml (¼ tsp) ground cumin
2 tuna steaks

PARMESAN POTATO CAKES

225 g (8 oz) potatoes, peeled and
chopped
15 g (½ oz) butter
20 g (¾ oz) freshly grated
Parmesan
½ egg yolk
salt and freshly ground black
pepper
milk, for brushing
15 g (½ oz) breadcrumbs
10 ml (2 tsp) chopped parsley

AVOCADO CREAM

½ ripe avocado, peeled
25 ml (1½ tbsp) soured cream
2.5 ml (½ tsp) lemon juice

TO GARNISH

olive oil flavoured with basil
spring onion, chopped
finely chopped basil, coriander
and/or parsley

1 Mix 15 ml (1 tbsp) olive oil, the soy sauce, lemon juice and cumin together in a shallow dish. Marinate the tuna steaks in the mixture for at least 1 hour.

2 Meanwhile, make the potato cakes. Boil the potatoes for 8–10 minutes until tender, drain and mash with the butter, 15 g (½ oz) of the Parmesan and egg yolk. Season and shape into 4 patties.

3 Brush the potato cakes with milk. Mix the breadcrumbs, remaining Parmesan and parsley together on a sheet of greaseproof paper and coat the potato cakes. Cover with cling film and refrigerate.

4 Make the avocado cream. In a small bowl, mash the avocado with a fork, and mix in the soured cream and lemon juice.

5 Heat a little olive oil in a frying pan and fry the potato patties for 3–4 minutes each side until golden brown.

6 Heat a little olive oil in a nonstick frying pan or wok, add the tuna and fry for 1–2 minutes each side.

7 Serve the tuna steaks on top of the potato cakes, topped with a dollop of avocado cream. Drizzle the basil oil over the spring onions, and use to garnish the plate, along with the fresh herbs.

anchovy–larded blue–fin tuna with green beans and wasabi vinaigrette

600 g (1 lb 5 oz) blue–fin tuna loin
8 salted anchovy fillets, rinsed
60 ml (4 tbsp) olive oil
60 ml (4 tbsp) chopped fresh herbs such as chives, parsley, chervil
salt and freshly ground black pepper
100 g (3½ oz) haricot verts, blanched

WASABI VINAIGRETTE
30 ml (2 tbsp) olive oil
15 ml (3 tsp) cider vinegar
5 ml (1 tsp) prepared wasabi paste, or horseradish

TO SERVE
Garlic Mash (see page 157)

1 Using a small larding needle, lard the tuna with the anchovy fillets. (Alternatively, pierce the tuna with a skewer and insert the anchovies.) Mix the olive oil with the herbs. Season the tuna and marinate in the oil and herb mixture for about 2 hours or overnight in the refrigerator. (Remove the tuna at least an hour before cooking.)

2 To make the vinaigrette, whisk the oil, vinegar and wasabi paste with seasoning until well blended.

3 Sear the tuna in a very hot dry sauté pan for a few minutes on each side. It should be still red in the middle. Using a sharp knife, cut into thin slices.

4 Toss the beans in a little of the vinaigrette and and arrange on serving plates. Place the sliced tuna on top of the beans and drizzle some vinaigrette around the plate. Serve with the garlic mash, shaped into patties with a 6 cm (2½ inch) biscuit cutter if you like.

chargrilled fennel tuna with red wine sauce and carnaroli rice

15 ml (3 tsp) fennel seeds
1 small clove garlic
sea salt and freshly ground black pepper
4 slices of tuna, about 120 g (4 oz) each
juice ½ lemon
30 ml (2 tbsp) olive oil
100 ml (3½ fl oz) red wine
30 ml (2 tbsp) chopped fennel tops
fennel tops or chervil, to garnish

RED WINE SAUCE
200 ml (7 fl oz) red wine
50 ml (2 fl oz) port or Madeira
200 ml (7 fl oz) light chicken stock
30 g (1 oz) unsalted butter, cubed

CARNAROLI RICE
100 g (3½ oz) carnaroli rice
400 ml (14 fl oz) chicken stock
20 ml (4 tsp) double cream
20 ml (4 tsp) mascarpone
15 ml (1 tbsp) chopped chives
15 ml (1 tbsp) chopped basil or chervil

TO SERVE
Wilted Radicchio (see page 163)
Confit Tomatoes (see page 165)

1 In a pestle and mortar, grind the fennel seeds, garlic and salt and pepper to a paste. Smear the paste over the tuna slices and place them in a shallow dish. Mix the lemon juice, oil, wine and fennel tops and pour over the tuna. Cover with cling film and marinate for at least 1 hour and up to 4 hours in the refrigerator.

2 Simmer the rice in the chicken stock for about 12 minutes or until just soft, stirring occasionally. Season and set aside.

3 Place the wine in a saucepan and bring to the boil. Reduce well until dark and syrupy. Deglaze with the port or Madeira. Add the chicken stock and reduce again until smooth and slightly thickened. Strain through muslin into a clean pan. Bring to the boil again and whisk in the butter gradually. Check the seasoning.

4 When ready to serve, heat a stove–top grill pan until extremely hot. Sear the tuna pieces for 1 minute on each side.

5 Gently reheat the rice, stirring in the cream, mascarpone and chopped herbs. Check the seasoning.

6 Place a small mound of carnaroli rice on each serving plate. Top with the tuna. Drizzle a little red wine sauce over. Garnish with fennel tops or chervil. Serve with wilted radicchio and confit tomatoes, lightly drizzled with the red wine sauce.

grilled salmon tails with gazpacho dressing

SERVES 2

2 salmon tails, lightly buttered

GAZPACHO DRESSING

50 g (2 oz) red pepper, finely chopped

50 g (2 oz) green pepper, finely chopped

¼ red onion, finely chopped

75 g (3 oz) cucumber, skinned, deseeded and finely chopped

2 tomatoes, deseeded and finely chopped

3 pieces sun-dried tomato, finely chopped

45 ml (3 tbsp) olive oil

30 ml (2 tbsp) oil from sun-dried tomatoes

15 ml (1 tbsp) cider vinegar

squeeze of lemon juice

salt and freshly ground black pepper

TO GARNISH

1 spring onion, finely chopped

few mint leaves, finely chopped

1 To make the dressing, mix all the ingredients thoroughly until well blended.

2 Heat a baking tray under the grill until it is very hot. Season the salmon tails, place on the hot baking tray and grill for 9 minutes.

3 Transfer the salmon to a serving dish with the gazpacho dressing. Garnish with finely chopped spring onion and mint leaves.

scottish salmon fillets with an asparagus and baby leek topping

SERVES 2

olive oil, for frying and brushing
120 g (4 oz) asparagus tips
120 g (4 oz) baby leeks, cut into strips
15 g (½ oz) red onion, chopped
1.25 ml (¼ tsp) grated orange zest
2 Scottish salmon fillets
salt and freshly ground black pepper

HERBY CRÈME FRAÎCHE

45 ml (3 tbsp) crème fraîche
10 ml (2 tsp) chopped tarragon
10 ml (2 tsp) chopped dill
10 ml (2 tsp) chopped flat–leaf parsley
10 ml (2 tsp) chopped chives
5 ml (1 tsp) grated orange zest

TO SERVE

Spring Onion Mash (see page 160)

1 Make the herby créme fraîche. Mix all of the ingredients together to blend thoroughly.

2 Heat a little olive oil in a frying pan or wok. Toss the asparagus tips, leeks and onion in the oil and stir in the orange zest. Stir fry until the vegetables are just tender.

3 Brush the salmon fillets with olive oil and season. Grill under a preheated hot grill for about 2 minutes on each side.

4 Serve the salmon fillets topped with the sautéed vegetables and herby crème fraîche, accompanied by spring onion mash.

main courses : fish & shellfish

couscous crusted salmon with asparagus

SERVES 2

120 g (4 oz) couscous
½ clove garlic, finely chopped
1.25 ml (¼ tsp) finely chopped
fresh root ginger
grated lemon zest
sprig of fresh coriander, finely
chopped
few fresh chives, finely chopped
pinch of paprika
pinch of ground cumin
2 salmon fillets
salt and freshly ground black
pepper
25g (1 oz) flour
1 egg, beaten
2 medium carrots
6 stalks asparagus
olive oil, for pan-frying

TARRAGON BUTTER SAUCE
25g (1 oz) butter
5 ml (1 tsp) finely chopped fresh
tarragon

1 Cook the couscous according to the packet instructions. Add the garlic, ginger, lemon zest, herbs and spices, and leave to infuse the flavours.

2 Cut the salmon fillets in half, remove the skin, and remove any small bones. Rub salt and pepper into the salmon, dip in the flour to coat, and then into the beaten egg.

3 Coat the salmon fillets with the spicy couscous mixture, pressing the couscous on with your fingers. Refrigerate until ready to use, to firm up the coating.

4 Slice the carrots, using a decorative cutter if you like. Steam the asparagus and carrots for about 4 minutes.

5 Meanwhile, make the tarragon butter sauce. Melt the butter in a small pan over a low heat and stir in the tarragon.

6 Heat a little olive oil in a frying pan and fry the salmon pieces for 1 minute on each side.

7 Arrange the fish, asparagus and carrots on the plates, and drizzle the tarragon butter over the carrots.

quartet of salmon

500 g (1 lb 2 oz) salmon fillet, skinned
salt and freshly ground black pepper
1 egg white
250 ml (9 fl oz) whipping cream
1 bunch watercress, coarsely chopped
4 small slices smoked salmon
vegetable oil, for greasing
12 baby new potatoes
24 baby carrots
12 stalks asparagus
250 ml (8 fl oz) fish stock
150 ml (¼ pint) dry white wine
50 g (2 oz) jar salmon caviar
flat–leaf parsley, to garnish

1 Using 7 x 3.5 cm (2⅔ x 1½ inch) ring moulds as a guide and a sharp knife, cut 4 circles of salmon. Slice horizontally to make 8 pieces. Season and set aside.

2 Purée the salmon trimmings in a food processor with the egg white and a good pinch of salt. Add about 150 ml of the cream and process to a smooth purée. Stir the watercress into the salmon mousseline and chill.

3 Cut 4 circles of smoked salmon from the slices using the ring moulds as before. Reserve.

4 Oil the ring moulds and place on an oiled baking tray. Place a circle of salmon fillet in each followed by about 10 ml (2 tsp) of mousseline, a circle of smoked salmon, another layer of mousseline and a final circle of salmon fillet. Season and brush with oil and cover with oiled kitchen foil. Chill until ready to cook.

5 Cook the potatoes in boiling salted water for 10 minutes, adding carrots 2 minutes before the end of cooking time and asparagus 1 minute before the end. Drain and keep warm.

6 Cook the salmon in a preheated oven at 230°C (450°F) mark 8 for 10 minutes or until the fish just turns opaque.

7 Meanwhile, make the sauce. Place the fish stock and wine in a pan over a medium heat and reduce by two thirds. Stir in the remaining cream and bring back to boil. Adjust the seasoning and keep warm. When ready to serve, stir in most of the caviar.

8 To serve, place the ring moulds in the centre of warmed plates. Run a knife around the edges and carefully slide off the ring moulds. Garnish with parsley and a little of the remaining caviar. Pour the sauce around the fish and arrange the vegetables on it.

main courses: fish & shellfish

fricassée of langoustine and monkfish with tarragon and baby vegetables

900 g (2 lb) langoustines (about 16)
450 g (1 lb) monkfish
1 small bunch tarragon, stalks and leaves separated
600 ml (1 pint) fresh fish stock
350 g (12 oz) mixed baby vegetables (e.g. carrots, courgettes, asparagus tips)
40 g (1½ oz) unsalted butter
30 ml (2 tbsp) sugar
300 ml (½ pint) double cream
salt and freshly ground black pepper

1 Remove the meat from the langoustine tails, and any meat you can scoop out from the legs. Cut the monkfish into equal–sized pieces, and refrigerate until needed.

2 Put the langoustine shells, tarragon stalks and fish stock into a large saucepan, cover and simmer for 20–30 minutes to infuse. Pass through a sieve, return to the heat and reduce to just under half the quantity.

3 Put the vegetables in a large saucepan with 25 g (1 oz) of the butter, the sugar and a little water. Cook over a high heat until tender. Drain and keep warm.

4 Melt the remaining butter in a large frying pan. Add the monkfish and then the langoustine, turning the pieces once. Add the fish stock and simmer for a moment. Remove the fish from the pan, and add cream and tarragon leaves. Bring to the boil to thicken the sauce. Season to taste. Just before serving, return the fish to the pan, cover and warm through over very low heat.

5 Place the vegetables, monkfish and langoustine tails on each plate, spoon the sauce over, and serve.

honey–glazed monkfish with a creamy pepper and caviar sauce

1 large monkfish tail, bones removed
5 ml (1 tsp) cracked black peppercorns, plus extra for coating
vegetable oil, for frying
20 ml (4 tsp) honey
20 ml (4 tsp) oyster sauce
150 ml (¼ pint) fish stock
75 ml (2½ fl oz) double cream
20 g (¾ oz) butter
1 cm (½ inch) cube fresh root ginger, peeled and grated
20 ml (4 tsp) rice wine
2 sprigs coriander, chopped
15 ml (1 tbsp) caviar

TO SERVE
sautéed potatoes
steamed asparagus, drizzled with butter
marinated enoki mushrooms

1 Roll the monkfish in the cracked peppercorns to coat. Heat the oil over a high heat and pan fry the monkfish, turning once, to seal. Add the honey and oyster sauce to the pan as a glaze. Transfer to a dish, cover with foil and place in a preheated 180°C (350°F) mark 4 oven for 10 minutes.

2 Meanwhile, make the sauce. Bring the stock to a boil, then lower the heat to a simmer. Add the cream, butter, ginger, rice wine and 5 ml (1 tsp) cracked black peppercorns. Stir until the sauce thickens. Add the coriander and caviar.

3 Slice the fish in 1 cm (½ inch) slices, drizzle the sauce over and serve with sautéed potatoes, asparagus and enoki mushrooms.

grilled fillet of orange roughy served on a potato rösti with a light orange sauce

SERVES 2

2 New Zealand orange roughy fillets, 150–175 g (5–6 oz) each
knob of butter, melted
juice of 2 large sweet oranges
2 large baking potatoes
vegetable oil, for frying
15 ml (1 tbsp) caster sugar
15 ml (1 tbsp) single cream

TO SERVE

steamed asparagus, baby carrots and mange-tout

1 Place the two fillets on a baking tray and smear with the butter. Drizzle the juice of 1 orange over the fish.

2 Peel both the potatoes and grate coarsely. Place the grated potato in a clean tea towel and squeeze to remove any excess water.

3 Place the fish under a preheated grill and cook for 7–8 minutes on each side or until opaque throughout and firm.

4 Heat a little vegetable oil in a frying pan and carefully spoon the potato mixture into the frying pan in 2 mounds. With a spatula, shape the potato into patties about 1 cm (½ inch) thick and the size of the fish fillets. Fry the potato patties for 4–5 minutes each side.

5 Meanwhile, put the remaining orange juice into a small saucepan and add the sugar and cream; heat gently until the sugar has dissolved, stirring constantly.

6 To serve, place the potato rösti in the centre of the warmed plates with the fish on top. Pour the hot orange sauce over and surround with the steamed vegetables.

main courses: fish & shellfish

monkfish and scallops in a lime leaf, chilli and coconut sauce on a bed of thai noodles

SERVES 2

2.5 cm (1 inch) piece fresh root ginger, peeled and chopped
1 red chilli, cored, deseeded and chopped
1 clove garlic, chopped
25 g (1 oz) coriander leaves, chopped
30 ml (2 tbsp) olive oil
3 lime leaves
1 lemon grass stalk, cut lengthways and lightly crushed
175 ml (6 fl oz) fish stock
175 ml (6 fl oz) coconut milk
5 ml (1 tsp) Asian fish sauce
350 g (12 oz) monkfish
4–6 scallops
50 g (2 oz) vermicelli noodles, cooked

TO GARNISH
mint leaves
chopped spring onion

1 Reserve about 1.25 ml (¼ tsp) of the ginger and red chilli. In a blender or food processor, purée the remainder of the ginger and chilli, the garlic, and coriander with the oil. Heat the purée in a frying pan over a moderate heat for 2 minutes adding the lime leaves and lemon grass stalk. Add the fish stock, coconut milk, fish sauce and the reserved ginger and chilli. Simmer for 10 minutes.

2 Add the fish to the fish sauce and poach lightly for about 2 minutes; add the scallops and poach for about 2 minutes more. The fish and shellfish should be just opaque throughout. Remove the fish with a slotted spoon and keep warm. Remove and discard the lime leaves and lemon grass stalks.

3 Reduce the sauce to a creamy consistency. Arrange the fish on the prepared noodles. Pour the sauce over and sprinkle with mint leaves and chopped spring onions.

smoked haddock in a cream sauce with pasta

SERVES 2
180 g (7 oz) smoked haddock
fillet, skinned
100 ml (3½ fl oz) double cream
50 g (2 oz) unsalted butter
10 g (¼ oz) parsley, chopped
2 egg yolks

PASTA
100 g (3½ oz) pasta flour
1 egg
5 ml (1 tsp) olive oil
salt

TO SERVE
Carrots with Sesame Seeds and
Honey (see page 162)
Sliced Green Beans with Bacon
(see page 164)

1 Make the pasta: place the flour on the work surface and make a well in it, crack the egg into it and add the olive oil and a pinch of salt. Gradually bring in the flour until you have a dough. Knead the dough for 10 minutes and wrap in cling film for 30 minutes. Pass the pasta dough through a pasta machine on its widest setting 6 or 7 times. Then pass it through on each thickness until it reaches its lowest setting. Pass the pasta through the pasta cutter and leave it to dry for 30 minutes.

2 Scald the fish in boiling water for a few seconds then place the fish in foil with the cream, butter and parsley and fold the foil to make a parcel. Bake for 20 minutes in a preheated oven at 200°C (400°F) mark 6. Remove the fish and keep it warm.

3 Pour the remaining cream and parsley mixture into a bain marie over simmering water and add the two egg yolks; simmer for 5 minutes, stirring frequently.

4 Cook the pasta in boiling salted water for 3 minutes and drain. Arrange the pasta on the serving plates. Flake the fish over the pasta, and pour the cream sauce over the top. Serve immediately with carrots with sesame seeds and green beans with bacon.

steamed fillet of hake with a red wine sweet and sour fish jus, served with garlic mussels and a warm salad

SERVES 2
salt and freshly ground black
pepper
2 fillets hake
squeeze of lemon juice
5 ml (1 tsp) olive oil

FISH JUS
50 g (2 oz) sugar
100 ml (3½ fl oz) balsamic
vinegar
425 ml (¾ pint) well-flavoured fish
stock
250 ml (8 fl oz) red wine

1 Season the hake fillets and sprinkle with lemon juice and olive oil. Wrap tightly in cling film and steam for 15–20 minutes, until the flesh flakes easily.

2 Meanwhile, make the jus. Heat a dry pan. Add the sugar and heat until caramelized; remove from heat and add the balsamic vinegar. Stir quickly to dissolve any sugar crystals. Add the fish stock and reduce as required. The longer reduced, the stronger the flavour. Then add the red wine and reduce further. Season well.

3 Prepare the mussels. Heat the olive oil in a saucepan over a medium heat. Add the onion, celery, bay leaf, lemon and garlic. Cook until golden brown and add the mussels. Cook for about a minute, then add about 125 ml (4 fl oz) of water, the white wine, and season well.

4 Simmer for 4–5 minutes until all the mussels have opened. Remove and discard the bay leaf.

MUSSELS
olive oil, for sautéeing
1 onion, roughly chopped
½ stick celery, roughly chopped
1 bay leaf, torn
½ lemon
½ bulb garlic, crushed
8 fresh mussels, washed and debearded
175 ml (6 fl oz) white wine

WARM SALAD
knob of butter
45 ml (3 tbsp) olive oil
¼ red onion, diced
¼ aubergine, diced
½ red pepper, cored, deseeded and diced
½ yellow pepper, cored, deseeded and diced
¼ cucumber, diced

TO SERVE
Roasted Braised Leeks (see page 162)
Cubed Sautéed Potatoes (see page 153)

5 For the warm salad, heat the oil and butter in a saucepan, and add the red onion. When it is starting to caramelize, add the aubergine. After 30 seconds add the peppers. Continue cooking for 1 minute, then add the cucumber. Stir, and remove from the heat.

6 Arrange the fish jus in the centre of the serving plates and place the hake on top. Arrange the warm salad around the edge and top with the mussels. Serve with roasted braised leeks and cubed sautéed potatoes.

pan—fried wild sea bass with samphire with scottish girolles in a cream sauce and pea purée

300 g (10 oz) floury potatoes, peeled
300 g (10 oz) fresh peas, shelled
sea salt and freshly ground black pepper
200 ml (7 fl oz) full fat milk
extra-virgin olive oil, for pan-frying
4 wild sea bass fillets, with skin
juice of 1 lemon
500 g (1 lb 2 oz) samphire
few whole black peppercorns
100 g (3½ oz) unsalted butter
500 g (1 lb 2 oz) Scottish girolles, thinly sliced
100 ml (3½ fl oz) dry white wine
200 ml (7 fl oz) double cream

TO GARNISH
small bunch of flat—leaf parsley, finely chopped
lemon slices

1 Bring a pan of salted water to the boil and boil the potatoes for 20 minutes until very tender.

2 Meanwhile, bring another pan of salted water to the boil and boil the peas for about 8 minutes until tender. Drain the potatoes and peas, and mash together with seasoning to taste. Warm the milk and add to the potato mixture; push the potato mixture through a sieve and keep warm.

3 Heat the olive oil in a frying pan and pan-fry the sea bass fillets. Drizzle half the lemon juice over the fish and season with salt and pepper. Cook until the fish is just opaque throughout.

4 Steam the samphire for 5 minutes with the remaining lemon juice, peppercorns and salt in the water.

5 In a large sauté pan, heat the butter and fry the Scottish girolles for 1 minute; add the wine and cook for 1 more minute. Take the pan off the heat and stir in the cream.

6 Place the fish on serving plates with the crisped skin on top, add the samphire and the mushrooms in cream sauce. Garnish with chopped parsley and slices of lemon and serve with the pea and potato purée.

sea bass with squat lobster sauce with wilted spinach

15 ml (1 tbsp) olive oil, plus extra for coating
25 g (1 oz) butter
2 large carrots, finely diced
1 medium leek, finely diced
3 shallots, finely diced
4 cloves garlic, finely chopped
24 squat lobsters
125 ml (4 fl oz) white wine
15 ml (1 tbsp) Pernod
4 fillets sea bass, 175 g (6 oz) each
freshly ground salt

WILTED SPINACH
450 g (1 lb) baby spinach
25 g (1 oz) butter
freshly grated nutmeg

TO SERVE
Lemon Garlic New Potatoes (see page 155)
Braised Fennel (see page 152)

1 Heat 15 ml (1 tbsp) oil and the butter in a large stockpot, and add the carrots, leek, shallots and garlic. Sweat for 5 minutes.

2 Tail and shell the squat lobsters, reserving the tail meat. Place the shells and heads in the stockpot and crush. Cook for a further 5 minutes over a medium heat. Add the wine, Pernod and 3.5 litres (6 pints) of water. Simmer for about 2 hours or until the stock is reduced by half. Strain the stock and then sieve through muslin into a clean pan. Over a high heat, reduce the volume of the stock until about 45 ml (3 tbsp). The sauce should now be a deep orange colour and like syrup in consistency.

3 Prepare the wilted spinach. Place the wet spinach in a pan with the butter and heat until the spinach wilts. Add nutmeg to taste. Squeeze the liquid from the spinach and place on the centre of 4 serving plates. Keep warm.

4 Rub the skin side of the fish fillets with olive oil and freshly ground salt. Place under a hot grill, skin side up, until the skin is crispy and slightly charred for about 4 minutes, turning once.

5 Meanwhile, place the reserved squat tails in the warm sauce and cook for 1 minute.

6 Place the fish fillets, skin side up, on the spinach and spoon the sauce and tails around the fish. Serve with lemon garlic new potatoes and braised fennel.

pan-fried sea bass on a bed of baby spinach with scallops, a green herb sauce and a lemon saffron oil

SERVES 2

10 leaves baby spinach
10 g (¼ oz) butter
30 ml (2 tbsp) olive oil
2 fillets sea bass
10 scallops

HERB SAUCE

425 ml (¾ pint) well-flavoured fish stock
3 sprigs parsley, roughly chopped
3 sprigs chervil, roughly chopped
3 sprigs tarragon, roughly chopped
3 sprigs coriander, roughly chopped
1 handful spinach, roughly chopped
salt and freshly ground black pepper

LEMON SAFFRON OIL

300 ml (½ pint) extra-virgin olive oil
½ lemon, cut into chunks or slices
1 bay leaf, torn
1 sprig thyme
2 black peppercorns
1 strand saffron
2.5 ml (½ tsp) salt

TO SERVE
Parisian Potatoes (see page 156)

1 Bring the stock to the boil in a saucepan. Add the chopped herbs and spinach and boil until reduced by half. Taste for seasoning and then process with a hand blender to a purée. Pass through a sieve and set aside.

2 Place all the ingredients for the lemon saffron oil in a saucepan. Bring to the boil for 1 minute, mashing the lemon with the back of a spoon, then strain and set aside.

3 Bring about 200 ml (7 fl oz) of water to the boil in a saucepan and add the spinach leaves. Blanche for 1 minute and then remove; plunge in cold water to refresh, and drain well. Place in the centre of 2 serving plates and keep warm.

4 Heat half the butter and oil in a frying pan and fry the fish, skin side down, about 3–5 minutes until opaque throughout. Take off the heat and place on the spinach. Re-heat the pan with the remaining butter and oil and fry the scallops quickly for 30 seconds until just opaque. Toss the scallops in the lemon saffron oil.

5 To serve, pour the herb sauce around fish and spinach and dot with the lemon saffron oil. Arrange the scallops on the plate. Serve with the Parisian potatoes.

crusted cod steaks

SERVES 2

100 ml (3½ fl oz) olive oil

zest and juice of 1½ lemons

2 cod fillets

10 g (¼ oz) freshly grated
Parmesan

15 g (½ oz) freshly toasted
breadcrumbs

5 g (1 tsp) chopped parsley

salt and freshly ground black
pepper

TO SERVE

Sweated Leeks (see page 163)
Roast Cherry Tomatoes with
Kohlrabi (see page 149)

1 Mix the olive oil with the lemon juice in a shallow dish and marinate the cod fillets in the refrigerator until ready to use.

2 Place the Parmesan, breadcrumbs, parsley, seasoning and lemon zest in a bowl and mix thoroughly.

3 Remove the fillets from the marinade and place in an ovenproof dish; spread 1½–2 cm (½–¾ inch) of the Parmesan breadcrumb crust over the fish, and place in a preheated oven at 200°C (400°F) mark 6 for 15–20 minutes or until crust is golden brown.

4 Serve with the juices drizzled over, on a bed of sweated leeks with the roast tomatoes and kohlrabi.

stuffed sole rolls

SERVES 2

1 carrot, grated

½ courgette, grated

30 ml (2 tbsp) wholewheat
breadcrumbs

juice of 1 lime

salt and freshly ground black
pepper

2 sole fillets

SAUCE

250 ml (8 fl oz) double cream

70 ml (4 tbsp) chopped parsley

70 ml (4 tbsp) dill

TO SERVE

broccoli and new potatoes

1 Mix the grated carrot and courgette together in a bowl, stir in the breadcrumbs and lime juice and season to taste.

2 Lay the fish fillets skin–side up and divide the stuffing between them, spreading it evenly. Roll up to enclose the stuffing and place the fish rolls in an ovenproof dish. Cover and cook in a preheated oven at 200°C (400°F) mark 6 for 30 minutes until the fish flakes easily.

3 Meanwhile, make the sauce. Place the double cream, parsley and dill in a saucepan and bring to the boil. When the fish is cooked, stir the juices from the baking dish into the sauce and simmer for 2 minutes.

4 Place a pool of sauce in the middle of each serving plate, then place the fish rolls in the middle. Serve with broccoli and new potatoes.

soufflé of dover sole, crab and scallops

785 g (3 oz) scallops
2.5 ml (½ tsp) salt
1 egg yolk
4 fillets of Dover sole, about 75 g
(3 oz) each
15 ml (1 tbsp) unsalted butter,
melted
juice of ½ lemon
salt and freshly ground black
pepper
30 ml (2 tbsp) white crabmeat
15 ml (1 tbsp) brown crabmeat
20 g (¾ oz) fresh root ginger,
peeled, blanched and diced
pinch of cayenne pepper
90 ml (3 fl oz) whipping cream
2 egg whites

LEMON GRASS AND GINGER
SAUCE
1 crab carcass, chopped
115 g (4 oz) butter
25 g (1 oz) fresh root ginger,
peeled and chopped
25 g (1 oz) lemon grass stalk
15 ml (1 tbsp) brown crab meat
400 ml (14 fl oz) well-flavoured
vegetable stock
60 ml (2 fl oz) whipping cream

POMME FONDANT
4 medium potatoes, peeled
50 g (2 oz) unsalted butter
salt and freshly ground white
pepper
25 ml (1 fl oz) vegetable stock

TO SERVE
Mediterranean Vegetables in Filo
Baskets (see page 150)

NOTE: you will need 4 ring moulds
each 4 cm (1½ inches) deep x 6 cm
(2½ inches) across.

1 To make the pomme fondant, cut a 4cm (1½ inch) thick slice from the largest section of each potato. Using a ring mould as a cutter, cut a 6 cm (2½ inch) ring out of each slice. In a heavy–based ovenproof frying pan, melt the butter over a low heat. Place the rings of potato in the butter and lightly brown on both sides. Season with the salt and pepper. Pour the vegetable stock over and transfer the pan to a preheated oven at 180°C (350°F) mark 4 and cook for about 30 minutes until the potatoes are cooked through.

2 Meanwhile, purée the scallops in a food processor with the salt and egg yolk until smooth. Transfer to a metal bowl and refrigerate for 30 minutes.

3 Make the sauce. Melt 25 g (1 oz) of the butter in a large pan and add the crab carcass. Sweat gently for 5 minutes. Add the ginger, lemon grass and crab meat and cook for 5 minutes. Cover with the vegetable stock and bring to the boil. Simmer for 10 minutes. Add the cream and cook for 2 minutes longer. Pass the sauce through a fine strainer, return to the heat and reduce by half. When ready to use, add the remaining butter.

4 Prepare the fillets of sole for the ring moulds. Score the skin side and lay the fillets side by side under a sheet of cling film. Cover with another sheet of cling film and flatten the fillets with a heavy knife so that they are 4 cm (1½ inches) wide. Grease the ring moulds with a little melted butter and cover the base and outside of the moulds with cling film.

5 Add half the lemon juice, and salt and pepper to the remaining melted butter and brush on the sole fillets. Press the fillets into the ring moulds, flesh side against the moulds, with the ends overlapping.

6 Mix together the white and brown crab meat and ginger in a small bowl. Season with salt and cayenne pepper. Set aside.

7 Remove the scallop soufflé mixture from the refrigerator and stand the bowl on ice. Gradually add the cream, whisking to incorporate as much air as possible.

8 In a separate bowl, whisk the egg whites with a pinch of salt to a soft peak consistency. Add the remaining lemon juice and beat until smooth and firm. Add a quarter of the scallop soufflé mixture then fold in the rest.

9 One quarter fill the sole-lined rings with scallop soufflé mixture and cover with 15 ml (1 tbsp) of the crab mixture. Top with remaining soufflé mixture and smooth the surface.

10 Place the filled rings in a roasting pan and pour in about 1 cm (½ inch) hot water. Cook in preheated oven at 230°C (450°F) mark 8 for 12 minutes.

11 Place the pomme fondant on the serving plates. Place the soufflés on baking tray, remove the cling film and lift off the ring moulds. With a fish slice, carefully place a soufflé on each plate of pomme fondant. Strain the juices from the potatoes into the sauce and pour the sauce around the soufflés. Serve with vegetables in filo baskets.

paupiette of dover sole with beurre blanc

SERVES 2

2 Dover sole, skinned and filleted
salt and freshly ground black pepper
2 tomatoes, skinned
3 sprigs of dill, finely chopped
2 eggs, separated
60 ml (2 fl oz) double cream
125 g (4 oz) shallots, peeled and chopped
30 ml (2 tbsp) dry white wine
60 g (2½ oz) butter
1 clove garlic, finely chopped or 1 tbsp garlic purée
juice of ½ lemon, or to taste
4 tiger prawns, peeled
1 sprig of chervil, to garnish

BEURRE BLANC

250 ml (8½ fl oz) dry white wine
50 ml (2 fl oz) double cream
finely grated zest and juice of 1 lemon
finely grated zest and juice of 1 lime
200 g (7 oz) butter, diced

TO SERVE

Creamed Potatoes with Soured Cream (see page 156)

1 Season 6 of the fish fillets with salt and pepper and place to one side.

2 Place the tomatoes, dill and the remaining fish fillets in a blender, add the egg whites, cream and seasoning and purée until smooth. Place a spoonful of the mixture on each fillet and roll each up, securing with toothpicks. Place the stuffed fish rolls on a baking tray.

3 Sprinkle the chopped shallots around the fish rolls and pour the wine over the top; grease a piece of baking paper with a little of the butter, and place over the fish. Bake in a preheated oven at 180°C (350°F) mark 4 for 20–25 minutes. The fish should be opaque throughout.

4 Meanwhile, melt the remaining butter with the garlic and lemon juice in a frying pan and sauté the prawns until opaque throughout.

5 For the beurre blanc: pour the wine into a small saucepan and reduce by boiling to half the amount. Add the cream and reduce by half again. Add the zest of the lemon and lime and a squeeze of lemon and lime juice to taste. Stir in the diced butter, season with salt and pepper and whisk into froth, taking care not to allow the sauce to boil once the butter is added.

6 Place the fish rolls on the serving plates, and pour the beurre blanc around them. Garnish with the prawns and chervil, and serve with creamed potatoes with soured cream.

roast cod with tapénade, tomato sauce, potato mayonnaise and french bean vinaigrette

vegetable oil, for brushing
4 thick pieces of cod fillet

FRENCH BEAN VINAIGRETTE
25 ml (5 tbsp) extra-virgin olive oil
15 ml (1 tbsp) red wine vinegar
salt and freshly ground black
pepper
200 g (7 oz) French beans

TOMATO SAUCE
350 g (12 oz) cherry tomatoes
15 ml (1 tbsp) sun-dried tomato
purée
15 ml (1 tbsp) tomato purée
10 ml (2 tsp) granulated sugar

TAPÉNADE
75 g (3 oz) stoned black olives,
drained and rinsed
4 anchovy fillets
30 g (1 oz) capers, drained and
rinsed
3 cloves garlic, peeled
75 ml (2½ fl oz) olive oil

POTATO MAYONNAISE
1 egg
10 ml (2 tsp) lemon juice
finely grated zest of ½ lemon
200 ml (7 fl oz) vegetable oil
100 ml (3½ fl oz) extra-virgin olive
oil
white pepper
600 g (1 lb 5 oz) new waxy
potatoes

TO GARNISH
rock salt
sprigs of basil

1 Make the vinaigrette with the oil, vinegar and seasoning. Cook the beans in boiling salted water for 4 minutes, drain, refresh in cold water and drain again. Toss the beans in vinaigrette to give a light coating.

2 For the tomato sauce, place the tomatoes in a food processor and process. Put through a sieve, return to the food processor with the tomato purées, sugar and a pinch of salt and process again. Chill.

3 For the tapénade, put the olives, anchovies, capers, and garlic into a food processor and process. Add the oil gradually with the machine still on to form a finely chopped mixture. Stir in some black pepper. Chill.

4 Make the mayonnaise. Place the egg, lemon juice and lemon zest in a food processor and process. Mix the two oils together and add to the egg in a steady stream with the processor still running. Add salt and white pepper to taste. Chill.

5 Cook the potatoes in boiling salted water until soft. Cut the potatoes in half lengthways and take off the skin. While still hot, toss in enough mayonnaise to give a light coating.

6 Heat a stove–top grill pan and oil it. Brush the cod with oil on both sides and sprinkle with salt. Place the cod on the hot grill, skin side down, and cook until the skin is crisp and nicely marked. Turn over and cook the other side until the flesh is just opaque all the way through.

7 Place a pile of potatoes in the centre of each plate, place the French beans on top, and the cod on top of them, skin–side up. Sprinkle with a little rock salt and decorate with a sprig of basil. Swirl a little tomato sauce around the edges of the plate, and place 15 ml (1 tbsp) tapénade on top of the sauce. Serve.

MAIN COURSES: VEGETARIAN

mataar panneer, jeeru chawal, and rathu with papaad and garlic and coriander naan bread

SERVES 2

240 ml (8 fl oz) vegetable oil
1 medium onion, chopped
2.5 ml (½ tsp) cayenne pepper
5 ml (1 tsp) green chillies, deseeded and finely chopped
4 ml (¾ tsp) garlic, very finely chopped
4 ml (¾ tsp) fresh root ginger, grated
1.25 ml (¼ tsp) turmeric
5 ml (1 tsp) garam masala
225 g (8 oz) tomatoes, skinned and chopped
100 g (3½ oz) panneer, cut into cubes
450 g (1 lb) frozen petit pois
150 g (5 oz) basmati rice
Ghee (clarified butter), for frying
cumin seeds, to taste
fresh coriander, chopped, to garnish

NAAN BREAD

200 g (7 oz) plain flour, plus extra for dusting
15 ml (1 tbsp) yeast
5 ml (1 tsp) salt
1.25 ml (¼ tsp) cayenne pepper
5 ml (1 tsp) dried mixed herbs
5 ml (1 tsp) fresh coriander, chopped
5 ml (1 tsp) vegetable oil
5 ml (1 tsp) margarine
5 ml (1 tsp) garlic purée
7.5 ml (1½ tsp) plain yogurt
120 ml (4 fl oz) warm milk
butter, for spreading

1 Make the dough for the naan bread: in a large bowl, mix the flour, yeast, salt and cayenne pepper, together with the herbs. Add the oil, margarine, garlic purée, and yogurt and rub in with your fingers. Gradually stir in 120 ml (4 fl oz) water and the milk and knead lightly to a dough. Set the dough aside to rest.

2 In a large saucepan, heat 60 ml (4 tbsp) of the oil, add the onion and cook, stirring occasionally, until browned. Add the cayenne pepper, chillies, garlic, ginger, turmeric and garam masala and cook for 1 minute, stirring. Add the tomatoes and cook over a medium heat until slightly reduced.

3 Heat the remaining oil in a deep frying pan and fry the panneer cubes until golden brown. Remove with a slotted spoon and drain on paper towels. Add the panneer to the pan with the tomatoes.

4 Soak the frozen petit pois in a bowl of hot water and set aside for a few minutes. Drain and add them to the pan with the tomatoes. Add 500 ml (16 fl oz) of water and stir gently.

5 Make the rathu: put the yogurt in a small bowl and stir in the chillies, coriander and cumin seeds, and the salt. Set aside.

6 Soak the rice in warm water. In a large saucepan heat a little clarified butter and fry the cumin seeds; stir until slightly darkened and then add the drained rice and 1 litre (2 pints) water. Bring to the boil, stir, and cook for 5 minutes. Cover and cook until all the water is absorbed.

7 Knead the dough and divide it into small round balls. Using a rolling pin, and working on a floured surface, roll each ball into a naan shape. Heat a frying pan until hot and cook each naan individually until brown, then cook the other side under a preheated grill until risen and brown. Butter each naan.

8 Remove the rice from the heat. Chop fresh coriander and add to the cooked maatar panneer. Serve the maatar panneer with the rice, naan bread, rathu and papaad.

RATHU
20 ml (4 tbsp) plain yogurt
1.25 ml (¼ tsp) deseeded and
very finely chopped green chillies
2.5 ml (½ tsp) each coriander and
cumin seeds, crushed
2.5 ml (½ tsp) salt

TO SERVE
green chilli poppadoms (papaad,
from specialist Asian shops)

NOTE: Mataar Panneer is a traditional Punjabi tofu cheese curried in a rich tomato and onion sauce, with peas.
Jeeru Chawal is boiled rice stir-fried in cumin seeds and clarified butter.
Rathu is an authentic-style yogurt with added spices.

main courses: vegetarian

mushroom and brie tartlets

SERVES 2

120 ml (8 tbsp) redcurrants

90 ml (6 tbsp) port

35 g (1½ oz) butter, plus extra for greasing

75 g (3 oz) plain flour, plus extra for dusting

5 ml (1 tsp) finely grated Parmesan

5 ml (1 tsp) olive oil

¼ red onion, finely chopped

150 g (5 oz) chestnut mushrooms, sliced

salt and freshly ground black pepper

75 g (3 oz) Brie, sliced

60 ml (4 tbsp) cranberry jelly

TO SERVE

Potato and Leek Patties (see page 160)

steamed medley of garden vegetables

1 Place the redcurrants in a small bowl and pour the port over. Set aside.

2 Make the pastry. Rub together the butter, flour and Parmesan. Add enough cold water to bind together to form a soft dough. Roll out the pastry on a lightly floured work surface.

3 Grease 2 loose–bottomed individual flan tins with butter and line with the pastry. Put the pastry cases in the refrigerator to chill for 20 minutes.

4 Heat the olive oil in a frying pan, add the onion and fry until soft. Add the mushrooms and season to taste.

5 Remove pastry cases from refrigerator and place on a baking tray, then bake them blind in a preheated oven at 200°C (400°F) mark 6 for 10 minutes. Remove from the oven; leave the oven on.

6 Put one quarter of the onion and mushroom mixture into each tartlet case, add half the Brie to each case, and then the remaining onion and mushroom. Replace the tartlets in the oven for approximately 20 minutes.

7 Meanwhile, in the frying pan, simmer the redcurrants in the port until softened. Add the cranberry jelly and stir gently.

8 Remove the tartlets from the oven, remove from the flan tins and place the tartlets on warmed plates. Strain a little redcurrant-cranberry sauce over the top of the tartlets, and serve any remaining sauce separately. Serve with potato and leek patties and steamed vegetables.

ravaya

SERVES 2

RAVAYA (POTATO AND ONION STUFFED AUBERGINES)
60 ml (4 tbsp) oil
1.25 ml (¼ tsp) poppy seeds
1 onion, finely diced
2 potatoes, finely diced
5 ml (1 tsp) garam masala
5 ml (1 tsp) salt
2.5 ml (½ tsp) green chillies, cored, deseeded and finely chopped
2.5 ml (½ tsp) garlic
2.5 ml (½ tsp) grated fresh root ginger
1.25 ml (¼ tsp) cayenne pepper
1.25 ml (¼ tsp) ground turmeric
4 small aubergines
fresh coriander, chopped, to garnish

KARRI (YELLOW SAUCE TO ACCOMPANY THE RICE)
60 ml (4 tbsp) yogurt
5 ml (1 tsp) chickpea flour
5 ml (1 tsp) dhana jeeru (optional)
2.5 ml (½ tsp) green chillies, cored, deseeded and finely chopped
1. 25 ml (¼ tsp) ground turmeric
1.25 ml (¼ tsp) salt
15 ml (1 tbsp) clarified butter
2.5 ml (½ tsp) cumin seeds

SALAD
6 iceberg lettuce leaves
2 carrots, grated
¼ cucumber, thinly sliced
1 tomato, thinly sliced

PILAU RICE
15 ml (1 tbsp) clarified butter
2.5 ml (½ tsp) cumin seeds

1 Heat the oil in a frying pan and cook the poppy seeds, When they have 'popped' add the onion and cook for about 3 minutes until brown; then add the potatoes. Add the garam masala, salt, chillies, garlic, ginger, cayenne and turmeric. Stir the mixture well and cook it for 10–15 minutes. Set aside to cool.

2 Make the karri. In a medium bowl, mix the yogurt, chickpea flour, dhana jeeru (if using), chillies, turmeric and salt. Stir the mixture until smooth. Add 125 ml (4 fl oz) water and whisk until frothy. In a small pan, heat the clarified butter and fry the cumin seeds for 2 minutes or until the colour of the seeds has darkened. Add the yogurt spice mixture and cook, stirring, for 5–6 minutes over a low heat. Set aside.

3 Make a deep cross–shaped cut from the base end of the aubergines without cutting all the way through to the stalk end, so that the aubergines are partly quartered. Stuff the potato and onion mixture into each aubergine, and replace the aubergines in the pan the stuffing was cooked in. Cook for 10–15 minutes over a moderate heat until the aubergines are soft and cooked through.

4 Make the salad: finely chop 3 of the lettuce leaves. Line a salad bowl with the remaining leaves, and layer the carrots, cucumber and tomato into the bowl, with the tomatoes on top.

5 Prepare the pilau rice; heat the clarified butter in a saucepan and add the cumin seeds. Let these change colour to a dark brown black; meanwhile soak the petit pois in hot water. Once the cumin seeds have changed colour, add the turmeric, green chillies and salt, then stir. Drain the peas and add to the saucepan. Stir well. Add the rice and stir to mix with the spices and peas. Pour on 1 litre (1¾ pints) boiling water and cook, covered, over a moderate heat for 25 minutes or until the water is absorbed.

6 Make the bhaji: heat the oil in a frying pan and add the onion. Fry until golden brown then add the spinach, chillies, salt and dhana jeeru (if using). Cook the spinach until halved in quantity.

7 Make the chapattis: put the flour in a bowl and rub in the oil and 150–200 ml (5–7 fl oz) water to form a stiff dough. Turn the dough onto a floured surface and knead until smooth and elastic. Heat a griddle until very hot. Take a small piece of dough and shape into a ball. Dip the ball of dough into some flour, then roll out on the floured surface to a round shape. Slap the chapatti onto the hot griddle and cook over a low heat; as soon as brown spots appear on the underside, turn it over and cook the other side. Turn the chapatti over again and, with a clean tea towel, press the edges of the chapatti to circulate the steam and make the chapatti puff up. Cook until the underside is golden brown. Brush the chapattis with butter.

8 Reheat the karri. Garnish the ravaya and spinach bhaji with freshly chopped coriander and serve with the pilau rice and karri sauce, accompanied by the salad and hot chapattis. NOTE: This recipe calls for Dhana jeeru, a spice mixture which may be hard to find. If so it may be omitted.

75 g (3 oz) frozen petit pois
1. 25 ml (¼ tsp) ground turmeric
1. 25 ml (¼ tsp) green chillies, cored, deseeded and finely chopped
salt, to taste
150 g (6 oz) basmati rice

BHAJI (CURRIED SPINACH)
60 ml (4 tbsp) oil
½ onion, finely chopped
450 g (1 lb) spinach,
5 ml (1 tsp) green chillies, cored, deseeded and finely chopped
5 ml (1 tsp) salt
2.5 ml (½ tsp) dhana jeeru (optional)
fresh coriander, chopped, to garnish

CHAPATTIS
200 g (7 oz) wholemeal flour, plus extra for dusting
45 ml (3 tbsp) oil
melted butter, for brushing

NOTE: This recipe calls for Dhana jeeru, a spice mixture which may be hard to find. If so it may be omitted.

spinach gnocchi with roasted capsicum and blue cheese sauces and stottie cake

SERVES 2

1 large baking potato
50 g (2 oz) plain flour, plus extra for dusting
1 egg
1 egg yolk
50 g (2 oz) steamed spinach
nutmeg, freshly grated

STOTTIE CAKE

450 g (1 lb) white bread flour, plus extra for dusting
50 g (2 oz) dried yeast
5 ml (1 tsp) salt
butter, to glaze

BLUE CHEESE SAUCE

275 ml (9 fl oz) milk
25 g (1 oz) butter
25 g (1 oz) plain flour
50 g (2 oz) blue cheese
1 egg yolk
salt and cayenne pepper
15 ml (1 tbsp) whipping cream

ROASTED CAPSICUM SAUCE

2 red peppers
oil, for pan frying
2 shallots, finely chopped
1 clove garlic, finely chopped
(4 fl oz) vegetable stock
salt and freshly ground black pepper

1 Bake the potato in a preheated oven at at 220°C (425°F) mark 7 for about 35 minutes.

2 Make the Stottie cake: in a large bowl, mix the flour, yeast and salt together. Add 300 ml (½ pint) warm water and mix to a soft dough. Transfer to a floured work surface and knead for 5 minutes. Roll out on a greased oven tray and prick the top of the dough several times. Bake in the preheated oven at 220°C (425°F) mark 7 for 35 minutes. Remove from the oven and glaze with butter.

3 Meanwhile, make the blue cheese sauce: warm the milk in a large pan. Melt the butter in a heavy–based pan, add the flour and mix well. Cook for a few minutes over a gentle heat without colouring. Gradually add the warmed milk and stir until smooth. Allow to simmer for approximately 10 minutes. Add the blue cheese, then remove from the heat. Add the egg yolk, season to taste with salt and cayenne, and mix well. Gently fold in the whipping cream. Set aside.

4 Make the roasted capsicum sauce; bake the peppers in the preheated oven at 220°C (425°F) mark 7, turning occasionally, until dark spots appear on the skin. Remove from the oven and allow to cool. When cool enough to handle, split the skin, remove the core and seeds, and roughly chop.

5 Heat the oil in a frying pan and gently sweat the shallots and garlic until soft but not browned. Add the peppers and cook for a further 5 minutes. Add the stock and simmer for 3 minutes. Transfer the mixture to a blender and purée. Check the seasoning and pour into a tian or grill–proof serving dish.

6 When the baked potato is cooked, remove the flesh from the skin and pass through a sieve into a bowl. Add the flour, egg, egg yolk, steamed spinach, nutmeg and seasoning while the potato is still hot and mix well. Roll out on a floured board to form a large sausage shape. Press with a fork to flatten slightly. Cut the roll into 2.5 cm (1 inch) pieces and drop into a large pan of boiling salted water; cook for 5 minutes. Drain and place in the serving dish on top of the capsicum sauce.

7 Pour the blue cheese sauce over the gnocchi in the dish, and grill under a preheated grill until golden brown.

A C C O M P A N I M E N T S

glazed baby onions

175 g (6 oz) baby onions, peeled
50 g (2 oz) butter
15 ml (1 tbsp) olive oil
2 sprigs of thyme
15 ml (1 tbsp) caster sugar

1 Heat the butter and oil in a large shallow pan and add the onions and thyme. Turn to coat and cook over a medium heat, turning gently, until golden.

2 Sprinkle with the caster sugar, cover with nonstick baking parchment and cook in a preheated oven at 180°C (350°F) mark 4 for 20 minutes, turning occasionally.

blackberry glazed shallots

16 shallots
50 g (2 oz) unsalted butter
5 ml (1 tsp) blackberry jelly
300 ml (½ pint) red wine
salt and freshly ground black pepper

1 Cook the shallots in boiling salted water for 2 minutes, then plunge into cold water, drain and dry on paper towels.

2 Melt the butter in a frying pan and fry the shallots, turning until coloured. Add the jelly and half the wine. Cook very slowly over low heat for about 30 minutes, adding the remaining wine when the liquid has evaporated. They are ready when the sauce is sticky and reduced to about 15 ml (1 tbsp). Serve on blanched cabbage leaves.

mediterranean vegetable gateau

1 aubergine, thickly sliced, then slices quartered
1 courgette, sliced
1 red pepper, cored, deseeded and cut into chunks
1 yellow pepper, cored, deseeded and cut into chunks
4 canned plum tomatoes
1 red onion, coarsely chopped
3 cloves garlic, halved
salt and freshly ground black pepper
60 ml (4 tbsp) olive oil
few sprigs of thyme
15 ml (1 tbsp) capers, plus a few to garnish
grated zest of ½ lemon

1 Place the aubergine, courgette and peppers in a roasting tin. Crush the tomatoes over the top. Add the chopped onion and garlic and mix into the other vegetables. Season, sprinkle the oil over, and turn with your hands to ensure the vegetables are well mixed. Tuck a few sprigs of thyme in and roast in a preheated oven at 230°C (450°F) mark 8 for 30 minutes. Remove from the oven and allow to cool.

2 Remove the woody stems of thyme. Remove the skins from the peppers. Stir in the capers and lemon zest. Place a square of nonstick baking parchment in the bottom of 4 dariole moulds and layer in the vegetables, starting with the red and yellow peppers. Cover with foil and heat in the preheated oven at 190°C (375°F) mark 5 for 20 minutes.

3 To serve, slide a knife around the inside of each mould and turn out on to the serving plates. Garnish with a few capers.

red onions and potato

900g (2 lb) peeled, cubed potatoes
2 red onions, cubed
60 ml (4 tbsp) olive oil
sprig of rosemary, chopped
sprig of thyme, chopped
salt and freshly ground black pepper

1 Bring a large pan of salted water to the boil. Add the potatoes and onions. Cook for 10–15 minutes until al dente. Drain and toss immediately in the oil, herbs and garlic. Check the seasoning.

2 Turn into an ovenproof dish and bake in a preheated oven at 220°C (425°F) mark 7 for 40 minutes.

roast cherry tomatoes with kohlrabi

SERVES 2
1 small kohlrabi, peeled and cut into 1cm (½ in) cubes
600 ml (1 pint) chicken stock made with a stock cube
100 g (3½ oz) vegetable oil
10–20 cherry tomatoes, halved

1 Parboil the kohlrabi for 10–15 minutes in the chicken stock, then drain.

2 Pour a 1 cm (½ in) layer of oil into a roasting tin. Place in a preheated oven at 200°C (400°F) mark 6 for 5 minutes. Being careful in case the hot oil splashes, remove the tin and place the kohlrabi and cherry tomatoes in the oil. Return the tin to the oven and cook for 10 minutes, or until the sides of the vegetables are golden brown. Serve immediately.

roasted vegetables

SERVES 2
½ aubergine, sliced into rounds
½ courgette, sliced into rounds
½ red pepper, cored, deseeded and cut into 1 cm (½ in) squares
45 ml (3 tbsp) olive oil
salt and freshly ground black pepper

1 Put the vegetables in a baking tin and pour on the olive oil. Cook in a preheated oven at 220°C (425°C) mark 7 for 30–40 minutes, turning the vegetables occasionally.

carrot and celeriac

225 g (8 oz) celeriac, cut into chunks
225 g (8 oz) carrots
175 g (6 oz) smoked bacon, finely diced

1 Blanch the celeriac and carrots in boiling water for 1 minute, then drain and refresh in cold water. Cut into 5 mm (¼ in) dice.

2 Heat 15 g (½ oz) of butter in a pan. Add the celeriac, carrots and bacon and sauté until tender.

mediterranean vegetables in filo baskets

2 courgettes, sliced diagonally
olive oil with herbs and garlic
1 red pepper, cored, deseeded and
halved
1 green pepper, cored, deseeded
and halved
½ aubergine, sliced and cut into
diamond shapes
8 small vine tomatoes
8 sheets of filo pastry
50 g (2 oz) unsalted butter, melted

1 Place the courgettes in a bowl with the olive oil and marinate for about 15 minutes.

2 Place the peppers under a hot grill, skin–side up, until the skin is blackened. Place peppers in a polythene bag to steam off the skins. Remove skin with a sharp knife then cut into diamond shapes.

3 Cut the filo sheets into 4 squares and brush each sheet with a little melted butter, keeping the others covered with cling film. Lightly brush 4 5 cm (2 in) fluted tartlet tins with melted butter and place a square of filo pastry in each. Continue adding layers of filo pastry at an angle, to make a flower shape, 4 layers in total. Bake in a preheated oven at 180°C (350°F) mark 4 for 6 minutes. Remove, cool and unmould.

4 Put 15 ml (1 tbsp) of the herb and garlic olive oil into a chargrill pan over a high heat. Add the aubergines and cook for 2 minutes. Add the courgettes and peppers and then the tomatoes and cook until tender and marked with the grill. Arrange the vegetables in the filo baskets and serve.

mixed vegetable stir-fry

SERVES 2

75 ml (5 tbsp) toasted sesame oil
100 g (3½ oz) carrots, thinly sliced
40 g (1½ oz) spring onions, sliced
35 g (1¼ oz) pak choi, cut into
strips
100 g (3½ oz) courgettes, sliced
30 g (1¼ oz) beansprouts
25 g (1 oz) sesame seeds, toasted

1 Heat the oil in a wok until hot. Add the carrots, spring onions, pak choi, courgettes and beansprouts in that order and stir-fry for 2–3 minutes.
2 While the vegetables are still crisp add the sesame seeds, stir-fry for a few seconds and then serve immediately.

baby roast vegetables

20 baby potatoes
30–45 ml (2–3 tbsp) extra virgin
olive oil
20 baby carrots
10 shallots
fresh or dried rosemary
salt and freshly ground black
pepper

1 Par-boil the potatoes for 5 minutes, then refresh under cold water.
2 Preheat a roasting tin with the olive oil in an oven at 220°C (425°F) gas 7. Place the carrots, potatoes and shallots in the pan, coating well with the olive oil. Add the rosemary (dried works better than fresh I think) and season well with salt and pepper. Roast for 45 minutes until the vegetables look crisp and almost well done.

braised fennel

4 bulbs of fennel, fronds reserved
and chopped
30 ml (2 tbsp) butter
30 ml (2 tbsp) olive oil
90 ml (3 fl oz) white wine

1 Peel and quarter the bulbs of fennel. Heat the butter and olive oil in a frying pan. Add the fennel and sauté for 4–5 minutes to colour. Transfer to an ovenproof dish, add the white wine and cook in a preheated oven at 190°C (375°F) mark 5 for about 30 minutes, or until just tender.
2 To serve, garnish with the chopped fronds.

camargue rice

SERVES 2

50 g (2 oz) Camargue red rice

1 Place the rice in a pan of salted boiling water and boil gently for approximately 30 minutes.
2 Drain and serve.

stir-fried summer vegetables

SERVES 2

4 asparagus spears
50 g (2 oz) mushrooms
50 g (2 oz) mange-tout
4 spring onions
¼ red pepper, cored and deseeded
¼ yellow pepper, cored and deseeded
15 ml (1 tbsp) sesame oil

1 Chop the vegetables into even-sized pieces.

2 Heat the pan or wok and add the oil.

3 Add the asparagus and stir-fry for 2 minutes. Add the remaining vegetables and stir-fry for a few minutes until evenly cooked but still crunchy. Serve immediately.

stir-fried vegetables

SERVES 2

1 dash of garlic oil
½ carrot, peeled and cut into julienne
¼ red pepper, cored, deseeded and cut into julienne
¼ green pepper, cored, deseeded and cut into julienne
½ leek, cut into julienne
salt and freshly ground black pepper

1 Heat the oil in a wok until hot.

2 Add the vegetables and stir-fry for a few minutes until just cooked, but still crisp. Season and serve immediately.

cubed sautéed potatoes

SERVES 2

2 medium Cyprus potatoes, peeled
15 ml (1 tbsp) olive oil
15 g (½ oz) butter
salt and freshly ground black pepper

1 Cut the potatoes into 1cm (½ in) thick slices. Then cut off the edges to form rectangles and cut the rectangles into 1 cm (½ in) squares. Wash and drain well.

2 Heat the oil and butter in an ovenproof frying pan and add the potatoes. Season well. Turn over a medium heat until the potatoes are evenly browned on all sides, then transfer the pan to a preheated oven at 180°C (350°F) mark 4 for 10 minutes or until the potatoes are tender.

griddled potatoes

500 g (1 lb 2 oz) Charlotte
potatoes, halved lengthways
salt
olive oil

1 Cook the potatoes in boiling salted water until soft.
2 Drain, cool slightly, then remove the skins. Sprinkle with olive oil.
3 Heat a ridged griddle pan until hot. Cook the oiled potatoes on it until marked with a ridged pattern and reheated.

dauphinoise potatoes

3 cloves garlic
1 tbsp Malden salt
300 ml (½ pint) double cream
300 ml (½ pint) milk
freshly ground white pepper
1 kg (2½ lb) potatoes, peeled and
finely sliced
butter, for greasing
50 g (2 oz) grated Parmesan

1 Crush the garlic into a paste with the salt. In a large pan, combine the garlic paste, cream, milk and white pepper. Add the sliced potatoes, turning in the cream mixture to ensure all the slices are evenly coated. Bring to the boil, then simmer for 15 minutes until the potatoes are tender and the mixture has thickened.
2 Gently pour the potatoes into a buttered ovenproof dish and level the top. Sprinkle over the grated Parmesan and place in a preheated oven at 150°C (300°F) mark 2 for about 1 hour, until the top is nicely golden.

garam masala pommes parisiennes

6 large potatoes, peeled
30 ml (2 tbsp) peanut oil
25 g (1 oz) butter
garam masala, to sprinkle
½ bunch of coriander, chopped
60 ml (4 tbsp) Greek yogurt

1 Scoop the potatoes into balls with a melon baller. Heat the oil in a sauté pan and add the butter. Add the potato balls and toss in the pan till well coated. Fry very slowly over low heat until they are browned and tender, shaking the pan frequently to prevent them sticking.
2 Drain well, sprinkle with garam masala and mix with the chopped coriander. Serve as a side dish with a spoonful of the yogurt.

herbed duchesse potatoes

SERVES 2
1 large potato, peeled and cut into
chunks
15 ml (1 tbsp) milk
15 ml (1 tbsp) cream
knob of butter
5 ml (1 tsp) fresh chopped herbs

1 Boil the potatoes in salted water for 20 minutes, or until tender. Drain well.
2 Mash the potato, then beat in the milk, cream, butter and herbs to give a smooth, creamy consistency.
3 Spoon the potato into a piping bag and pipe rosettes onto a baking sheet lined with nonstick baking parchment. Bake in a preheated oven at 180°C (350°F) mark 4 for 15–20 minutes, or until golden.

lemon garlic new potatoes

450 g (1 lb) new potatoes
salt and freshly ground black pepper
2 cloves garlic, crushed
25 g (1 oz) butter
juice of ½ lemon

1 Boil the new potatoes in salted water for 12 minutes, until just cooked.
2 Drain and add the garlic, butter and lemon juice. Cover and leave to stand for 5 minutes before serving. Season with salt and freshly ground black pepper.

layered stilton potatoes and leeks

SERVES 2
2 large potatoes, peeled and halved
3 leeks, sliced in half lengthways, then finely slice across into half rings
15 ml (1 tbsp) cream
50 g (2 oz) Stilton, grated
salt and freshly ground black pepper
vegetable oil, for brushing

1 Parboil the potatoes in salted water for 4–5 minutes. Drain and leave to cool. Grate coarsely into a bowl.
2 Place the leeks in a bowl. Add the cream and Stilton. Season with pepper but very little salt and mix thoroughly.
3 Wash and dry 2 small empty 'spaghetti rings' tins with the labels removed. Stand on a baking sheet. Place a layer of potato in each tin, season, and press down.
4 Place a layer of the leek mixture on top of the potato.
5 Repeat the layers of potato and leek, finishing with a layer of potato. Brush the tops with oil, then fluff the tops with a fork. Bake in a preheated oven at 190°C (375°F) mark 5 for 20–25 minutes, or until well browned.

mustard soufflé jackets

4 jacket potatoes
7.5 ml (1½ tsp) Dijon mustard
50 ml (2 fl oz) milk
25 g (1 oz) butter
1 egg yolk
2 egg whites
10 ml (2 tsp) chopped chives
salt and freshly ground black pepper

1 Cut one end off each potato so that they stand up. Bake in a preheated oven at 220°C (425°F) mark 7 until soft.
2 Slice off the other end of each potato and scoop out the inside, being careful not to damage the skins. Add the milk and butter to the potato and mash until soft.
Mix in the egg yolk and mustard. Whip the egg whites into peaks and fold into the mash with the chives and seasoning.
3 Spoon the mixture back into the potato skins and bake in a preheated oven at 220°C (425°F) mark 7 for 20–25 minutes until the soufflé is firm.

parisian potatoes

SERVES 2
8 medium Jersey new potatoes
425 ml (¾ pint) water
5 ml (1 tsp salt)
5 ml (1 tsp) olive oil
freshly ground black pepper

1 Scoop the potatoes into balls with a parisienne cutter. Bring a pan of water to the boil and add the salt and the potatoes. Boil for 5–10 minutes, then drain.

2 Heat the oil in a frying pan. Add the potatoes and sauté for 3–4 minutes, turning until golden on all sides. Season, then remove from heat and serve.

creamed potatoes with soured cream

SERVES 2
450 g (1 lb) potatoes, peeled
salt and freshly ground black pepper
25 g (1 oz) butter
25 ml (1 fl oz) milk
75 ml (2½ fl oz) sour cream

1 Boil the potatoes in salted water until tender. Drain and mix in the butter, milk and sour cream. Season with salt and pepper. Mash the potatoes, then whisk using a hand blender until light and fluffy.

2 Spoon the creamed potatoes into a piping bag and pipe rosettes or other shapes onto a greased baking sheet. Place under a hot grill until lightly browned.

pommes savoyarde

2 cloves garlic, crushed
50 g (2 oz) unsalted butter
1 kg (1¼ lb) peeled potatoes, thinly sliced
2 shallots, chopped
salt and freshly ground black pepper
ground nutmeg
50 g (2 oz) grated Gruyère
50 g (2 oz) grated Parmesan
450 ml (¾ pint) double cream

1 Rub a gratin dish with the garlic and grease with half the butter. Layer the potatoes with the shallots, seasoning, nutmeg and cheeses, reserving 15 ml (1 tbsp) of Parmesan. Heat the cream in a pan until almost boiling, then pour over the potatoes. Sprinkle with the remaining cheese and dot with the remaining butter. Cover with foil.

2 Bake for 1 hour in a preheated oven at 180°C (350°F) mark 4. Remove the foil and cook for another 20 minutes, until golden outside and soft in the middle.

horseradish mashed potatoes

700 g (1½ lb) potatoes, peeled
40 g (1½ oz) butter
10 ml (2 tsp) fresh horseradish, grated
salt and freshly ground black pepper

1 Cook the potatoes in a large pan of boiling salted water for 20 minutes. Drain well.

2 Add the butter, grated horseradish and plenty of black pepper. Mash the potatoes until smooth, check the seasoning and serve.

carrot and fennel purée

50 g (2 oz) butter
1 fennel bulb, finely sliced
450 g (1 lb) carrots, chopped
1 onion, sliced

1 Melt half the butter in a nonstick pan. Add the fennel, carrots and onion and turn in the butter to ensure all the vegetables are coated. Sauté gently for about 30 minutes until the vegetables are tender, stirring regularly, and adding the remaining butter if the vegetables become dry.
2 Place the mixture in a food processor and purée.
3 To serve, form quenelles of the purée with 2 spoons, placing them on a warmed serving dish

creamed celeriac

1 large celeriac, cut into 2.5 cm
(1 in) cubes
600 ml (1 pint) chicken stock
30 ml (2 tbsp) double cream
25 g (1 oz) unsalted butter
salt and freshly ground mixed
pepper

1 Place the celeriac in a pan with the chicken stock, bring to the boil and simmer until tender. Drain, reserving the stock. Mash the celeriac in the pan and dry out over a low heat.
2 Boil the reserved stock until reduced to a syrup. Add to the celeriac with the cream and butter and mix well, seasoning to taste. Reheat gently and serve on blanched cabbage leaves.

garlic mash

600 g (1¼ lb) Maris Piper
potatoes, peeled and cubed
4–5 cloves garlic, peeled
150 ml (¼ pint) milk
knob of butter
salt and freshly ground black
pepper

1 Place the potatoes, garlic and milk in a pan. Add enough water to cover. Bring to the boil and simmer until the potatoes are tender.
2 Drain the potatoes, reserving about 150 ml (¼ pint) of the cooking liquid. Mash the potatoes and garlic with the reserved liquid and butter, adding salt and pepper to taste.

goats' cheese mash

SERVES 2
2 large potatoes, peeled and cut
into chunks
salt and freshly ground black
pepper
100 g (3½ oz) goats' cheese
75 g (3 oz) butter
60 ml (4 tbsp) double cream

1 Boil the potatoes in salted water until tender. Drain, then add the goats' cheese on top of the potatoes and allow to soften for a few minutes. Mash the potato with the cheese, adding the butter and cream. Season well with salt and pepper.

accompaniments

himmel und erde with sage

800 g (1¾ lb) floury potatoes, peeled and cut into chunks
salt and freshly ground black pepper
400 g (14 oz) Bramley apples, peeled, cored and chopped
25 g (1 oz) unsalted butter
15–30 ml (1–2 tbsp) double cream
15–30 ml (1–2 tbsp) fresh chopped sage

1 Cook the potatoes in boiling salted water until tender, then drain.

2 Rinse the apples and cook with just the water that clings to them, until soft.

3 Mash the potatoes with the butter and cream. Purée the apples and stir into the mashed potato. Stir in the sage and add season to taste.

parmesan mashed potatoes

SERVES 2

2 large potatoes, peeled and
halved
salt and freshly ground black
pepper
60 ml (4 tbsp) double cream
15 ml (1 tbsp) butter
50 g (2 oz) grated Parmesan

1 Cook the potatoes in a large pan of boiling salted until tender.

2 Drain the potatoes and transfer to a bowl. Mash the potatoes, mixing in the cream, butter and Parmesan.

3 Season well before serving.

puréed parmesan potatoes with nutmeg

SERVES 2

2 baking potatoes
vegetable oil
melted duck fat, if available
salt and freshly ground black
pepper
25 g (1 oz) grated Parmesan
15 g (½ oz) butter
5 ml (1 tsp) nutmeg

1 Wash and prick the potatoes. Put in the microwave on high (full) for 15 minutes then leave to stand for 5 minutes. Brush with oil, then bake in a preheated oven at 200°C (400°F) mark 6 for 15 minutes, until soft inside.

2 Cut the potatoes in half and scoop out the cooked potato into a bowl. Brush the potato skins with melted duck fat or oil and sprinkle with salt. Put crinkled foil inside the skins to hold their shape and return to the oven for 15–20 minutes until crisp. Cream the cooked potato with the Parmesan, butter, nutmeg and seasoning. Keep warm.

3 When the shells are crisp fill with the creamed potato and return to the oven for 15 minutes, until lightly browned on top.

spring onion mash

SERVES 2

450 g (1 lb) potatoes, peeled
salt and freshly ground black
pepper
75 g (3 oz) butter
60 ml (2 fl oz) double cream
about 60 ml (2 fl oz) single cream
bunch of spring onions, finely
chopped

1 Cook the potatoes in boiling salted water until tender, then drain. Mash the potatoes, adding the butter and double cream. Beat in enough single cream to give a smooth, soft consistency. Mix in the chopped spring onions and season to taste.

mushroom, bacon and spinach rösti

SERVES 2

225 g (8 oz) potatoes, peeled
salt and freshly ground black
pepper
vegetable oil
50 g (2 oz) bacon, trimmed and
chopped finely
50 g (2 oz) fresh baby spinach,
shredded
50 g (2 oz) mushrooms, sliced
knob of butter

1 Use the medium blade of a mandolin to shred the potatoes. Wrap the shredded potato in a clean tea towel and squeeze out all excess moisture. Season the potatoes.

2 Heat a blini pan or small omelette pan, adding just enough oil to coat the pan thinly. Place a thin layer of potato in the pan, bring the potato up the sides of the pan. Layer the bacon, spinach and mushroom in this well. Finish with a layer of potato and the knob of butter.

3 Cook the rösti over a low heat. When the base is golden brown, turn with a spatula and cook the other side. Shake the pan slightly during cooking to give a good shape to the rösti.

parmesan potato croquettes

SERVES 2

2 large potatoes, peeled and
quartered
30 ml (2 tbsp) milk
knob of butter, plus extra for
greasing
1 sprig of parsley, finely chopped
30 ml (2 tbsp) flour
1 egg, beaten
50 g (2 oz) grated Parmesan
50 g (2 oz) breadcrumbs

1 Place the potatoes in a pan of cold salted water, bring to the boil and cook until tender. Drain, then mash the potatoes with the milk and butter and mix in the parsley.

2 Place the flour, egg, and Parmesan and breadcrumbs mixed, in 3 separate dishes. Using 2 dessertspoons, shape the potatoes into rounded ovals. Dip each as shaped into the flour, then egg, then cheese and breadcrumb mix, to coat all sides. Place each croquette when coated onto a greased baking sheet.

3 Place the croquettes under a hot grill until crisp and browned, turning to brown all sides.

potato and leek patties

SERVES 2

4 medium-sized potatoes, peeled
and cut into small chunks
salt and freshly ground black
pepper
½ leek, thinly sliced
large knob of butter, plus extra for
gsreasing
30 ml (2 tbsp) milk
50 g (2 oz) grated Cheddar

1 Cook the potatoes in salted boiling water until tender, then drain. Cook the leek in boiling salted water until just tender, then drain.

2 Mash the potatoes with the butter and milk. Season to taste. Grease 4 individual patty tins. Fold the leeks into the mashed potatoes and put the mixture into the tins. Top each one with grated cheese.

3 Bake in a preheated oven at 200°C (400°F) mark 6 for 10 minutes. Remove from the oven and place under a hot grill for 3–5 minutes until the cheese is golden. Turn out of tins to serve.

caramelized shallots

SERVES 2
NOTE: the shallots should be cooked in the meat juices left from pan-frying lamb or beef steaks. Otherwise add 15 ml (1 tbsp) lamb stock to the pan.
6 shallots
10 ml (2 tsp) sugar

1 Blanch the shallots in boiling water for about 15 minutes. Remove and refresh in cold water. Dry on paper towels.

2 Heat the meat juices (see note) or lamb stock in a frying pan. Add the shallots, sprinkle with the sugar and cook gently until tender and the sugar has caramelized, turning frequently.

carrots with sesame seeds and honey

3 carrots, cut into matchstick strips
1 tsp sesame seeds
5 ml (1 tsp) runny honey
5 ml (1 tsp) unsalted butter

1 Cook the matchstick carrots in boiling water for 10 minutes, then drain. Place the carrots in a pan with the sesame seeds, honey and butter and cook for another 5 minutes, stirring occasionally.

roasted braised leeks

2 large leeks, split lengthways, but not through the root
15 g (½ oz) butter
salt and freshly ground black pepper

1 Place a very large saucepan of salted water over a high heat. Place the leeks in the boiling water, half cover with a lid and simmer for 20 minutes. Drain well.

2 Place a knob of butter in 2 ramekins and season. Place the leeks on a board. Cut off the white base of one leek, discarding the leaves. Cut it in half. Roll up one half and stand it upright. Remove and discard the inner section of the other leek half. Wrap the outer section tightly around the rolled up section and place in a ramekin. Place another knob of butter on top and season again. Repeat with the other leek.

3 Place the ramekins on a baking sheet and roast in a preheated oven at 190°C (375°F) mark 5 for 15–20 minutes.

parsnip purée

6 parsnips, peeled and cut into chunks
salt and freshly ground black pepper
8 cloves garlic, peeled
100 ml (3½ fl oz) double cream

1 Place the parsnips in a pan of salted boiling water with the garlic. Cook until the parsnips are very soft, about 45 minutes. Drain well and whisk with the cream, adding plenty of pepper.

2 Spoon the purée into a heatproof serving dish and place under a hot grill until browned on top.

spinach creams

500 g (1 lb 2 oz) fresh spinach, stalks removed
butter
2 egg yolks
75 ml (2½ fl oz) double cream
pinch of ground nutmeg
salt and freshly ground black pepper

1 Blanch 6–8 of the largest spinach leaves in boiling salted water for 10 seconds, then refresh in cold water and lay out to drain on paper towels. Cook the remaining spinach in boiling water for 1 minute and drain. Cool, and squeeze out as much water as possible.

2 Butter 4 small moulds and line with the whole leaves, leaving enough hanging over the edge to cover the filling.

3 Process the spinach in a food processor with the egg yolks, cream, nutmeg, salt and pepper. Fill the moulds nearly to the top with this mixture, fold over the spinach leaves to cover, and brush with melted butter.

4 Poach in a large shallow pan of barely simmering water for 10 minutes. Turn out to serve.

sweated leeks

SERVES 2
100 g (3½ oz) butter
2 cloves garlic, sliced
3 leeks, sliced crossways into circles

1 Melt the butter in a pan and add the garlic. Add the leeks and cover. Cook over a low heat for 5–10 minutes, checking occasionally that the leeks are not sticking. Add a little water if necessary. When the leeks are tender serve immediately.

rocket and apple salad

1 granny smith apple, peeled,cored and chopped
10 ml (2 tsp) lemon juice
20 g (¾ oz) rocket
20 g (¾ oz) mixed salad leaves

DRESSING
30 ml (2 tbsp) olive oil
5 ml (1 tsp) cider vinegar
salt and freshly ground black pepper

1 Toss the apple in a salad bowl with the lemon juice. Add the rocket and salad leaves.

2 Mix the olive oil and vinegar to an emulsion then season.

3 Pour the dressing over the salad, toss and serve.

wilted radicchio

1 head radicchio, leaves separated
10 ml (2 tsp) extra–virgin olive oil
salt and freshly ground black pepper

1 Heat a chargrill then add the radicchio leaves and leave until the purple fades. Remove from the grill, toss the leaves in oil and seasoning and place in an ovenproof dish. Wilt further in a preheated oven at 140°C (275°F) mark 1 for 5–10 minutes.

shiitake risotto

SERVES 2
20 g (¾ oz) butter
20 ml (4 tsp) olive oil
½ small onion,sliced
½ clove garlic, sliced
65 g (2¾ oz) carnaroli risotto rice
5 ml (1 tsp) ground cumin
800 ml (1½ pints) vegetable stock
400 ml (14 fl oz) coconut milk
30–40 coriander leaves, chopped
40 g shiitake mushrooms, sliced

1 Heat the butter and oil in a pan. Add the onion and garlic and sauté for a few minutes.
2 Add the rice and cumin and then add a ladleful of stock and stir until absorbed. Keep adding stock and stirring until the rice is almost cooked, about 20 minutes. Then start to add the coconut milk gradually, stirring until absorbed. When all the liquid has been absorbed and the rice is tender, remove from the heat and stir in the mushrooms and coriander. Stir well and serve.

sliced green beans with bacon

6 stringless green beans, sliced
3 rashers of smoked back bacon
15 ml (1 tbsp) vegetable oil

1 Cook the beans in a pan of boiling water for 10 minutes or until tender, then drain.
2 Meanwhile, heat the oil in a frying pan, add the bacon and fry until crispy. Drain on paper towels, then chop the bacon into small pieces and mix into the beans.

summer vegetables

2 courgettes, finely sliced
1 orange pepper, cored, deseeded and finely sliced
1 red chilli, deseeded and chopped
225 g (8 oz) fresh spinach, chopped
1 beetroot, peeled and finely sliced
125 g (4 oz) coriander leaves, chopped

DRESSING
175 ml (6 fl oz) olive oil
60 ml (2 fl oz) white wine vinegar
5 ml (1 tsp) honey
5 ml (1 tsp) Dijon mustard
10 ml (2 tsp) coriander seeds, toasted

1 Combine all the ingredients for the dressing and whisk well.
2 Lightly steam the courgettes, pepper and chilli for 5 minutes. Add the spinach and steam for a further 4–5 minutes.
3 Toss the steamed vegetables in a bowl with the raw beetroot and coriander. Add the dressing and mix well until all the vegetables are coated.

timbale of summer vegetables

450 g (1 lb) carrots, diced
450 g (1 lb) cauliflower, diced
450 g (1 lb) spinach, stems removed
5 ml (1 tsp) butter, melted, plus extra for greasing

1 Steam the carrots and cauliflower until just cooked. Wilt the spinach briefly by adding washed leaves to the melted butter in a heavy–based pan over a low heat.
2 Layer the hot vegetables in 4 lightly buttered timbales and keep warm until ready to serve. Turn out to serve.

NOTE: choose any 3 different coloured vegetables.

butternut squash

SERVES 2
1 ripe butternut squash, peeled and cut into cubes
15 ml (1 tbsp) butter
5 ml (1 tsp) sugar
pinch of ground cinnamon

1 Bring a pan of water to the boil, add the squash and cook for 10 minutes or until soft.
2 Drain the squash, transfer to a bowl and mash with the butter until smooth. Stir in the sugar and cinnamon and mix well.

carrot gratin

15 g (½ oz) unsalted butter
120 g (4 oz) carrots, grated
½ clove garlic
10 ml (2 tsp) lemon juice
30 ml (2 tbsp) double cream
15 ml (1 tbsp) dried breadcrumbs
15 g (½ oz) melted butter
parsley sprigs, to garnish

1 Melt the butter in a nonstick pan. Add the carrots and garlic and cook over a low heat for 5 minutes. Add the lemon juice and cream and stir to mix. Season well, and spoon into 2 ramekin dishes. Mix the breadcrumbs with the melted butter and spoon on top of the ramekins.
2 Put the ramekins on a baking sheet and bake in a preheated oven at 190°C (375°F) mark 5 for 20 minutes. Turn out onto warm plates and garnish with parsley.

confit tomatoes

6 large plum or other flavoursome tomatoes
olive oil
sea salt

1 Blanch and skin the tomatoes, then halve and deseed them. Cut the tomatoes into squares and lay, skinned–side up, in a shallow baking tin. Drizzle with olive oil and season with salt.
2 Place in a preheated oven at 110°C (225°F) mark ¼ for 1–1½ hours, until softened but not collapsed. Remove from the oven and cover until ready to serve.

NOTE: These are also delicious served as part of a salad, with spring onions, if you have any left over.

fricassée of mushrooms

50 g (2 oz) butter
1 shallot, finely chopped
225 g (8 oz) mixed mushrooms, wild if possible
2 plum tomatoes, peeled, deseeded and diced
5 ml (1 tsp) snipped chives

1 Melt half the butter in a pan, add the shallots, cover and sweat until soft. Add the mushrooms and cook until liquid appears. Drain and add the remaining butter. Cook for a further 1–2 minutes then mix in the diced tomatoes and chives. Warm through and serve.

NOTE: inspired by Marco Pierre White, Chef/Patron, Harvey's Battersea

chargrilled mediterranean vegetables

1 aubergine, cut into small chunks
1 red pepper, cored, deseeded and cut into chunks
1 yellow pepper, cored, deseeded and cut into chunks
2 courgettes, chopped
4 baby plum tomatoes, halved
1 red onion, cut into chunks
45 ml (3 tbsp) basil-infused olive oil
salt and freshly ground black pepper

1 Place the vegetables in a bowl and add the olive oil. Stir well to mix and season to taste. Leave to marinate for 30 minutes.
2 Heat a griddling pan or large frying pan. Place the vegetables in the pan, in batches if necessary, and fry on each side for about 3-4 minutes. The tomatoes should be added last. The vegetables should not be too hard, and should have black grill marks on them. Transfer to an ovenproof dish as they are cooked, and keep warm in a low oven until ready to serve.

seasonal green vegetables

SERVES 2
50 g (2 oz) fresh peas
50 g (2 oz) haricots verts
50 g (2 oz) small broccoli florets
50 g (2 oz) sugar snaps
50 g (2 oz) broad beans
50 g (2 oz) courgettes

TO SERVE
melted butter

1 Cut the courgettes into 7.5 cm (3 inch) pieces and then slice them thinly lengthways.
2 Place all the vegetables in a pan of lightly-salted boiling water for 2–3 minutes, until just done.
3 Drain and toss in a little melted butter to serve.

D E S S E R T S

almond sourdough cake with plum compote and orange curd ice cream

This is based on a recipe by Kim O'Flaherty in *A Modernistic View of Plated Desserts*

SOURDOUGH STARTER (SEE NOTE)
5 ml (1 tsp) dried yeast
150 ml (¼ pint) lukewarm water
80 g (3¼ oz) plain flour

ALMOND SOURDOUGH CAKE
50 g (2 oz) marzipan
40 g (1½ oz) caster sugar
40 g (1½ oz) unsalted butter, softened
⅓ vanilla pod, split and seeds reserved
2 eggs, slightly beaten
25 g (1 oz) sourdough starter (about 2 tbsp)
40 g (1½ oz) plain flour
7.5 ml (1½ tsp) baking powder
pinch of salt

PLUM COMPOTE
5 red plums, cut into 1 cm (½in) dice
80 ml (5½ tbsp) raspberry purée
200 g (7 oz) sugar
100 ml (3½ fl oz) orange juice
1 vanilla pod, split and scraped
5 ml (1 tsp) lemon juice

ALMOND TUILES
15 g (½ oz) marzipan
5 ml (1 tsp) finely grated lemon zest
85 g (3¼ oz) sugar
75 g (3 oz) plain flour
1 egg

ORANGE CURD ICE CREAM
180 ml (6 fl oz) milk
65 ml (4 tbsp) double cream

1 To make the starter, place the yeast in a non-metal container with the water and stir until dissolved. Mix in the flour. Cover loosely with cling film and leave to sit at room temperature for 2–3 days, stirring occasionally.

2 To make the cake, grease and line a 20 cm (8in) square cake tin. Process the marzipan and sugar in a food processor until fine. Add the butter and vanilla seeds and beat until pale and creamy. Slowly add the lightly beaten eggs. Add the sourdough starter. Sift in the flour, baking powder and salt and fold until combined.

3 Transfer the mixture to the cake tin and smooth the top. Bake in a preheated oven at 170°C (325°F) mark 3 for about 20 minutes, until golden and a skewer inserted into the centre comes out clean.

4 To make the compote, combine all the ingredients in a pan and cook over medium heat for 10–15 minutes, so that the plums are cooked but do not lose their shape. Strain the plums, removing the vanilla pod, and reserve the syrup.

5 To make the tuiles, process the marzipan, zest and sugar in a food processor until fine. Add the flour and process briefly. Add the egg with the machine running and process until well–mixed. The batter should be the consistency of thick double cream.
Strain through a sieve to remove any lumps.

6 Spoon the batter into a piping bag and pipe right-angled triangles measuring 18 cm (7 in) x 10cm (4 in) with a lattice pattern onto a non-stick baking sheet. Bake in a preheated oven at 175°C (325°F) mark 3 for 5–6 minutes, until light golden. Remove the tuiles immediately and wrap round a rolling pin. Leave to cool until set.

7 To make the ice cream, bring the milk, cream and vanilla to the boil in a small pan. Whisk the sugar, yolks and zest to the ribbon stage in a bowl. Pour the milk onto the yolks, whisking all the time, and return to the pan. Heat slowly until the mixture thickens, but do not allow it to boil.

8 Strain the mixture through a fine sieve, then whisk in the orange curd and crème fraîche. Cool, then transfer to an ice-cream machine and churn for 30–40 minutes. Transfer to the freezer until ready to serve.

9 To assemble, warm the plums in the syrup. Cut out four 7cm (3in) circles from the cake and place one in the centre of each plate. Top with some of the plum compote. Arrange some of the plums to one side. Place 2 small scoops of ice cream on the compote and top with a tuile. Drizzle some syrup around the plate.

NOTE: Sourdough starters can be kept alive indefinitely, as long as they are regularly fed. Once a week, remove from the refrigerator. In a bowl place

5 ml (1 tsp) vanilla extract
60 g (2¼ oz) sugar
2 egg yolks
grated zest of 1 orange
4 heaped tsp orange curd
200 g (7 oz) crème fraîche

8 fl oz (250ml) of the starter (discard the rest), 8 fl oz (250ml) water and 175 g (6 oz) plain flour. Stir to combine, cover and leave at room temperature for about 12 hours. A healthy starter should have the consistency of pancake batter, with lots of bubbles. The longer the starter is left out of the refrigerator the more sour it becomes. Return to the fridge. To use the starter in a recipe, combine 1 part starter, 1 part water and 1½ parts flour and leave at room temperature for 1-3 days before using. A wonderful source of information on sourdough, including recipes, can be found on the Internet in newsgroup: rec.food.sourdough.

bread and butter pudding with forest fruits and a vanilla custard

SERVES 2
200 ml (7 fl oz) milk
150 ml (¼ pint) double cream
3 drops of vanilla essence
50g (2 oz) butter
8 slices thick white bread, crusts removed
3 eggs
50 g (2 oz) caster sugar
50 g (2 oz) raisins
50 g (2 oz) sultanas
grated zest of 1 lemon
15 ml (1 tbsp) demerara sugar
5 ml (1 tsp) ground cinnamon

VANILLA CUSTARD
300 ml (½ pint) double cream
2 egg yolks
50 g (2 oz) caster sugar
4 drops of vanilla essence

COULIS
50 g (2 oz) raspberries
45 ml (3 tbsp) water
30 ml (2 tbsp) granulated sugar

TO DECORATE
5 ml (1 tsp) icing sugar
1 pinch of cinnamon
25 g (1 oz) fresh raspberries
25 g (1 oz) fresh blueberries

1 Place the milk, cream and vanilla essence in a pan and bring almost to the boil. Butter the bread and cut into quarters diagonally. Whisk the eggs and sugar together until the mixture is pale and thick, and forms a ribbon. Add the hot milk and whisk again.

2 Layer the bread in a shallow baking dish with the dried fruit and zest. Strain the hot egg sauce over the bread and leave to stand for 20 minutes. Sprinkle with the sugar and cinnamon.

3 Place the pudding in a preheated oven at 180°C (350°F) mark 4 for 35 minutes.

4 To make the custard, heat the double cream in a pan. Whisk together the egg yolks, caster sugar and vanilla essence. When the cream is almost boiling pour it onto the eggs and mix well. Return the custard to the pan and heat until it is thick enough to coat the back of a spoon, but do not allow it to boil. Remove from the heat.

5 To make the coulis, place the ingredients in a pan and boil until glossy and all the sugar has dissolved.

6 To serve, spoon some custard on each plate. Use a mould to cut 4 rounds out of the bread and butter pudding. Place a round in the centre of each plate and sprinkle with icing sugar and cinnamon. Dot the custard with the coulis and decorate with the fresh fruits.

orange and almond brioche bread and butter pudding

150 g (5 oz) unsalted butter, plus extra for greasing
½ x 450 g (1 lb) jar of marmalade
4 brioche rolls
grated zest of 1 orange
100 g (3½ oz) marzipan
75 ml (2½ fl oz) almond liqueur
30 ml (2 tbsp) thick single cream
50 ml (2 fl oz) milk
4 large eggs
50 g (2 oz) vanilla sugar
200 ml (7 fl oz) double cream
60 ml (4 tbsp) Cointreau

1 Butter an ovenproof dish, approximately 25 cm (10 in) x 20 cm (8 in).

2 Heat the marmalade in a pan with a little water until the jelly melts, then strain, reserving the jelly. Cut the brioche into 1 cm (½ in) thick slices, then cut each slice into 2 or 3 strips. Mix the butter with the orange zest and spread on the slices. Then spread the slices with the marmalade jelly, reserving 30 ml (2 tbsp) for glazing.

3 Line the bottom of the dish with half the brioche slices. Mix the marzipan and almond liqueur to a smooth runny paste and pour on top of the slices in the bowl. Top with the remaining slices. Place the single cream, milk, eggs and half the vanilla sugar in a bowl. Whip well, then pour the mixture over the brioches. If possible, leave the pudding for about 1 hour so that the mixture soaks in completely.

4 Bake the pudding in a preheated oven at 190°C (375°F) mark 5 for 40–45 minutes, until set and brown. Meanwhile, mix the double cream, Cointreau and remaining vanilla sugar in a jug. Cover and chill.

5 To serve, warm the reserved marmalade jelly in a small pan. Take the pudding out of the oven and cut out 4 rounds about 7 cm (3 in) in diameter. Place a round in the centre of each plate. Brush with the warmed jelly and pour the cream around the base. The pudding can also be decorated with orange segments if you like.

desserts

brioche and butter pudding with mascarpone ice cream

knob of butter
4 small brioche rolls
50 g (2 oz) sultanas soaked in
50 ml (2 fl oz) Amaretto
250 ml (8 fl oz) double cream
250 ml (8 fl oz) milk
1 vanilla pod
4 large eggs
pinch of grated lemon zest
50 g (2 oz) vanilla sugar
icing sugar, for dusting
15 ml (1 tbsp) apricot purée,
to serve

MASCARPONE ICE CREAM
125 g (4 oz) caster sugar
120 ml (4 fl oz) water
30 ml (2 tbsp) lemon juice
4 large egg yolks
450 g (1 lb) mascarpone

1 Butter an oval gratin dish. Slice the brioches and arrange in a single layer over the bottom of the dish. Sprinkle on the sultanas and the liqueur.

2 Place the cream, milk and vanilla pod in a pan and bring to a simmer to infuse. Beat the eggs with the sugar in a bowl and add the lemon zest. Add the warm cream and stir. Strain carefully over the brioches. Place the dish in a bain-marie. Cook in a preheated oven at 160°C (325°F) mark 3 for 30–40 minutes. The pudding should be just set in the middle.

3 To make the ice cream, place the sugar and water in a small pan and bring to the boil. Add the lemon juice and stir until a syrup has formed. Whisk the egg yolks in a bowl until pale then trickle the syrup in slowly. Add the cheese and mix well. Transfer the mixture to an ice-cream maker and churn until frozen.

4 To serve, use a round cutter to divide the pudding into 4 portions. Place each portion on a plate and dust with icing sugar. Brown with a blowtorch if desired. Dot around a little apricot purée and serve with the ice cream.

NOTE: Inspired by Anton Mosimann's dining club at The Belfrey.

chocolate pudding with a fudge sauce

SERVES 2

25 g (1 oz) butter, plus extra for greasing
50 g (2 oz) dark chocolate
45 ml (3 tbsp) water
25 g (1 oz) caster sugar
1 medium egg
40 g (1½ oz) chopped dried apricots
50 g (2 oz) chopped walnuts
15 g (½ oz) self-raising flour

FUDGE SAUCE

25 g (1 oz) butter
45 ml (3 tbsp) syrup
60 ml (4 tbsp) double cream
15 ml (1 tbsp) cocoa powder
icing sugar, to sprinkle
10ml (2 tsp) double cream, to decorate

1 Grease 2 ramekin dishes. Fill a roasting tin with hot water and put in the oven at 220°C (425°F) mark 7.

2 Place the butter and chocolate in a small pan and melt over a medium heat. Add the water and caster sugar and heat, stirring until the sugar has dissolved. Remove from the heat, transfer to a bowl and leave to cool.

3 Separate the egg and whisk the egg white. Add the egg yolk, apricots and walnuts to the chocolate mixture and mix well. Fold the flour and egg whites into the chocolate mixture.

Pour the mixture into the ramekins.

4 Place the ramekins in the roasting tin filled with water. The water should come halfway up the sides of the dishes – if necessary, top up with more hot water. Cook in the preheated oven for 20 minutes.

5 To make the fudge sauce, place the butter, syrup, double cream and cocoa powder in a small pan. Stir over a medium heat until the ingredients have melted and are well mixed.

6 To serve, turn out the puddings in the centre of each plate and pour the sauce around. Sprinkle icing sugar over the pudding. Place a teaspoonful of cream on top of the fudge sauce and 'feather', using a skewer or wooden cocktail stick.

carrot halva sponge with nutmeg cream

125 g (4 oz) self-raising flour
5 ml (1 tsp) baking powder
1.25 ml (¼ tsp) salt
1 large egg
75 g (3 oz) granulated sugar
90 ml (3 fl oz) vegetable oil
1 large desiccated carrot
50–90 ml (2–3 fl oz) rose water
8 green cardamom pods, opened
and seeds ground
sliced kumquats, to decorate
roasted pistachios and almonds, to
serve

NUTMEG CREAM
6 egg yolks
100 g (3½ oz) caster sugar
200 ml (7 fl oz) milk
300 ml (½ pint) double cream
2.5 ml (½ tsp) ground nutmeg
pinch of ground cinnamon

1 Mix the flour, baking powder and salt in a bowl. Beat the egg in another bowl, gradually adding the sugar, then beat in the oil a little at a time. Add the carrot, rose water and cardamom and liquidize. Do not overwork the mixture. Fold the flour into the mixture.

2 Spoon the mixture into 4 greased ramekins and bake in a preheated oven at 170°C (325°F) mark 3 for 40 minutes, or until the sponge has cooked through. Turn out the sponges and trim into a diamond shape.

3 To make the nutmeg cream, whisk the egg yolks in a bowl. Add the sugar and whisk until the mixture is pale and forms the ribbon. Put the milk, cream, nutmeg and cinnamon in a pan and bring to the boil. Pour the mixture onto the eggs, whisking continuously. Return the mixture to the pan and heat gently, stirring continuously, until it is thick enough to coat the back of a wooden spoon. Strain into a bowl and stand on ice to cool as quickly as possible.

4 To serve, place each sponge on a plate and decorate with the kumquats – any contrasting coloured fruit will give the right result. Pour the nutmeg cream around and sprinkle with pistachios and almonds.

ginger pudding with whisky ice cream

225 g (8 oz) self-raising flour
120 g (4 oz) soft brown sugar
2.5 ml (½ tsp) bicarbonate of soda
10 ml (2 tsp) ground ginger
2.5 ml (½ tsp) ground cinnamon
120 g (4 oz) butter, plus extra for greasing
150 ml (¼ pint) milk
60 ml (4 tbsp) black treacle
2 eggs
1 jar of stem ginger

WHISKY ICE CREAM
30 ml (2 tbsp) water
50 g (2 oz) caster sugar
5 cl (2 fl oz) whisky, or to taste
300 ml (½ pint) whipping cream

1 Sieve all the dry ingredients into a bowl. Place the butter, milk and treacle in a pan and heat gently until they are all melted (use a warm spoon when adding the treacle). Add the eggs to the dry ingredients and mix until smooth, then whisk in the contents of the pan.

2 Pour the mixture into 4 well-greased individual pudding tins and bake in a pre-heated oven at 180°C (350°F) mark 4 for 30–40 minutes, or until a good crust appears on top.

3 To make the ice cream, place the water and caster sugar in a pan and heat gently to form a syrup (do not let it boil). Remove from the heat, add the whisky, then leave the syrup to cool.

4 Place the cream and cooled syrup in a bowl and whisk until it holds a clear trail, or until fairly firm. Transfer the mixture to an ice-cream maker and churn for about 30 minutes, or until the mixture takes on an ice–cream texture. If you do not have an ice-cream maker, whisk the cream and syrup together as above, place in a shallow container and freeze until the sides turn solid (about 1½ hours). Whisk well again and freeze for about 4 hours before serving.

5 To serve, turn out the puddings onto individual plates and drizzle the syrup from the stem ginger jar on the top. Add scoops of the whisky ice cream.

orange-scented manjari chocolate mousse wrapped in a striped sponge with citrus fruit salad and chocolate and orange sorbets

SPECIAL EQUIPMENT
tiling adhesive spreader with serrated end
30 cm (12in) length of plastic pipe about 4 cm (1½ in) in diameter
acetate sheet

CHOCOLATE PASTE
50 g (2 oz) butter
50 g (2 oz) icing sugar
2 egg whites
40 g (1½ oz) flour, sifted
15 g (½ oz) cocoa powder

CHOCOLATE SORBET
200 ml (7 fl oz) water
50 ml (2 fl oz) milk
60 g (2½ oz) sugar
30 g (1 oz) liquid glucose
60 g (2½ oz) Manjari chocolate, chopped

MANJARI CHOCOLATE MOUSSE
125 g (4 oz) Valrhona Manjari Chocolate, chopped
3 egg whites
60 g (2½ oz) caster sugar
2 egg yolks
1 tsp finely grated orange zest
15 ml (1 tbsp) Cointreau
75 ml (5 tbsp) whipping cream, lightly whipped

ORANGE SORBET CONES
130 g (4½ oz) sugar
50 ml (2 fl oz) water
1 tsp grated orange zest
350 ml (12 fl oz) fresh orange juice

1 To make the chocolate paste, cream the butter and icing sugar in a bowl, then slowly add the egg white until well combined. Mix in the flour and cocoa powder. Line a baking sheet with nonstick baking parchment and mark out a 32 cm (13 in) x 20 cm (8 in) rectangle. Spread the paste evenly over the rectangle. Working lengthways, scrape off half the paste using the tile adhesive spreader so that you end up with very fine chocolate stripes. Freeze for about 30 minutes.

2 To make the chocolate sorbet, place the water, milk, sugar and glucose in a pan and bring to the boil. Pour over the chocolate in a bowl and stir with a whisk until completely amalgamated. Strain and leave to cool. Transfer to an ice-cream maker and churn until frozen.

3 To make the chocolate mousse, first line the plastic pipe with nonstick baking parchment. Cut out a rectangle slightly longer and wider than the pipe, roll up and slide inside the pipe. Make small cuts at each end and fold back to secure. Cover one end. Place the chocolate in a bowl over a pan of hot water until it melts. Spoon 1 tablespoon of the melted chocolate into a small piping bag and pipe 4 small zigzags onto a piece of acetate. Whisk the egg whites until risen then still whisking slowly add the sugar. Continue whisking until firm. Mix the yolks with the orange zest and Cointreau. Stir the yolks into the melted chocolate, then the cream. Fold in the egg whites. Reserve 2–3 tablespoons of the mousse for later. Using a piping bag, pipe the rest of the mousse into the lined plastic pipe and freeze for about 1 hour.

4 To make the orange sorbet, place the sugar, water and zest in a pan and bring to the boil. Remove from the heat and allow to cool completely, then add the orange juice. Strain and transfer to an ice-cream maker. Churn until frozen. Make 4 cones measuring 10 cm (4 in) x 4 cm (1½ in) out of acetate and fill with the sorbet. Place in the freezer.

5 To make the striped sponge, place the icing sugar, almonds and whole egg in a bowl and beat to the ribbon. In a separate bowl beat the egg white and caster sugar until well risen and firm. Fold the butter then flour into the whole–egg mixture. Fold in a-third of the whites to loosen the mixture, then gently fold in the rest. Don't over-mix. Using a palette knife spread the mixture over the area covered with the chocolate paste ribbons to a thickness of about 3–5 mm (¼ in). Bake in a preheated oven at 250°C (500°F) mark 10 for about 3 minutes, until the sponge is just firm to the touch. Don't overcook or it will be too dry. Dust the top of the sponge lightly with flour and invert on to a piece of nonstick baking parchment. Allow to cool slightly then carefully remove the nonstick baking parchment.

6 To make the tuile baskets, mix the butter and icing sugar in a bowl until

STRIPED SPONGE
40 g (1½ oz) icing sugar
40 g (1½ oz) ground almonds
1 egg plus 1 egg white
5 g (¼ oz) caster sugar
8 g (¼ oz) butter, melted and cooled
10 g (½ oz) flour

TUILE BASKETS
100 g (3½ oz) soft unsalted butter
100 g (3½ oz) icing sugar, sifted
100 g (3½ oz) egg whites (about 3 large) at room temperature
75 g (3 oz) flour, sifted
½ tsp finely grated orange zest

TO DECORATE
mixed citrus fruits such as orange, blood orange, grapefruit, clementine etc., pith removed and cut into segments

well combined. Slowly mix in the egg whites and then the flour and zest. Mix to a smooth paste. Place teaspoonfuls of the paste on a nonstick baking sheet and spread out to make 10cm (4 in) circles. Bake in a preheated oven at 180°C (350°F) mark 4 for about 4 minutes. Immediately lift each circle off the tray and mould over the base of a small ramekin or glass to make a basket. Leave to cool.

7 To assemble, trim the sponge to 30 cm (12 in) x 12 cm (5 in). Lay the sponge on a board, striped side down, and spread on a thin layer of the reserved mousse, softening it if necessary to give a sticky consistency. Remove the chocolate mousse from the tube by pulling out with the paper. Peel off the paper then wrap the mousse in the sponge, trimming as necessary. Using a sharp knife, square off the ends. Cut the tube into 2 equal lengths, then cut each length diagonally. Stand a mousse on each plate and place a tuille basket alongside. Fill the basket with a scoop of chocolate sorbet. Add an orange sorbet cone and top with a chocolate zigzag. Arrange the pieces of citrus fruit salad around.

summer pudding with greek honey and yogurt

SERVES 2
1½ brioche loaves
1 kg (2¼ lb) mixed fresh summer berries
15–30 ml (1–2 tbsp) water
500 ml (16 fl oz) Greek yoghurt
200 ml (7 fl oz) clear honey
mint sprigs and fresh berries, to decorate

1 Thinly slice the brioche and gently roll the slices with a rolling pin. Line an earthenware dish with some overlapping slices of brioche.

2 Place the mixed fruits in a pan with the water and cook over gentle heat until slightly soft. Remove from the heat and layer in the dish with the remaining slices of brioche, adding the juice from the fruit to colour the brioche. Finish with a layer of brioche. Weigh down heavily with another earthenware dish, with weights on top. Refrigerate for as long as possible, preferably overnight, to ensure that the brioche is soaked through with juices.

3 To serve, turn out the pudding onto a large plate. Mix the yoghurt and honey together and spoon over the pudding. Decorate with a few fresh berries and mint sprigs.

warm chocolate pudding with belgian chocolate sauce and an orange cream swirl

125 g (4 oz) organic white self-raising flour
5 ml (1 tsp) baking powder
2 organic eggs (large)
125 g (4 oz) caster sugar
125 g (4 oz) Olivio margarine or organic butter, at room temperature
12 ml (2½ tsp) cocoa powder

BELGIAN CHOCOLATE SAUCE
175 g (6 oz) Belgian milk chocolate (cooking chocolate)
25 g (1 oz) Belgian dark chocolate (cooking chocolate)
knob of butter
30–45 ml (2–3 tbsp) cream or milk

ORANGE CREAM
50 g (2 oz) organic double cream
50 g (2 oz) orange curd
50 g (2 oz) Greek yogurt

TO SERVE
finely grated orange zest
cocoa powder or icing sugar

1 Grease 4 individual aluminium pudding basins, and place a circle of non-stick baking parchment in the bottom of each one.

2 Sift the flour and baking powder into a large bowl. Add all the other ingredients and beat until creamy, 2–3 minutes. Spoon into the basins so that each is almost half full. Place in a bain-marie, or a roasting tin half filled with water, and bake in a preheated oven at 190°C (375°F) mark 5 for 20 minutes. Test for doneness with a skewer, then remove from the oven.

3 To make the chocolate sauce, break up the chocolate and place in a bowl over a pan of barely simmering water (do not allow water to touch the bowl). When the chocolate has melted, mix in the butter and enough milk or cream to give it a pouring consistency. Remove from the heat but stir occasionally to keep smooth.

4 To make the orange cream, gently fold together the ingredients just before serving.

5 To serve, turn out the puddings onto 4 plates, then turn again so that the crisp top is uppermost. Pour some sauce around each pudding. Swirl on some cream and decorate with orange zest. Dust each plate with cocoa powder.

warm chocolate and pecan tarts

This is an adaptation of an Anton Edelmann recipe from *Perfect Pastries, Puddings and Desserts*

100 g (3½ oz) plain flour
65 g (2½ oz) unsalted butter, cut into pieces, plus extra for greasing
25 g (1 oz) caster sugar
1 egg yolk
15 ml (1 tbsp) cold water
icing sugar and cocoa powder, for dusting

FILLING
150 g (5 oz) pecans
150 g (5 oz) plain dark chocolate, broken up
2 egg yolks
1 egg
30 g (1¼ oz) caster sugar
100 g (3½ oz) unsalted butter, softened

VANILLA ICE CREAM
1 vanilla pod, seeds scraped out
190 ml (6 fl oz) milk
45 g (1¾ oz) granulated sugar
3 egg yolks
100 ml (3½ fl oz) double cream

1 Put the flour and butter in a food processor and process until mixture is like fine breadcrumbs. Add the sugar and process for a few seconds. Add the egg yolk and water and process until the mixture sticks together in small lumps. Turn the mixture into a bowl and gather into a ball. Chill for 30 minutes.

2 Roll out the pastry and use to line 4 greased 7.5–10 cm (3–4 in) tartlet tins. Leave to rest in the refrigerator for 30 minutes. Line the pastry cases with nonstick baking parchment and baking beans. Bake blind in a pre-heated oven at 200°C (400°F) mark 6 for 15 minutes. Remove the paper and beans and return to the oven for 2–3 minutes. Remove from oven and leave to cool. Reduce the oven temperature to 180°C (350°F) mark 4.

3 To make the filling, divide the pecans between the pastry cases and spread over the bottom of each. Place the chocolate in a heatproof bowl set over a pan of simmering water (do not allow the water to touch the bowl) and leave to melt, or melt in the microwave. Remove from the heat and allow to cool slightly. Beat the egg yolks, whole egg and sugar together in a bowl until creamy. Slowly pour on the melted chocolate, stirring all the time. Beat in the butter. Pour the filling into the pastry cases and bake in the pre-heated oven for 10–12 minutes, until just firm.

4 To make the ice cream, place the vanilla pod in a pan with the milk and half the sugar. Bring to the boil. Whisk the egg yolks and remaining sugar together, then pour the milk onto the egg in a steady stream, whisking all the while. Cook over a low heat, stirring constantly, until the mixture is thick enough to coat the back of a wooden spoon. Pour into a bowl and leave to cool. Remove the vanilla pod and stir in the cream. Pour into an ice-cream maker and churn until frozen.

5 To serve, cool the tarts to just above room temperature and serve dusted with icing sugar and cocoa powder. Serve a scoop of the ice cream with each tart.

warm chocolate puddings with white and dark chocolate sauces

SERVES 2

50 g (2 oz) unsalted butter, plus
extra for greasing
50 g (2 oz) dark chocolate
1 egg
1 egg yolk
25 g (1 oz) caster sugar
7 g (¼ oz) plain flour

WHITE CHOCOLATE SAUCE

120 ml (4 fl oz) double cream
50 g (2 oz) white chocolate
drop of vanilla essence

DARK CHOCOLATE SAUCE

120 ml (4 fl oz) double cream
30 g (1¼ oz) caster sugar
7 g (¼ oz) unsalted butter
pinch of salt
25 g (1 oz) dark unsweetened
chocolate
drop of vanilla essence

TO SERVE

crème fraîche
icing sugar, for dusting

1 Grease 2 dariole moulds. Place the butter and chocolate in a bowl set over a pan of simmering water and leave to melt.

2 Place the egg, egg yolk and sugar in a bowl and whisk until they just hold a trail. Whisk in the melted butter and chocolate. Fold in the plain flour. Pour the mixture into the moulds and bake in a preheated oven at 160°C (325°F) mark 3 for 10–12 minutes, or until just firm. Remove from the oven and unmould.

3 To make the white chocolate sauce, bring the cream to the boil in a pan. Place the chocolate in a bowl and pour over the boiling cream. Cover with cling film and leave to stand for about 5 minutes, or until the chocolate has melted.

Whisk until smooth. Stand the bowl in very cold water to reduce the temperature quickly. Stir in the vanilla essence.

4 To make the dark chocolate sauce, heat the cream, sugar, butter and salt in a pan until the sugar has dissolved. Bring to the boil. Place the chocolate in a bowl and pour over the boiling cream mixture. Cover with cling film and leave to stand for about 5 minutes, or until the chocolate has melted. Whisk until smooth. Stand the bowl in very cold water to reduce temperature quickly. Stir in the vanilla essence.

5 To serve, turn out the puddings on 2 plates. Pour around the white and dark chocolate sauces. Spoon a dollop of crème fraîche on each plate and dust with icing sugar.

steamed lemon sponge pudding with caramelized orange and vanilla ice cream

125 g (4 oz) unsalted butter, plus extra for greasing
150 g (5 oz) caster sugar
grated zest and juice of 1 lemon
2 eggs
1 egg yolk
200 g (7 oz) self-raising flour, sifted

VANILLA ICE CREAM
425 ml (15 fl oz) double cream
150 ml (¼ pint) whole milk
1 vanilla pod, scraped
6 egg yolks
75 g (3 oz) caster sugar

CARAMELIZED ORANGE
125 g (4 oz) caster sugar
juice of 2 large oranges
15 ml (1 tbsp) Cointreau
grated zest of 1 orange
segments of 1 orange

1 Place the butter, sugar and lemon zest in a bowl and beat until pale, light and fluffy. Beat in the eggs one at a time, followed by the egg yolk. Mix in the flour then add the lemon juice and beat until well combined. Spoon the mixture into four 150 ml (¼ pint) greased moulds until about three-quarters full. Cover with buttered foil and place in a steamer over boiling water for 35–40 minutes or until well risen. Remove from the steamer and leave to cool slightly.

2 To make the ice cream, place the cream and milk in a pan with the vanilla pod and its seeds. Bring to the boil. In a bowl, beat together the eggs and the sugar until pale and light in texture. Add the cream mixture stirring continuously until well blended. Allow to cool, leaving the vanilla pod in the mixture. When cool, remove the pod and place half the mixture in an ice-cream maker. Churn for about 20 minutes, or until the ice cream is thick. Churn the remaining mixture, then transfer the ice cream to the freezer and leave until 10 minutes before serving.

3 To make the caramelized orange, place the sugar and 15ml (1 tbsp) of orange juice in a pan over a gentle heat until the sugar starts to dissolve, then turn up the heat to caramelize the mixture. Remove from the heat, add the Cointreau and the remaining juice and mix thoroughly. Add the orange zest and the orange segments and stir gently to coat the segments.

4 To serve, place a sponge pudding in the centre of each plate and arrange 3 spoonfuls of ice cream around the sponge. Place the orange segments in between the spoonfuls of ice cream and spoon the orange sauce over the pudding and the ice cream.

traditional bread and butter pudding with seville orange marmalade

SERVES 2

4 slices of white bread

30 g (1¼ oz) butter, softened, plus extra for greasing

22 ml (1½ tbsp) Seville orange marmalade

15 ml (1 tbsp) candied peel

140 ml (4½ fl oz) whole milk

30 ml (2 tbsp) double cream

2 eggs

40 g (1¼ oz) sugar

15 ml (1 tbsp) demerara sugar

clotted cream, to serve

1 Grease a baking dish. Butter the slices of bread on one side, then spread the marmalade on two slices. Put the other 2 slices on top to make 2 rounds of sandwiches. Spread the remaining butter over the top of each sandwich, then cut into quarters to make triangles or squares. Sprinkle the candied peel at the bottom of the baking dish.

2 Arrange the sandwiches, buttered side up, overlapping in the baking dish. Whisk the milk, cream, eggs and sugar together in a bowl and pour over the bread. Sprinkle the top with the demerara sugar and bake in a pre-heated oven at 180°C (350°F) mark 4 for about 40 minutes, or until golden and puffed up.

3 Serve the pudding with clotted cream

desserts

caramelized lemon tart

125 g (4 oz) plain flour
25 g (1 oz) icing sugar
50 g (2 oz) unsalted butter,
softened, plus extra for greasing
pinch of salt
1 small egg, separated
2 tsp water

FILLING
2 eggs
50 g (2 oz) caster sugar
grated zest and juice of 2 lemons
60 ml (2 fl oz) whipping cream

PASSION FRUIT SORBET
200 g (7 oz) caster sugar
150 ml (¼ pint) water
25 ml (1 fl oz) liquid glucose
325 g (11 oz) passion fruit pulp

MERINGUE MUSHROOMS
1 egg white
75 g (3 oz) caster sugar
pinch of cream of tartar
drinking chocolate, to sprinkle

TO SERVE
15 g (½ oz) Demerara sugar
15 g (½ oz) caster sugar

1 Put the flour, sugar, butter, salt and egg yolk in a food processor and process until it forms a firm dough. Place in a polythene bag and chill for 30 minutes. Heat a baking sheet in the oven at 200°C (400°F) mark 6.

2 Lightly grease four 10 cm (4 in) fluted tartlet tins. Roll out the pastry and use to line the tartlet tins. Prick the bases, lightly whisk the egg white and brush over the pastry. Bake on the baking sheet for about 6 minutes, on the middle shelf of oven. Remove from the oven and reduce oven temperature to 180°C (350°F) mark 4.

3 To make the filling, whisk the eggs and the sugar very lightly in a bowl. Add the lemon juice, zest and cream and whisk until combined. Pour the mixture into the pastry cases and bake for 8–10 minutes, or until the filling is set.

4 To make the sorbet, combine the sugar, water and glucose in a small pan and bring to the boil. Boil for 1 minute, skimming off any impurities, then remove from the heat and leave to cool.

5 Mix the cooled syrup into the passion fruit pulp. Pour into an ice-cream maker and churn for about 20–25 minutes, until frozen. Transfer to the freezer until ready to serve.

6 To make the meringues, line a baking sheet with nonstick baking parchment. Whisk the egg white in a bowl with the cream of tartar until soft peaks form. Gradually beat in the sugar until mixture has thickened. Spoon the meringue into a piping bag with a 1 cm (½ in) nozzle and pipe assorted-sized rounds onto the paper. Pipe the stalks by squeezing a little meringue out onto the sheet, lifting to a peak. Dust the caps with a little drinking chocolate. Bake for 1 hour in a preheated oven at 150°C (300°F) mark 2. Remove from the heat and leave to cool. Hollow out the caps and push a stalk into each one.

7 To serve, sprinkle the tarts with the sugars and glaze with a blow torch until the sugar caramelizes. Place a scoop of sorbet and a meringue mushroom on each plate.

champagne rhubarb cheesecake with a compote of strawberries and rhubarb

175 g (6 oz) unsalted butter
225 g (8 oz) packet of digestive biscuits, crushed
450 g (1 lb) rhubarb
50–75 g (2–3 oz) caster sugar, to taste
juice of ½ lemon
175 ml (6 fl oz) double cream, whipped to just hold its shape
225 g (8 oz) cottage cheese
1½ leaves of gelatine
a few fresh strawberries, to decorate

COMPOTE
125 g (4 oz) strawberries, hulled
125 g (4 oz) rhubarb, chopped
25–50 g (1–2 oz) sugar

1 Melt 125 g (4 oz) of the butter in a small pan, add the biscuits and mix well. Transfer either into a 20 cm (8 in) loose-bottomed cake tin or 4 individual tart tins. Press the biscuit base evenly over the bottom.

2 Place the rhubarb and remaining butter in a pan and poach carefully over gentle heat until it has reduced by about half (10–15 minutes). Add sugar and lemon to taste. Meanwhile, soak the gelatine in a little warm water until softened, then add to the rhubarb. Put the rhubarb, whipped cream and cottage cheese in a processor and process briefly, then press through a fine sieve to remove lumps. Cover the biscuit base carefully with the rhubarb mixture, level the top and place in the refrigerator to set.

3 To make the compote, place one-third of the strawberries in a small pan with the rhubarb and sugar. Bring to a simmer and as soon as the rhubarb is tender remove from the heat. Using a slotted spoon remove about half the rhubarb and add to the remaining strawberries. Transfer the cooked rhubard and strawberry mixture to a food processor and blend. Leave to cool a little, then pour over the fresh fruit mixture and refrigerate.

4 To serve, remove the cheesecake from the tin and decorate with half a fresh strawberry on top. Serve a little compote with each serving.

NOTES: In the summer, after rhubarb has lost that real rosiness, the juice from a few redcurrants will improve the colour without altering the flavour. Inspiration from Chris Barber, Chef/Patron of The Goose, Britwell Salome.

baked cheesecakes with blackberry sauce

SERVES 2

50 g (2 oz) plain flour, sifted
125 g (4 oz) caster sugar
2.5 ml (½ tsp) grated lemon zest
50 g (2 oz) butter, softened, plus
extra for greasing
½ egg yolk, lightly beaten
drop of vanilla essence
single cream, to serve

FILLING

300 g (10 oz) cream cheese
2.5 ml (½ tsp) plain flour
125 g (4 oz) caster sugar
10 ml (2 tsp) lemon juice
5 ml (1 tsp) grated lemon zest
drop of vanilla essence
2–3 eggs
1 egg yolk
60 ml (2 fl oz) double cream

BLACKBERRY SAUCE

225 g (8 oz) blackberries
10 ml (2 tsp) icing sugar

1 Combine the flour, sugar and lemon zest in a bowl. Add the butter and work in until the mixture resembles breadcrumbs. Mix in the egg and vanilla. Pat onto the greased base of two 7 cm (3 in)–wide deep tart tins. Line with nonstick baking parchment and baking beans and bake blind in a preheated oven at 200°C (400°F) mark 6 for 7 minutes, then remove the paper and beans and leave to cool. Increase the oven temperature to 220°C (425°F) mark 7.

2 To make the filling, place the cheese, flour, sugar, lemon juice, lemon zest and vanilla in a bowl and cream until light and smooth. Whisk in the eggs and yolk one at a time, then fold in the double cream. Pour the filling into the tart cases and bake for 5 minutes. Reduce the temperature to 180°C (350°F) mark 4 and bake for another 7 minutes. Remove from the oven immediately and unmould.

3 To make the sauce, purée the blackberries in a food processor until smooth. Push through a sieve then mix in the icing sugar.

4 Serve the cheesecakes warm with the blackberry sauce and some single cream.

NOTE: The cheesecakes will continue to cook when they come out of the oven, so don't be tempted to leave them in any longer.

chocolate and walnut tart with praline ice cream

25 g (1 oz) ground almonds
75 g (3 oz) plain flour
50 g (2 oz) butter
125 g (4 oz) caster sugar
1 egg yolk
30 ml (2 tbsp) milk

FILLING
100 g (3½ oz) dark cooking chocolate (70% cocoa solids), broken up
50 g (2 oz) unsalted butter
15 ml (1 tbsp) walnut oil
50 g (2 oz) pulverized walnuts
30 ml (2 tbsp) cream

PRALINE ICE CREAM
200 ml (7 fl oz) milk
200 ml (7 fl oz) cream
2 egg yolks
125 g (4 oz) sugar
200 ml (7 fl oz) crème fraîche
12–15 whole blanched almonds
25 ml (1 fl oz) water

1 Process the ground almonds, flour, butter, sugar and egg yolk in a food processor. Add the milk gradually until a moist pastry is formed. Wrap the pastry in cling film and chill for 20 minutes. Roll out the pastry and use to line 4 small greased tart cases, or one 20 cm (8 in) case. Line with non-stick baking parchment and baking beans and bake blind in a preheated oven at 180°C (350° F) mark 4 for 15 minutes. Remove from the oven and allow to cool.

2 To make the filling, melt the chocolate in a small pan over a very low heat with the butter and walnut oil. Add the walnuts and cream and stir to mix well. Pour the mixture into the cooled pastry cases. Leave to set for 1 hour.

3 To make the ice cream, warm the milk and cream in a pan. Beat the egg yolks and sugar in a bowl. Pour on the milk mixture, then return to the pan and heat gently, stirring continuously, until the mixture is thick enough to coat the back of a wooden spoon. Stir in the crème fraîche then remove from the heat and allow to cool.

4 Toast the whole almonds in a hot dry pan. Remove the almonds to a baking sheet, then add the sugar and water to the pan to form a syrup. Increase the heat until the syrup turns a dark golden colour, or sets hard when dropped into cold water. Pour the syrup over the almonds and leave to set. When the praline is hard smash it into small pieces with a rolling pin and grind briefly in a food processsor. Add the praline to the cream and place in an ice-cream maker. Churn for 30 minutes.

5 To serve, unmould the tarts and serve with a spoonful of the ice cream.

chocolate tart with apricot sorbet and peach coulis

150 g (5 oz) butter, plus extra for greasing
300 g (10 oz) plain flour
150 g (5 oz) caster sugar
pinch of salt
1 egg
1 egg yolk
cocoa powder, to sprinkle

CHOCOLATE BATTER
175 g (6 oz) crème fraîche
60 g (2½ oz) breakfast milk
200 g (7 oz) bittersweet chocolate (at least 70% cocoa solids), broken up
1 large egg and 1 egg yolk or 2 medium eggs

APRICOT SORBET
75 g (3 oz) granulated sugar
75 g (3 oz) soft brown sugar
300 ml (½ pint) water
175 g (6 oz) dried apricots
3 strips of lemon zest
225 g (8 oz) dry white wine
125 g (4 oz) fresh lemon juice

PEACH COULIS
2 peaches
15 ml (1 tbsp) water
30 ml (2 tbsp) sugar
10 ml (2 tsp) lemon juice

1 Place the butter, flour and sugar in a food processor and blend until the mixture resembles breadcrumbs. Add a pinch of salt. Mix the egg and egg yolk together, add to the mixture and blend together, about 30 seconds. Press pastry together to form a ball. Wrap in cling film and refrigerate for at least 20 minutes.

2 To make the chocolate batter, heat the crème fraîche and milk together in a pan until it comes to a simmer. Add the chocolate and stir until dissolved, then remove from the heat and allow to cool slightly. Mix together the egg and egg yolk, then add to the chocolate sauce, mixing all the time. Leave to cool.

3 Roll out the pastry and use to line a greased 23 cm (9 in) tart tin. Prick with a fork all over and line with foil and baking beans. Bake blind in a pre-heated oven at 190°C (375°F) mark 5 for 15 minutes. Remove from the oven and remove foil and beans. Add the chocolate batter to the pastry case and cook for another 10–12 minutes. The tart should still wobble slightly in the middle. Remove from the oven and leave to cool to room temperature.

4 To make the sorbet, combine the sugar and water in a pan over medium heat. Bring to the boil and stir until sugar has dissolved. Add the lemon zest. Add the apricots and cook until soft, about 10 minutes. Take out all but 1 strip of lemon zest. Purée the apricot mixture in a food processor. Add the wine and lemon juice and blend for 30 seconds. Transfer to a bowl and leave to cool completely, then churn in an ice-cream maker until frozen.

5 To make the coulis, poach the peaches with the water and sugar until soft. Skin and pit the peaches, then blend the peaches and syrup wth the lemon juice.

6 To serve, sprinkle the tart with cocoa powder and cut into thin wedges. Serve with a scoop of apricot sorbet and the coulis poured round.

amaretti pear and almond tart with a poire williams sauce

250 g (9 oz) plain flour
pinch of salt
175 g (6 oz) unsalted cold butter, cut into cubes, plus extra for greasing
75 g (3 oz) icing sugar
2 egg yolks

FILLING
250 g (9 oz) unsalted butter, softened
250 g (9 oz) caster sugar
125 g (4 oz) blanched whole almonds
150 g (5 oz) Amaretti biscuits
2 eggs
4 ripe comice pears, peeled, cored and halved

SAUCE
200 g (7 oz) sugar
60 ml (2 fl oz) water
15 ml (1 tbsp) liquid glucose
200 g (7 oz) unsalted butter
200 ml (7 fl oz) double cream
60 ml (2 fl oz) Poire Williams liqueur

1 Place the flour, salt and butter in a food processor and process until the mixture resembles coarse breadcrumbs. Add sugar, then the egg yolks, and process again until mixture leaves the side of the bowl. Wrap the pastry in cling film and chill for 1 hour.

2 Coarsely grate pastry into a greased loose-bottomed 23 cm (9 in) fluted flan tin and press it evenly onto the bottom and sides. Bake blind in a pre-heated oven at 180°C (350°F) mark 4 for 20 minutes until light brown. Remove from the oven and leave to cool. Reduce the oven temperature to 150°C (300°F) mark 2.

3 To make the filling, cream the butter and sugar in a bowl until the mixture is pale and light. Put the almonds and Amaretti into a food processor and chop until fine. Add the butter and sugar and blend well. Beat in the eggs one by one. Arrange the pears, core side down, in the tart case and pour the mixture over the pears. Bake for 40 minutes or until the filling is firm. Remove from the heat.

4 To make the sauce, combine the sugar, water and glucose in a pan. Bring to the boil and cook until the syrup turns a light caramel colour. Remove from the heat and beat in the butter a little at a time. Stir in double cream then add the liqueur.

5 To serve, unmould the tart onto a plate. Strain the sauce through a fine sieve and serve warm.

chocolate flans with strawberry sorbet, candied peel and ginger cream

60 g (2½ oz) butter, plus extra for greasing
60 g (2½ oz) caster sugar
5 cm (2 in) piece of fresh ginger root, peeled and chopped
120 g (4 oz) plain flour
pinch of salt
1 egg, beaten
5 ml (1 tsp) water
cocoa powder or icing sugar, to sprinkle

CHOCOLATE FILLING
130 g (4½ oz) dark chocolate (60% cocoa solids), broken up
80 ml (2½ fl oz) milk
120 ml (4 fl oz) double cream
1 large egg, beaten

STRAWBERRY SORBET
½ unwaxed lemon, chopped
200 g (7 oz) caster sugar
450 g (1 lb) strawberries
juice of ½ lime (optional)
50 ml (2 fl oz) red wine

CANDIED ORANGE PEEL
1 orange
sugar syrup made with
50 g (2 oz) sugar and 100 ml (3½ fl oz) water
zest of ½ a lemon

GINGER CREAM
4 cm (1½ in) length of fresh ginger root, peeled and very finely chopped
10 ml (2 tsp) caster sugar
120 ml (4 fl oz) double cream

1 Place butter, sugar and ginger in a food processor and process until smooth and well combined. Add just under half the egg and process again. Add the flour and salt and process until a crumbly dough is formed. Remove the dough and knead into a ball, wrap in cling film and leave to rest in the refrigerator for at least 20 minutes.

2 On a floured board, roll the pastry out very thinly and use to line 4 individual greased loose-bottomed flan tins. Fill any cracks with pastry trimmings and reserve the rest of the trimmings in the refrigerator. Prick the bases, line with nonstick baking parchment and baking beans and chill for 20 minutes.

3 Place the tarts on a baking sheet and bake blind in a preheated oven at 180°C (350°F) mark 4 for 10 minutes, or until the pastry is lightly set. Remove the paper and beans. Again cover any cracks with pastry trimmings if necessary. Return the cases to the oven for about 5–6 minutes, until lightly coloured. Remove from the oven and reduce the temperature to 140°C (275°F) mark 1. Mix the remaining beaten egg with the water and use to glaze the tarts. Return them to the oven until the glaze is set.

4 To make the chocolate filling, place the chocolate in a bowl and bring the milk and cream just to the boil in a pan. Pour the cream mixture over the chocolate and whisk well until all the chocolate has melted and the mixture is smooth. Whisk the egg and whisk into the chocolate mixture. Strain through muslin if you like to make it extra smooth.

5 Fill the flan cases with the chocolate mixture, stand cases on a baking sheet and bake in a preheated oven at 140°C (275°F) mark 1 for 10–15 minutes until just set. Switch off the heat and leave the flans in the oven for 20–25 minutes to cool down gradually. Remove when cool and chill until ready to serve.

6 To make the sorbet, process the lemon and sugar in a food processor until the mixture resembles cake icing. Purée the strawberries in a blender. Combine the two mixtures and taste. The result should be very sweet, to complement the chocolate flan filling. Depending on tartness, add the lime juice. Add the red wine and chill for 5–10 minutes. Transfer the mixture to an ice-cream maker and churn until frozen, or freeze in a shallow container in the freezer, whisking every hour to break down the ice crystals.

7 To make the candied peel, peel the orange thinly and cut into very fine julienne strips. Blanch the peel in boiling water for 1 minute, drain and refresh in cold water. Dry on paper towels. Pour the syrup into a pan with the lemon zest and bring to the boil. Add the blanched peel and simmer for 10 minutes. Remove the peel with a slotted spoon and spread it out on a tray lined with nonstick baking parchment. Place the tray in a very low oven or an airing cupboard for 30 minutes to dry out.

8 To make the ginger cream, combine the chopped ginger with the sugar

and cream in a bowl. Cover and leave to infuse in the refrigerator for at least 1 hour.

9 To serve, unmould a tart onto each plate. Whip the ginger cream and form into small quenelles between 2 teaspoons. Place a few quenelles on each plate and top with candied peel. Serve 3 scoops of sorbet on each plate. Sprinkle each plate with cocoa powder or icing sugar.

NOTE: The tart recipe is adapted from one by Gordon Ramsay. The sorbet recipe is adapted from *The River Café Cook Book*.

fresh walnut tart with armagnac glaze and clove ice cream

200 g (7 oz) plain flour
50 g (2 oz) castor sugar
pinch of salt
(130 g) 4½ oz unsalted butter, diced, plus extra for greasing
2 egg yolks
15–20 ml (3–4 tsp) cold water

FILLING
450 g (1 lb) walnuts
300 ml (½ pint) double cream
125 g (4 oz) caster sugar
2 drops of vanilla essence
2 egg whites
30 ml (2 tbsp) icing sugar
15 ml (1 tbsp) Armagnac

CLOVE ICE CREAM
125 ml (4 fl oz) milk
250 ml (8 fl oz) whipping cream
18 cloves
3 egg yolks
15 ml (1 tbsp) granulated sugar

1 Place the flour, caster sugar, salt, butter and egg yolks in a food processor and process until the mixture comes together to form a ball. Only add the water if necessary for the mixture to combine. Wrap the pastry in cling film and leave to rest in the refrigerator for 30 minutes.

2 Allow the pastry to come to room temperature for 5 minutes before rolling out to fit a greased 23 cm (9 in) loose-bottomed tart tin. Prick the pastry with a fork, line with nonstick baking parchment and baking beans. Place on a baking sheet and bake in a preheated oven at 180° (350°F) mark 4 for 10 minutes. Remove the baking beans and paper and bake for a further 5 minutes. Remove from the oven.

3 To make the filling, crack the walnuts to give 175 g (6 oz) of shelled nuts. Place in a food processor and grind until finely chopped. Place in a large bowl, add the cream, sugar and vanilla essence and mix well. Whip the egg whites until just stiff, then fold into the walnut mixture. Pour the filling into the tart shell and bake in the preheated oven at 180° (350°F) mark 4 for 30–35 minutes. The top of the tart should be lightly golden brown and feel springy to the touch. Remove the tart from the oven and allow to cool slightly before mixing the icing sugar and Armagnac and spreading on top of the tart.

4 To make the ice cream, place the milk, cream and cloves in a pan. Bring to the boil and leave to infuse for 10 minutes. Meanwhile, beat the yolks and sugar until light and creamy.

Strain the milk mixture onto the eggs, then return to the pan and cook over a low heat, stirring continuously, until the mixture is thick enough to coat the back of a wooden spoon. Pour into an ice-cream maker. Allow to cool then churn for about 30 minutes until frozen.

5 Serve the tart warm, with scoops of the clove ice cream.

NOTE: The ice cream is adapted from *Ices – The Definitive Guide* by Caroline Weir and Robin Waddle.

lemon tart with pistachio ice cream and raspberry coulis

PASTRY
225 g (8 oz) plain flour
30 ml (2 tbsp) icing sugar
pinch of salt
150 g (5 oz) unsalted butter,
softened, plus extra for greasing
1 egg yolk

FILLING
4 eggs
175 g (6 oz) caster sugar
finely grated zest and juice of 2
lemons
150 ml (¼ pint) double cream
45 ml (3 tbsp) icing sugar

PISTACHIO ICE CREAM
240 ml (8 fl oz) semi-skimmed
milk
75 g (3 oz) pistachios (shelled and
unsalted)
75 g (3 oz) vanilla sugar
3 eggs
175 ml (6 fl oz) double cream

RASPBERRY COULIS
225 g (8 oz) raspberries, defrosted
if frozen
15 g (½ oz) icing sugar
5 ml (1 tsp) lemon juice

1 First make the ice cream. Put the milk and pistachios in a pan and bring to the boil. Transfer to a food processor and process until smooth, then push through a fine sieve. Beat together the sugar and eggs in a bowl. Bring the cream to the boil in a small pan, pour onto the egg mixture, and whisk until smooth. Add the pistachio purée, mix well and leave to cool. Once cool, transfer the mixture to an ice-cream maker and churn until frozen. Place in the freezer until ready to serve.

2 To make the pastry, sieve the flour and sugar into a bowl and add a pinch of salt. Rub in the butter until the mixture resembles breadcrumbs. Mix in the beaten egg yolk to form a soft dough. Roll out and use to line a greased 23cm (9 in) flan dish. Line with nonstick baking parchment and baking beans. Bake blind in a preheated oven at 180°C (350°F) mark 4 for 15 minutes, then remove the paper and beans and leave to cool.

3 To make the filling, beat together the sugar and eggs in a bowl until smooth, then add lemon zest and juice. Whisk in the cream. Fill the pastry case with the mixture and bake in a preheated oven at 180°C (350°F) mark 4 for about 1 hour, or until firm. Allow to cool, then sprinkle over the icing sugar and place under a hot grill or use a blowtorch until the top has caramelized.

5 To make the coulis, push the raspberries through a fine sieve. Add icing sugar and lemon juice to taste, then chill.

strawberry and mascarpone torte

800 g (1 lb 12 oz) fresh
strawberries
400 g (14 oz) mascarpone
100 g (3½ oz) condensed milk
60 ml (4 tbsp) Grand Marnier
3 eggs, separated
75 g (3 oz) caster sugar
1 leaf gelatine, soaked in cold
water
1 ripe mango, flesh cut up
10 g (½ oz) icing sugar

SHORTBREAD
140 g (4½ oz) butter
50 g (2 oz) caster sugar
100 g (3½ oz) plain flour
80 g (3¼ oz) cornflour

1 To make the shortbread, cream the butter and sugar until soft and pale, add the flour and cornflour and knead into a dough. Roll out the dough to a 3 mm (⅛ in) thick square. Place on a baking sheet lined with nonstick baking parchment and bake in a preheated oven at 150°C (300°F) mark 2 for 30 minutes.

2 Blend half the strawberries and sieve. Slice the remaining strawberries and toss to coat with the juice.

3 Beat half the cheese, stir in the condensed milk and half the Grand Marnier.

Whisk the egg yolks with half the sugar over a pan of hot water until lukewarm and pale, then add the gelatine and whisk until fluffy. When cool beat in the remaining mascarpone and add to the milk and cheese mixture. Whisk the egg whites with the remaining sugar. Add one more tablespoon of Grand Marnier to the cheese mixture then fold in the egg whites.

4 Assemble the tortes in four 7 cm (3 in) deep moulds. Cut out rounds of shortbread to fit the moulds. Fill the moulds with alternate layers of shortbread, torte mixture and strawberry slices and leave in the refrigerator to set.

5 Blend the mango with remaining Grand Marnier and sieve.

6 To serve, cut remaining shortbread into 5 cm (2 in) triangles and place around torte on centre of plate. Between the shortbreads place strawberry sauce on one half of the plate and the mango sauce in the other. Dust with icing sugar.

tarte tatin

SERVES 2
75 g (3 oz) puff pastry
3 Granny Smith apples
45 g (1¾ oz) unsalted butter
105 g (3¼ oz) caster sugar

1 Roll out the puff pastry to 2–3 mm (⅛ in) thickness and cut out a circle slightly larger than the mould or frying pan. Refrigerate pastry until needed.
2 Peel and core the apples. Cut into quarters, leaving one half apple. Put the apple pieces into a bowl of water to stop them going brown.
3 Put 70 g (3 oz) of caster sugar into the bottom of a metal dish or small frying pan, and place over a medium heat for 3–5 minutes until the sugar turns a dark caramel colour. Turn off the heat and stir in 30 g (1¼ oz) of the butter. Arrange the apple quarters rounded side down around the edge of the mould. Put the half apple in the middle. Press the pieces down and make sure that there are no gaps. Dot with the remaining butter and sprinkle with remaining sugar. Bake in a preheated oven at 190°C (375°F) mark 5 for 25 minutes.
4 Remove from the oven and lay the pastry on top, tucking the edges of the pastry inside the mould. Cook for another 30 minutes. Allow to cool for 15 minutes then carefully turn out onto a serving dish.

tarte tatin with plums

SERVES 2
150 g (5 oz) caster sugar
25 g (1 oz) unsalted butter
40 g (1½) oz puff pastry
3 firm plums, halved and stoned

1 Place 2 small ovenproof frying pans on a medium heat and add the sugar gradually, dividing it between them. Heat until the sugar caramelizes.
2 Roll out the pastry thinly into 2 rounds the size of the pans and prick with a fork. Add half the butter to each pan, then add 3 plum halves, skin side down. Arrange the pastry over the pans, tucking in the edges, and bake in a preheated oven at 190°C (375°F) mark 5 for 15 minutes.
3 Remove from the heat and turn the tarts out onto 2 plates.

TARTE TATIN ILLUSTRATED OPPOSITE

thick lemon tart

PASTRY
175 g (6 oz) plain flour
45 g (1¾ oz) icing sugar
85 g (3¼ oz) butter, plus extra for
greasing
pinch of salt
1 egg yolk
15 ml (1 tbsp) water
egg white, for brushing

FILLING
3 eggs
2 egg yolks
85 g (3¼ oz) caster sugar
zest and juice of 4 lemons
150 ml (¼ pint) whipping cream

LEMON SYRUP/COMPOTE
150 g (5 oz) caster sugar
100 ml (3½ fl oz)water
1 lemon, zest removed and
reserved, roughly chopped
225 g (8 oz) raspberries

TO SERVE
60 ml (4 tbsp) crème fraîche
icing sugar, to dust

1 Place all the pastry ingredients in a food processor and process to a firm dough. Knead lightly then wrap in cling film and refrigerate for 30 minutes. Roll out the pastry thinly and use to line 4 individual greased tartlet tins. Prick the bases with a fork, brush the pastry with egg white and line with nonstick baking parchment and baking beans. Bake blind in a preheated oven at 200°C (400°F) mark 6 until crisp and very lightly browned, about 12 minutes. Reduce the oven temperature to 180°C (350°F) mark 4.

2 To make the filling, place the ingredients in a bowl and whisk lightly. Pour the filling into the tartlet cases and bake until set and springy in the middle, about 20 minutes. Allow to cool but do not refrigerate.

3 To make the lemon syrup and compote, dissolve the sugar in the water, bring to the boil and simmer for 2 minutes. Remove 60 ml (4 tbsp) of the syrup, mix with the raspberries and set aside. Add the roughly chopped lemon to the remaining syrup. Simmer for 10 minutes, then strain and return the syrup to the pan. Cut the lemon zest into fine strips and simmer in the syrup for 5 minutes until tender. Allow to cool.

4 To serve, dust the lemon tarts with icing sugar and top with a spoonful of crème fraîche. Decorate with the candied lemon zest and serve with the lemon syrup and raspberry compote.

flambéd bananas, honey ice cream and biscuits

SERVES 2

FLAMBÉD BANANAS
30 g (1¼ oz) soft brown sugar
30 g (1¼ oz) unsalted butter
2 bananas, peeled
30 ml (2 tbsp) brandy
30 ml (2 tbsp) orange juice

HONEY ICE CREAM
284 ml (9½ fl oz) whipping cream
50 g (2 oz) Tasmanian
leatherwood honey
4 tsp honeycomb, broken up

BISCUITS
100 g (3½ oz) unsalted butter
100 g (3½ oz) caster sugar
1 egg yolk
2.5 ml (½ tsp) almond essence
175 g (6 oz) plain flour
5 ml (1 tsp) baking powder
20 flaked almonds

1 To make the flambéd bananas, heat the sugar and butter in a frying pan until the butter has melted. Add the two bananas. Warm the brandy in a small pan then pour over the bananas and set alight. Remove bananas. Add the orange juice to remaining liquid to form a sauce.

2 To make the ice cream, mix all the ingredients together and pour into an ice-cream maker. Churn for 20–30 minutes, then place in the freezer for 30–60 minutes to complete freezing.

3 To make the biscuits, cream the butter and sugar in a food processor, then add the other ingredients, except the almonds, and process for about 2 minutes. Form the mixture into balls, using 5 ml (1 tsp) of mixture per biscuit and press a flaked almond into each biscuit. Bake in a preheated oven at 200°C (400°F) mark 6 for 10 minutes or until golden.

NOTE: Biscuit recipe from *the Magimix and Food Processor Cookery Book* by Marika Hanbury Tenison, published by ICTC.

gulab jambo exotic delight

175 g (6 oz) sugar
1 litre (1¾ pints) water
125 g (4 oz) milk powder
2.5 ml (½ tsp) baking powder
50 g (2 oz) fine semolina soaked
in 25 ml (5 tsp) cold water
50 g (2 oz) self-raising flour
1 tbsp ghee
½ tsp *elaichi* (cardamom seeds)
90 ml (3 fl oz) milk
185 ml (6 fl oz) vegetable oil
saffron
fruits such as kiwi and mango,
peeled and cut into chunks

1 Put the sugar in a pan with the water. Bring slowly to the boil, stirring to dissolve the sugar. Boil rapidly for 5 minutes then remove from the heat and set aside.

2 In a bowl, mix together the milk powder, baking powder, semolina, self-raising flour, ghee and elaichi. Stir into a soft dough with the milk. Knead the dough until smooth, then wrap in cling film. Roll the dough into smooth balls (golf ball size).

3 Meanwhile, heat the oil in a deep-fat fryer to 190°C (375°F) mark 5 and add the balls in batches. Deep-fry for a few seconds then reduce the heat and fry on low heat until golden brown, 8–10 minutes. Remove with a slotted spoon and drain on paper towels until cold.

4 Add the balls to the cold sugar syrup. Let them soak for a good 15–20 minutes.

5 To serve, thread the julab jambo onto 4 skewers, alternating with pieces of fruit.

mango & cardamom gratins (with biscotti and coconut sauce)

1 large or 2 medium mangoes
5–6 green cardamom pods
125 g (4 oz) caster sugar
2 eggs
200 ml (7 fl oz) half–fat crème fraîche
100 ml (3½ fl oz) double cream
4 basil sprigs, to garnish

BISCOTTI
75 g (3 oz) plain flour
75 g (3 oz) caster sugar
2.5 ml (½ tsp) baking powder
1 egg
zest of 1 lime
100 g (3½ oz) unsalted pistachios

COCONUT SAUCE
75 ml (2½ fl oz) mascarpone
75 ml (2½ fl oz) coconut cream
15 ml (1 tbsp) caster sugar, or to taste
a pinch of lime zest

1 Peel the mangoes, cut into small slices and put in a bowl. Remove the cardamom seeds and grind to a powder in a pestle and mortar with 45 ml (3 tbsp) of the sugar. Mix the cardamom sugar with the mango slices and leave to marinate for up to 2 hours (optional).

2 Whisk together the eggs, crème fraîche and cream in a bowl. Arrange the mangoes in 4 ramekin dishes, pour the cream-egg mixture over and sprinkle with the remaining sugar. Place in a bain-marie, or a roasting tin half-filled with hot water and bake in a preheated oven at 180°C (350°F) mark 4 for 30 minutes. Remove the ramekins from the oven and place under the grill for about 5 minutes until dark brown speckles appear. Remove, cool in a bain-marie, then chill until ready to serve.

3 To make the biscotti, in a mixing bowl combine the flour, sugar and baking powder. Beat the egg and slowly add about half to the bowl, mixing well. Add a little more egg until you have a cohesive mixture, not too wet (you will probably not need all the egg). Add the lime zest and pistachios. Using your hands (wet if necessary), shape the mixture into a sausage, about 3 cm (1½ in) in diameter. Place on a baking sheet lined with nonstick baking parchment and flatten slightly. Bake in a preheated oven at 180°C (350°F) mark 4 until golden brown, about 30 minutes. (It is important to have the mixture properly cooked at this stage, or else it will be too sticky to cut.) Leave to cool and firm for at least 10 minutes. Lower the oven temperature to 140°C (275°F) mark 1. Using a serrated knife, cut the sausage into thin slices and return to the baking sheet. Bake for 10–12 minutes, then turn and bake for another 10–12 minutes until browned. Remove and leave to cool on wire racks.

4 To make the coconut sauce, place the mascarpone, coconut cream and sugar in a bowl and beat well until smooth. Chill until ready to serve. Stir in the lime zest just before serving.

5 To serve, unmould the gratins from the ramekins onto 4 plates, smoothing the tops if necessary. Place a tablespoon of coconut sauce and 3 biscotti on each plate. Decorate with basil sprigs.

NOTES: Adapted from Sophie Grigson in *Independent on Sunday*.
These biscotti are very good dipped in vin santo, Marsala or coffee if you have any left over, and they store well, so it is well worth doubling the recipe and keeping some for later use.

pear and almond upside-down cake with amaretto crème anglaise

165 g (5½ oz) butter, melted
175 g (6 oz) caster sugar
175 g (6 oz) brown sugar
4 ripe pears, peeled, cored and halved
100 g (3½ oz) flaked almonds

BATTER

300 g (10 oz) caster sugar
175 g (6 oz) butter
250 g (9 oz) plain flour
7.5 ml (1½ tsp) baking powder
10 ml (2 tsp) salt
5 ml (1 tsp) ground cinnamon
2.5 ml (½ tsp) ground nutmeg
3 eggs
250 ml (8 fl oz) buttermilk

CRÈME ANGLAISE

500 ml (16 fl oz) milk
½ vanilla pod
5 egg yolks
120 g (4 oz) caster sugar
20 ml (4 tsp) Amaretto

1 Pour the melted butter into a 25 cm (10 in) cake tin. Stir the sugar into the butter, then arrange the pears in the tin and sprinkle on the almonds.

2 To make the batter, cream the butter and sugar in a bowl, sift in the dry ingredients and mix well. Add the eggs and mix well. Slowly add the buttermilk, mixing until well incorporated. Pour the batter over the pears and bake in a preheated oven at 180°C (350°F) mark 4 for 40 minutes. Remove from the oven and leave to settle for 10 minutes, then turn out onto a serving dish.

3 To make the crème anglaise, put the milk and vanilla pod in a pan and bring to the boil. Remove from the heat and leave to infuse. Whisk the egg yolks and sugar in a bowl until the mixture is pale and the sugar has dissolved. Remove the vanilla pod, then slowly pour the milk onto the egg mixture and whisk well. Return the mixture to the pan over a low heat, stirring continuously until thick enough to coat the back of a wooden spoon. Add the Amaretto then pour through a fine sieve.

4 To serve, put a slice of the cake on each plate and pour over some crème anglaise.

poached pear with mascarpone and amaretto ice cream and a port jus

4 dessert pears
25 g (1 oz) caster sugar
1 cinnamon stick
zest of 1 small orange
600 ml (1 pint) port

ICE CREAM
juice of 1 lemon
juice of 1 lime
35 g (1¼ oz) caster sugar
125 g (4 oz) mascarpone
250 g (9 oz) organic natural yogurt
100 ml (3½ fl oz) double jersey cream
75 ml (2½ fl oz) Amaretto

BASKETS
50 g (2 oz) unsalted butter, plus extra for greasing
50 g (2 oz) golden syrup
50 g (2 oz) soft brown sugar
50 g (2 oz) plain flour
pinch of ground ginger

TO SERVE
cocoa powder, for dusting
raspberries, to decorate
icing sugar, for dusting

1 Peel the pears and cut about 1 cm (½ in) off the large end so the pears can stand up on the plate. Put pears in a pan with 25 g (1 oz) of sugar, the cinnamon stick and the orange zest. Cover with the port and simmer (not boil) for about 30 minutes, stirring occasionally, until the pears are cooked but still firm. Remove the cinnamon and zest and leave the pears to cool in the port for 1 hour so as to take on the port's colour.

2 Remove the pears with a slotted spoon and reduce the port on a moderate heat by two-thirds until it is thick enough to coat the back of a spoon, and almost syrup-like. Keep warm.

3 To make the ice cream, place the lemon and lime juices in a food processor with the sugar. Blend until well mixed and the sugar is dissolved. Add the mascarpone and blend again. Transfer the mixture to a bowl, add the yogurt and cream and stir. Add the Amaretto. Put the mixture in an ice-cream maker and churn for 20 minutes until thick but not hard as this makes it grainy. Transfer to the freezer until ready to serve.

4 To make the baskets, melt the butter in a pan, add the syrup and sugar and stir until the butter has melted and the sugar has dissolved. Remove from the heat, add the flour and ginger and mix well. Grease and line a baking sheet. Spoon the mixture onto the baking sheet in 4 heaps, spaced well apart, and spread out thinly. Bake in a preheated oven at 180°C (350°F) mark for 4–6 minutes until done, but still soft. Allow to cool for about 30 seconds, then gently remove and ease into greased moulds. Put another mould of the same shape on top and press on top to form the shape. Leave until set.

5 To serve, stand a pear on each plate, put a basket filled with a scoop of the ice cream next to it. Dust very sparingly with cocoa powder and pour some of the port jus over the pear and to one side. Arrange the raspberries on the plate, spoon over some jus and dust with icing sugar.

raspberry clafoutis

SERVES 2
1½ eggs
25 g (1 oz) caster sugar
20 g (¾ oz) caster sugar and 40 g
(1½ oz) butter (to butter and sugar
ramekins)
80 g (3½ oz) self-raising flour
pinch of salt
150 ml (¼ pint) milk
125 g (4 oz) raspberries

FOREST FRUIT COULIS
100 g (3½ oz) soft fruit
150 g (5 oz) raspberries
sorbet syrup, made by boiling 75 g
(3oz) icing sugar with 150 ml
(¼ pint) water

1 Whisk the eggs and sugar in a bowl until light and fluffy. Fold in the flour and salt, then mix in the milk. Butter and sugar 2 ramekins and fill halfway with the batter. Cook in a preheated oven at 180°C (350°F) mark 4 for 15 minutes.

2 Remove the ramekins and fill with raspberries and the remaining batter. Cook for another 20 minutes.

3 To make the coulis, purée the fruit, then add the sorbet syrup and blend.

4 To serve, turn the clafoutis out of the ramekins and serve with the fruit coulis.

RASPBERRY CLAFOUTIS ILLUSTRATED OVERLEAF

rhubarb and ginger clootie dumplings

SERVES 2

4 stalks of fresh rhubarb (trimmed and chopped)
120 ml (4 fl oz) ginger wine
4 pieces of stem ginger, thinly chopped
50 g (2 oz) caster sugar

PASTRY

50 g (2 oz) fresh grated suet
125 g (4 oz) plain flour, plus extra for flouring
25 g (1 oz) ground ginger
20 ml (4 tsp) water

LEMON CUSTARD

6 egg yolks
300 ml (½ pint) double cream
50 g (2 oz) caster sugar
zest and juice of 1 lemon

1 Place the rhubarb in a pan with the ginger wine, stem ginger and sugar and soften over gentle heat for 10–15 minutes so that the rhubarb holds its shape. Remove from the heat and leave to cool.

2 Mix together the suet, flour and ground ginger in a bowl. Add the water and mix to form a soft dough. Cover and refrigerate for at least 30 minutes.

3 On a floured board place 2 muslin cloths. Divide the pastry and roll out into 2 rounds. Place a round in the centre of each cloth. Spoon 30 ml (2 tbsp) of the fruit into centre of the rounds. Gather up the cloth by the corners to form the dumplings and secure with string.

4 Bring a large pan of water to the boil. Drop the dumplings into the boiling water and cook for 20 minutes, then remove and drain.

5 To make the custard, in a bain-marie whisk together the egg yolks, cream and sugar. Add lemon juice and zest and continue to whisk for a further 5–7 minutes or until the custard thickens.

6 To serve, remove the cloth, turn out the dumplings onto 2 plates and serve with the lemon custard.

sautéed peppered pears and china tea sorbet

SERVES 2

2 ripe pears
45 ml (3 tbsp) pear liqueur
30 ml (2 tbsp) crushed mixed peppercorns
50 g (2 oz) butter

CHINA TEA SORBET

300 ml (½ pint) China tea, cooled
185 ml (6 fl oz) sugar syrup
juice of ½ lemon
1 egg white, lightly whisked

1 With skins left on, cut the pears into 8 even lengths and core each segment. Place the pears in a dish and sprinkle with the liqueur and peppercorns. Refrigerate for 15 minutes.

2 Melt the butter in a heavy-based sauté pan. Add the pears and sauté until golden brown.

3 To make the sorbet, mix together the tea, sugar syrup and lemon juice. Pour into an ice-cream maker, then add the egg white. Churn until frozen.

4 Serve the pears on individual plates, with a scoop of sorbet.

soufflé omelette

SERVES 2

½ orange
½ lemon
300 ml (½ pint) water
1 stick cinnamon
95 g (3½ oz) sugar
3 large basil leaves, chopped
1 generous pinch of grated fresh
ginger
300 g (10 oz) mixed berries
3 large eggs, separated
15 ml (1 tbsp) olive oil
50 g (2 oz) Greek yogurt
10ml (2 tsp) ground ginger
25 g (1 oz) icing sugar

TO SERVE

1 strawberry, halved
½ kiwi fruit, sliced
2 sprigs of mint

1 Squeeze the orange and lemon into a pan with the water and add the skins of the squeezed fruit. Add the cinnamon and 75 g (3 oz) of the sugar. Bring to the boil and cook until reduced by half. Strain and return the syrup to the pan. Add the basil and ginger. Add the berries and simmer gently until the syrup is dark and rich in colour and the berries still intact. Remove from the heat, strain, reserving the syrup, and mash the berries.

2 Whisk the egg whites until peaks form. Beat the egg yolks with 20 g (¾ oz) of sugar and fold into the egg whites. Lightly oil a non-stick omelette pan with olive oil. Heat the pan until hot, pour in half the egg mixture and cook for 30 seconds or until the underside is golden. Place under a hot grill and brown the top lightly for a further 30 seconds or until just golden. Place some berries on the centre of the omelette, fold and slide onto a plate. Dust with icing sugar. Heat a skewer and mark the omelette in a criss-cross fashion. Repeat with the remaining omelette mixture.

3 To serve, place some berries and syrup at the side of each omelette. Add a heaped spoonful of yogurt and sprinkle with ginger and icing sugar. Decorate with half a strawberry, a slice of kiwi fruit and a sprig of mint.

summer berries in a tuile basket with lemon balm ice cream

125 g (4 oz) self-raising flour
3 egg whites
160 g (5½ oz) icing sugar
225 g (8 oz) butter, melted
pinch of salt
225–350 g (8–12 oz) assorted
summer berries, rinsed

LEMON BALM ICE CREAM
350 ml (12 fl oz) double cream
175 ml (6 fl oz) single cream
175 ml (6 fl oz) milk
150 g (5 oz) lemon balm leaves
6 egg yolks
175 g (6 oz) caster sugar

1 Place the flour and sugar in a bowl, add the egg whites and butter and mix together with a pinch of salt. Chill for 30 minutes.

2 Spread the mixture in 4 rounds onto a baking sheet lined with nonstick baking parchment. Bake in a preheated oven at 150°C (300°F) mark 2 for about 3 minutes, or until lightly coloured. Remove from the oven, and shape into a basket shape using a brioche tin or an upturned cup. Leave to cool.

3 To make the ice cream, place the cream and milk in a pan and bring to the boil. Add the lemon balm, remove from the heat and leave to infuse for 10 minutes. Whisk together the egg yolks and sugar. Remove the lemon balm with a slotted spoon and place in a food processor. Pour the cream mixture over the eggs and stir to mix. Return the mixture to the pan and heat gently for 2–3 minutes, stirring continuously, to thicken. Pour into the food processor with the lemon balm and process. Strain and allow to cool. Place in an ice-cream maker and churn until frozen.

4 To serve, fill the baskets with the berries and serve with lemon balm ice cream.

petal basket filled with summer fruits, rose water cream and summer berry coulis

SERVES 2

75 g (3 oz) plain flour
75 g (3 oz) icing sugar
75 g (3 oz) unsalted butter,
melted, plus extra for greasing
2 whisked egg whites
acetate stencil in the shape of a
flower

ROSE WATER CREAM

120 ml (4 fl oz) double cream
10 ml (2 tsp) caster sugar
15 ml (1 tbsp) rose water

COULIS

175 g (6 oz) blackcurrants
50 g (2 oz) raspberries
125 g (4 oz) caster sugar

TO SERVE

225 g (8 oz) mixed strawberries,
raspberries, blueberries,
loganberries, blackberries, sliced
kiwi fruit

1 To make the baskets, sift the flour and icing sugar into a bowl and mix in the melted butter and egg white. Lay the stencil on a greased baking sheet. Put 15 ml (1 tbsp) of mixture in the cut-out stencil and spread evenly. Remove the stencil. Repeat to make a second shape. Bake in a preheated oven at 210°C (410°F) mark 6½ for 10 minutes. Remove and shape over a small bowl.

2 To make the rose water cream lightly whip the cream in a bowl, then whip in the sugar and rose water.

3 To make the coulis, purée the fruit with the icing sugar, then push through a sieve.

4 To serve, divide the rose water cream between the 2 baskets, then add the fruit. Put a basket on each plate and spoon round the coulis.

chocolate and banana crème brûlée

SERVES 2

1 banana

5 ml (1 tsp) Cointreau

75 g (3 oz) good quality dark chocolate, broken up

50 g (2 oz) caster sugar

3 egg yolks

300 ml (½ pint) double cream

SHORTBREAD

50 g (2 oz) butter, plus extra for greasing

25 g (1 oz) caster sugar, plus extra for dusting

75 g (3 oz) plain flour, plus extra for flouring

1 Slice the banana and divide between 2 ramekins. Sprinkle with the Cointreau. Place the chocolate in a bowl set over a pan of simmering water. Leave until melted, without stirring, then remove from the heat.

2 In a separate bowl whisk together 25 g (1 oz) caster sugar and the egg yolks. Gently heat the cream in a pan until almost simmering. Pour half the cream onto the egg mixture, and stir, then return the mixture to the pan. Cook over gentle heat, stirring continuously, until mixture is thick enough to coat the back of a wooden spoon. Remove from the heat immediately and stir in the melted chocolate. Divide the mixture between the ramekins and place in the refrigerator to set, about 1 hour. When set, sprinkle the tops with the remaining sugar. Clean the tops of the ramekins and blowtorch until golden brown.

3 To make the shortbread, cream the butter and caster sugar in a bowl until soft and creamy. Gradually add the flour to the mixture. Knead the dough into a ball, but do not over handle. Turn the dough onto a floured board and roll out to a 5 mm (¼ in) thickness. Cut into rounds and place on a greased baking sheet. Bake in a preheated oven at 160°C (325°F) mark 3 for 12 minutes until pale golden. Cool on a wire cooling rack and dust with caster sugar.

4 Serve the ramekins on individual plates with a shortbread round.

baked lemon custards

juice of 4 lemons
zest of 1 lemon
125 g (4 oz) caster sugar
200 ml (7 fl oz) double cream
100 ml (3½ fl oz) milk
3 eggs, plus 3 yolks
5 ml (1 tsp) cornflour
butter for greasing moulds
sugar for dusting moulds

ORANGE SAUCE
juice of 3 oranges
zest of 1 orange
40 g (1½ oz) sugar, or to taste
2.5 ml (½ tsp) arrowroot

CARAMEL ABSTRACTS
100 g (3½ oz) lump sugar
60 ml (4 tbsp) water
10 ml (2 tsp) liquid glucose

1 Place the lemon juice and zest and 100 g (3½ oz) of the sugar in a pan and heat gently to form a syrup. Heat the cream and milk to boiling point. Whisk the eggs and egg yolks in a bowl with the cornflour and remaining sugar. Add the strained syrup to the eggs, then add the cream. Stir well and strain through muslin.

2 Butter 4 individual moulds and dust with caster sugar. Fill the moulds with the custard.

Place the moulds in a roasting tin half-filled with warm water. Bake in a pre-heated oven at 150°C (300°F) mark 2 for about 25 minutes, or until just set. Remove from the oven and allow to cool, then chill.

3 To make the orange sauce, heat the orange juice and zest in a small pan, reduce by half and strain through muslin. Add sugar to taste – the sauce should be sweeter than the lemon custards. Mix the arrowroot with a little cold water and gradually mix into the simmering juice until just thickened. Chill.

4 To make the caramel, heat the lump sugar and water very slowly in a small pan until dissolved. Add the liquid glucose and raise the heat to bring the sugar to the boil. Boil until the colour is a light caramel. Brush the sides of the pan with cold water if the sugar starts to crystallize at the edges. Remove from the heat, allow to stand for a minute then with a fork or spoon drizzle the caramel onto nonstick baking parchment to form shapes.

5 To serve, turn out the custards onto 4 plates, pour over the orange sauce and decorate with the caramel shapes.

NOTE: Variation on a recipe by Nico Ladenis. Basic idea for caramel shapes from Michel Roux.

biscotti with chocolate cream

SERVES 2

75 g (3 oz) almonds

7.5 ml (½ tbsp) coriander seeds

50 g (2 oz) butter, plus extra for greasing

100 g (3½ oz) sugar

1 beaten egg

finely grated zest of ½ orange and ½ lemon

5 ml (1 tsp) baking powder

2.5 ml (½) tsp salt

175 g (6 oz) plain flour

40 g (1½ oz) semolina

CHOCOLATE CREAM

150 g (5 oz) double cream

50 g (2 oz) white chocolate, broken up

75 g (3 oz) dark chocolate, broken up

25 g (1 oz) butter

15 ml (1 tbsp) liqueur

125 g (4 oz) fresh raspberries

1 Put the almonds on a baking sheet and toast for 5–10 minutes in a hot oven. Allow to cool, then crush with the coriander seeds.

2 Cream the butter and sugar in a bowl. Beat in the egg, orange and lemon zest, baking powder and salt. Stir in the flour, semolina, almonds and coriander seeds. Form into a dough and knead until smooth. Divide the dough into 4 equal pieces and roll into 5cm (2 in) squares, 1.5 cm (¾in) deep. Place on greased baking sheets. Bake in a preheated oven at 170°C (325°F) mark 3 for 35 minutes, then remove from the oven, cut into fingers and bake for another 10 minutes.

3 To make the chocolate cream, put the cream in a pan and bring to the boil. Place the chocolate and butter in a bowl then pour the cream over. Stir until the chocolate and butter are melted then add the liqueur. Refrigerate for 30 minutes.

4 Beat the chocolate mixture until thick and creamy. Pour into 4 individual oiled moulds and push raspberries into the centre. Refrigerate until ready to serve.

5 To serve, turn out the chocolate creams onto individual plates and arrange biscotti around.

chilled hazelnut soufflé with bitter chocolate sauce

120 ml (4 fl oz) milk
400 ml (14 fl oz) whipping cream
1 vanilla pod
4 egg yolks
15 ml (1 tbsp) granulated sugar
pinch of salt
cocoa powder, for dusting

BITTER CHOCOLATE SAUCE
125 (4 oz) dark chocolate (70% cocoa solids), broken up
90 ml (3 fl oz) boiling water
15 ml (1 tbsp) unsalted butter
2 drops of vanilla essence

PRALINE PASTE
125 g (4 oz) shelled hazelnuts
125 g (4 oz) caster sugar

1 First make the praline paste. To remove the skins from the hazelnuts, bake in a preheated oven at 200°C (400°F) mark 6 for 10 minutes, then gently rub in a tea towel until the skins are removed. Place the sugar and the hazelnuts in a heavy-bottomed pan over a low heat until the sugar melts. Turn with a spoon until the sugar has lightly caramelized and the nuts are evenly coated. Turn into an oiled tin and allow to cool. Once cooled, break up the praline with a rolling pin and blend to a paste in a food processor.

2 Bring the milk, 50 ml (2 fl oz) of the cream and the vanilla pod almost to the boil in a pan. Remove from the heat and leave to infuse for 10 minutes. Meanwhile, prepare 4 ramekins by wrapping lengths of foil around to form a collar at least 5 cm (2in) above the rim. Secure with elastic bands.

3 Beat the egg yolks, sugar and salt together in a bowl until light and creamy. Remove the vanilla pod from the pan, then stir the hot milk into the whipped egg. Return the mixture to the pan and cook over a low heat, stirring continuously, until the mixture is thick enoughs to coat the back of a wooden spoon. Remove from the heat and leave to cool.

4 Once the mixture is cool, stir in 125 g (4 oz) of the praline paste. Whip the remaining cream and fold into the mixture. Divide the mixture between the ramekins, gently smoothing the surface, and place in the freezer for about 90 minutes.

5 Meanwhile, make the bitter chocolate sauce. Place the chocolate in a bowl and pour over the boiling water. Stir to ensure it is evenly melted. Beat in the butter and vanilla essence.

6 To serve, remove the soufflés from the freezer, carefully remove the foil collars and place on individual plates. Dust with cocoa powder and pour the chocolate sauce over the soufflés.

chocolate honeycomb mousse served with a redcurrant and orange sauce

SERVES 2

HONEYCOMB
30 ml (2 tbsp) sugar
15 ml (1 tbsp) golden syrup
7.5 ml (1½ tsp) bicarbonate of
soda

MOUSSE
80 g (3¼ oz) plain chocolate
(70% cocoa solids), broken up
15 ml (1 tbsp) water
15 ml (1 tbsp) rum
15 ml (1 tbsp) icing sugar
20 g (¾ oz) unsalted butter
55 ml (2½ fl oz) double cream
grapeseed oil

SAUCE
30 ml (2 tbsp) redcurrant jelly
juice of 1 orange
30 ml (2 tbsp) rum

TO DECORATE
grated chocolate, mint leaves or
sprigs of fresh redcurrants

1 To make the honeycomb, line a baking sheet with nonstick baking parchment. Heat the sugar and golden syrup in a small pan, stirring frequently. Cook until the sugar has completely dissolved and the mixture is a pale golden colour, and is bubbling. Add the bicarbonate of soda and stir well. Quickly transfer the mixture to the lined baking sheet and leave to dry. As soon as it has set, put the honeycomb into a plastic bag and lightly crush with a rolling pin. Keep airtight.

2 To make the mousse, place the chocolate in a bowl over a bain-marie with the water, rum, and icing sugar until it is a thick cream. Remove from the heat. Add the butter to the warm chocolate mixture and stir well. Leave to cool.

3 Whip the cream until thick and fold it into the chocolate mixture. Line the bottom of 2 ramekins with nonstick baking parchment, and oil the sides with grapeseed oil. Fill the ramekins with the chocolate mousse. Add 10 ml (2 tsp) of broken honeycomb pieces to the mousse and press in gently with a teaspoon. Refrigerate for 30 minutes.

4 To make the sauce, put the ingredients in a small pan and simmer gently over a low heat for about 20 minutes, until reduced to a syrup. Leave to cool.

5 To serve, loosen the sides of the mousse with a knife. Turn out onto individual plates and pour the sauce around. Decorate with grated chocolate, mint leaves or fresh redcurrants.

chocolate terrine with white chocolate ice cream

DARK LAYER

125 g (4 oz) good quality plain chocolate, broken up

25 g (1 oz) unsalted butter

⅔ egg yolk

240 ml (8 fl oz) double cream, whipped

25 g (1 oz) milk chocolate, chopped

WHITE LAYER

50 g (2 oz) white chocolate with natural vanilla flavouring

15 g (½ oz) unsalted butter

⅓ egg yolk

120 ml (4 fl oz) double cream, whipped

WHITE CHOCOLATE ICE CREAM

1 egg yolk

30 g (1¼ oz) caster sugar

150 ml (¼ pint) milk

150 ml (¼ pint) double cream

50 g (2 oz) white chocolate, broken up

1 To make the dark and white layers, melt the plain and white chocolate in separate bowls over pans of simmering water. Once melted, remove from the heat and stir in the butter until combined. Leave mixtures to cool, but ensure that they remain liquid. Once cool, add egg yolk to each bowl and beat well. Fold in the whipped cream. Add the chopped milk chocolate to the dark layer.

2 To assemble the terrine, line a plastic box, measuring 12 cm (5 in) x 10 cm (4 in) and 6 cm (2½ in) deep, with nonstick baking parchment. Spoon half the dark mixture into the container and smooth flat with the back of a spoon. With care spoon on the white mixture, use minimal pressure to smooth flat. Repeat with the remaining dark mixture. Cover with cling film and refrigerate until ready to serve.

3 To make the ice cream, whisk the egg yolk and sugar in a bowl until combined. Bring the milk and cream to the boil in a pan. Add the chocolate and stir until melted. Pour the boiling liquid onto the egg yolk and stir until well combined. Remove from the heat and leave to cool, stirring from time to time to prevent the chocolate coming to the top. When the mixture is cool transfer to an ice-cream maker and churn until frozen. Put into the freezer until ready to serve.

4 To serve, turn out the terrine and cut into slices. Serve with scoops of the white chocolate ice cream.

coconut ice cream with tangy lime syrup

SERVES 2

3 egg yolks

5 ml (1 tsp) cornflour

100 g (3½ g) caster sugar

5 ml (1 tsp) vanilla essence

150 ml (¼ pint) milk

150 ml (¼ pint) coconut milk

150 ml (¼ pint) double cream

TANGY LIME SYRUP

100 ml (3½ fl oz) water

100 g (3½ oz) granulated sugar

3 limes

15 ml (1 tbsp) arrowroot

1 In a bowl whisk together the egg yolks, cornflour, sugar and vanilla essence.

2 Heat the milk and coconut milk in a pan until it just comes to the boil. Pour over the egg yolk mixture and whisk. Return the mixture to the pan and stir over a low heat for a few minutes until it is thick enough to coat the back of a wooden spoon. Stir in the double cream then remove from the heat and leave to cool.

3 Put the cooled mixture in an ice-cream maker and churn to freeze.

4 To make the lime syrup, place the water in a pan with the sugar and strips of zest from 1 lime. Bring to the boil and cook until the sugar is dissolved, then lower the heat and leave to simmer.

5 Meanwhile squeeze the juice from the 3 limes and mix into the arrowroot in a bowl. Stir into the syrup and leave to thicken for about 5 minutes. Pour the syrup into a jug and refrigerate until cooled.

6 Serve scoops of the ice cream with the tangy lime syrup dribbled over.

dark fruit fool with biscuits and chocolate leaves

SERVES 2–4

250 g (9 oz) prunes, stoned
100 g (3½ oz) seeded raisins
50 g (2 oz) seeded currants
100 ml (3½ fl oz) ruby port
½ egg white

BISCUITS

100 g (3½ oz) butter
75 g (3 oz) sugar
1 egg
5 ml (1 tsp) vanilla essence
75 g (3 oz) self-raising flour

CHOCOLATE LEAVES

50 g (2 oz) plain cooking
chocolate, broken up
4 fresh bay leaves

1 Place the fruit in an ovenproof dish and cover with water. Add the port and place in a preheated oven at 140°C (275°F) mark 1 for 3 hours. Sieve the fruit, reserving the liquid, and purée in a food processor. Put the liquid in a pan over medium heat until reduced by three-quarters, then stir into the purée. Whip the egg white and gently fold into the purée. Refrigerate for 1 hour.

2 To make the biscuits, place the butter, sugar, egg, vanilla and flour in a food processor. Blend to a soft dough. Place teaspoonfuls of the mixture, spaced well apart, on a greased baking sheet. Bake in a preheated oven at 190°C (375°F) mark 5 for 10 minutes, or until golden brown. Remove and allow to cool.

3 To make the chocolate leaves, melt the chocolate in a bowl set over a pan of simmering water. Carefully paint the bay leaves on one side with chocolate, then refrigerate until chocolate has set. When set, peel away chocolate from each leaf.

4 Serve the fruit fool on individual plates. Place 2 biscuits on each plate and decorate with a chocolate leaf.

ice coffee soufflé wrapped in chocolate

50g (2 oz) amaretti biscuits,
crushed
50g (2 oz) caster sugar
2 eggs, separated
30 ml (2 tbsp) extra strong warm
coffee
300 ml (½ pint) double cream
15 ml (1 tbsp) Amaretti liqueur
125 g (4 oz) dark plain chocolate,
broken up

STRAWBERRY, BERRY AND MINT
SALSA

25g (1oz) strawberries, chopped
25g (1oz) redcurrants
25g (1oz) raspberries
15 ml (1 tbsp) chopped fresh mint
50g (2 oz) caster sugar
150 ml (¼ pint) water

1 Line 4 individual moulds with the crushed amaretti biscuits. Whisk the sugar and egg yolks in a bowl until thick and pale. Gradually whisk in the warm coffee and liqueur. Whip the cream and fold into the coffee mixture. Whisk the egg whites until stiff and fold into the mixture. Spoon the mixture into the moulds and freeze for 2 hours.

2 Unmould each soufflé by dipping quickly into boiling water, then turn out. Melt the chocolate in a bowl set over a pan of simmering water. Cut strips of nonstick baking parchment, their length being the diameter of the soufflé base and slightly taller than each soufflé. Paint each piece of paper with the melted chocolate. Wrap a strip around each soufflé and return to the freezer for 30 minutes.

3 To make the salsa, combine the fruit and mint in a bowl. Place the sugar and water in a pan and bring to the boil. Boil until the sugar has dissolved, 2–3 minutes. Leave to cool, then mix well with the berries and mint. Chill for 2 hours.

4 To serve, peel the paper from each soufflé and place them on individual plates. Drain the salsa and place a spoonful on each plate.

kheer

SERVES 2
600 ml (1 pint) milk
75 g (3 oz) roasted vermicelli
4 green cardamom pods
75 g (3 oz) sugar
10 almonds, grated
10 cashew nuts, grated

1 Heat the milk in a pan to a simmer. Add the roasted vermicelli with the cardamom pods and simmer gently for 10–15 minutes. Add the sugar with the grated nuts, and stir to dissolve the sugar. Remove from the heat and leave in the pan to cool.

2 Pour into 2 serving dishes and serve cool.

kiwi soup with passion fruit ice cream

120 ml (4 fl oz) passion fruit juice,with a few seeds for decoration
185 g (6½ oz) caster sugar
500 ml (16 fl oz) whole milk
½ vanilla pod
6 egg yolks
120 g (4 oz) caster sugar
12 kiwi fruit, peeled
juice of 2 lemons

1 Place the passion fruit juice in a pan and heat gently with 80 g (3¼ oz) of the caster sugar until dissolved, then sieve. Keep some of the seeds to decorate.

2 To make the ice cream, heat the milk in a pan with the vanilla pod until just simmering. Whisk the egg yolks and sugar in a bowl until pale and creamy. Remove the vanilla pod, then pour the milk onto the egg mixture and stir well. Return the mixture to the pan and stir gently over low heat until the mixture is thick enough to coat the back of a wooden spoon. Add half the passion fruit juice. Leave to cool, then place in an ice-cream maker and churn until frozen.

3 Purée the kiwi fruit in a food processor and add the remaining sugar and the lemon juice. Push through a sieve, then chill for 1 hour.

4 To serve, place a ladle of kiwi soup in each bowl. Place a scoop of ice cream in the centre and drizzle with the remaining passion fruit juice. Decorate with a few passion fruit seeds.

layered coffee and vanilla set cream with apricot and brandy sauce and raspberry purée

8 g (¼ oz) gelatine leaves
170 ml (5½ fl oz) milk
1 vanilla pod, cut lengthwise
90 g (3 oz) caster sugar
400 ml (14 fl oz) double cream
10 g (¼ oz) instant coffee
10 ml (2 tsp) boiling water
300 g (10 oz) raspberries
mint leaves, to decorate

APRICOT AND BRANDY SAUCE
200 g (7 oz) dried apricots,
coarsely chopped
20 ml (4 tsp) water
100 g (3½ oz) apricot glaze
60 ml (4 tbsp) brandy

1 Soak the gelatine leaves in cold water for about 10 minutes. Put the milk, vanilla pod and the sugar in a pan and bring to the boil, then remove from the heat. Drain the gelatine and add it to the hot milk, stirring until it dissolves completely. Remove the vanilla pod and add the double cream.

2 Pour the mixture into 2 separate bowls. Make some very strong coffee using the instant coffee and boiling water and add to one of the bowls. Half-fill 4 individual pudding bowls with the white mixture and leave to set in the refrigerator for 1 hour. Once set, add the coffee mixture to each bowl and chill for another hour.

3 To make the apricot sauce, put the dried apricots in a pan with the water and the apricot glaze. Cook gently for 10 minutes, until soft, then add the brandy and remove from the heat.

4 Put the raspberries in a bowl and stir with a fork to make a purée. Push through a sieve to remove the seeds.

5 To serve, dip one bowl at a time in hot water for a few seconds, then turn upside down over a plate and shake gently to unmould. Arrange the warm apricot sauce around it and cover one side of the set cream with the raspberry purée. Decorate with a few mint leaves.

peach marsala crème brûlée

SERVES 2
2 fresh peaches
60 ml (2 fl oz) sweet Marsala
60 g (2½ oz) caster sugar
2 vanilla pods
5 egg yolks
150 ml (¼ pint) double cream
60 ml (2 fl oz) milk
30 ml (2 tbsp) neige decor (very fine confectionery sugar)

1 Place peaches in boiling water for a few minutes, then remove skins. Chop the flesh into small pieces. Poach the peaches with the Marsala, 25 g (1 oz) of the sugar and 1 vanilla pod, until the Marsala and sugar have made a thick syrup and the peaches are tender. Remove the pod. Divide between 2 ramekins.

2 Cream the egg yolks and remaining sugar in a bowl. Bring the cream, milk and 1 vanilla pod to the boil in a pan, then remove the pod and pour onto the egg yolks and whisk well. Place in a clean saucepan and return to the heat. Stir continuously until the mixture is thick enough to coat the back of a wooden spoon. Carefully spoon over the peaches and refrigerate.

3 To serve, sprinkle the neige decor over the top of each ramekin, making sure they are completely covered. Lightly grill or blowtorch until golden brown.

passion fruit mousse with caramel crack and mango sauce

MOUSSE
1 egg white
60 g (2½ oz) sugar
15 ml (1 tbsp) water
2 leaves gelatine
8–10 passion fruit
50 g (2 oz) whipping cream
4 physalis fruits, to decorate

CARAMEL CRACK
100 g (3½ oz) granulated sugar
15 ml (1 tbsp) water

SAUCE
1 large ripe mango
juice of 2 limes
sugar, to taste

1 First prepare the caramel crack. Oil a large sheet of foil and stretch tightly over a marble slab. Oil four 7 cm (3 in) ring moulds and place on the foil. Put the sugar in a heavy pan with the water. Dissolve the sugar over a low heat, then raise the heat and boil until it turns golden brown. Pour a thin layer into each mould and twist to cover base. Allow to cool, then lift off moulds.

2 To make the sauce, cut the flesh from the mango and purée in a food processor with lime juice until a pouring consistency is obtained. Sweeten to taste if necessary.

3 To make the mousse, beat the egg white until it forms soft peaks. Boil the sugar and water until it reaches 120°C (248°F) on a sugar thermometer. Pour the boiling syrup in a thin stream onto the egg white while still whipping. Continue whipping until cold.

4 Soak the gelatine in cold water for 5 minutes, then strain. Cut the fruit open and scrape out juice and seeds into a bowl. Warm in a microwave and add the softened gelatine. Stir until gelatine is fully dissolved. Whip the cream until it forms soft peaks. Combine fruit juice and seeds, cream and egg white mixture by folding gently and pour into four chilled 7 cm (3 in) rng moulds lined with nonstick baking parchment and standing on a foil-lined baking sheet. Chill thoroughly until set.

5 To serve, unmould each mousse and place in the centre of a plate. Place a caramel crack on top and a physalis fruit on top of the caramel. Drizzle mango sauce around the mousse.

lemon and lime soufflé custard with lemon syllabub in almond tuiles

SERVES 2

100 g (3½ oz) caster sugar

15g (½ oz) butter

25 g (1 oz) plain flour

2 eggs, separated

zest and juice of 2 limes and 1 lemon

250 ml (8 fl oz) milk

LEMON SYLLABUB

25 g (1 oz) caster sugar

juice of ¼ lemon

7.5 ml (½ tbsp) brandy

15 ml (1 tbsp) sherry

155 ml (5 fl oz) double cream

TUILES

25 g (1 oz) unsalted butter

25 g (1 oz) icing sugar

grated zest of ½ lemon

7.5 ml (½ tbsp) flour, sifted

25 g (1 oz) flaked almonds, chopped

1 Place caster sugar, butter, flour, egg yolks, zest and juice into a food processor. Blend, and while blending, pour the milk in through the funnel. Pour custard into a large measuring jug.

2 Whisk the egg whites until soft peaks form. Fold into the custard mixture with a metal spoon until smooth.

3 Place 4 greased ramekins in a roasting tin. Fill with mixture, sharing it out equally. Pour boiling water into the roasting tin, until it comes halfway up the outsides of the ramekins. Bake in a preheated oven at 180°C (350°F) mark 4 for 15-20 minutes or until risen and golden brown.

4 To make the syllabub, place the caster sugar, lemon juice, brandy and sherry in a large bowl and stir until all the sugar has dissolved. Add the cream and whisk until the mixture forms stiff peaks. Chill the mixture for 1 hour at least.

5 To make the tuiles, cream together the butter, icing sugar and lemon zest in a bowl until light, pale and fluffy. Sieve in the flour, add the almonds and stir the mixture until combined well.

6 Place 2.5 ml (½ tsp) blobs of the mixture on a nonstick baking sheet, spacing well apart – only 3 or 4 blobs on a sheet. Spread out into small discs. Bake in a preheated oven at 180°C (350°F) mark 4 for 4–5 minutes, or until golden and bubbling. Remove from the heat and mould round small pudding moulds. Leave to cool and set.

7 To serve, place a ramekin on each plate with tuiles filled with lemon syllabub.

peanut butter mousse wrapped in chocolate with raspberry jelly and chocolate sauce with a happy clown face presentation

SPECIAL EQUIPMENT

two 20 cm (8 in) lengths of plastic pipe about 3 cm (1¼ in) in diameter and acetate sheet

PASTRY CREAM

30 ml (2 tbsp) cornflour

250 ml (8 fl oz) milk

1 To make the pastry cream, whisk the cornflour with about 60 ml (4 tbsp) milk until smooth. Whisk in the egg and yolk until blended. In a pan heat the remaining milk and the sugar until the sugar is dissolved. Bring to the boil. Gradually whisk about 120 ml (4 fl oz) of the milk into the egg mixture until well blended. Return it to the pan and bring to the boil, whisking constantly. Simmer for about 12 minutes, whisking continuously. Whisk in the butter and vanilla. Cover the surface with cling film and leave to cool.

2 To make the peanut mousse, cut 2 rectangles of nonstick baking parch-

1 egg
1 egg yolk
30 g (1¼ oz) sugar
15 ml (1 tbsp) unsalted butter
2.5 ml (½ tsp) vanilla extract

PEANUT BUTTER MOUSSE
1 quantity of Pastry Cream (see above)
180 g (6½ oz) smooth peanut butter
250 ml (8 fl oz) whipping cream

CHOCOLATE SAUCE
50 g (2 oz) plain chocolate, broken up
40 ml (2½ tbsp) milk
15 ml (1 tbsp) double cream
7.5 ml (½ tbsp) caster sugar
7.5 ml (½ tbsp) unsalted butter, diced

RASPBERRY JELLY
125 g (4 oz) sugar
170 ml (5½ fl oz) dry white wine
2 sheets gelatine, soaked in cold water
15 ml (1 tbsp) raspberry eau-de-vie
200 g (7 oz) fresh raspberries

CHOCOLATE BANDS
20 g (¾ oz) white chocolate, broken up
75 g (3 oz) plain chocolate, broken up

TO SERVE (OPTIONAL)
whipped cream
chopped peanuts

ment and use to line the plastic pipes , folding back the ends. Cover one end of each pipe. Place the pastry cream in a bowl and beat for about a minute until smooth. Gradually beat in the peanut butter until smooth. Whip the cream to soft peaks. Fold one-third of the cream into the peanut butter mixture, then fold in the rest. Using a piping bag, pipe the mousse into the prepared plastic pipes and freeze for about 1 hour until firm.

3 To make the chocolate sauce, melt the chocolate in a bowl set over a pan of simmering water. In a pan bring the milk, cream and sugar to the boil, stirring gently. Pour into the melted chocolate, stirring continuously. Return the mixture to the pan and let it bubble for a few seconds. Off the heat, beat in the butter a little at a time until well mixed. Pass through a fine sieve.

4 To make the raspberry jelly, put the sugar and wine in a pan and dissolve the sugar over a gentle heat. Remove from the heat and dissolve the soaked gelatine in the liquid. Add the eau-de-vie. Distribute the raspberries between 4 oiled dariole moulds and fill with the jelly. Leave to set in the refrigerator.

5 To make the chocolate bands, cut out 8 acetate shapes measuring 5 cm (2 in) x 11 cm (4½ in). Place on a baking sheet covered with nonstick baking parchment. Melt the white chocolate in a bowl set over a pan of simmering water. Using a small paper cone pipe thin zigzags of chocolate (or whatever other pattern you like) across each shape. Place in the refrigerator for 30 minutes to set.

6 Melt the plain chocolate in a bowl set over a pan of simmering water. Spread a thin layer of the plain chocolate over each of the shapes. Allow to firm up for about 5 minutes at room temperature before wrapping the mousses.

7 Remove the mousses from the tubes by pulling out with the baking paper. Gently peel off the baking paper. Cut the mousses into eight x 5 cm (2 in) lengths and wrap in the acetate shapes coated with chocolate. Secure with rubber bands or paper clips. Place each one in the refrigerator while wrapping the other mousses.

8 To assemble, remove the acetate and stand 2 mousse towers on each plate for the eyes. Dip each dariole mould briefly in hot water to unmould the jellies. Use the jelly as a nose and drizzle the chocolate sauce around as a mouth. If liked, top each mousse tower with whipped cream and chopped peanuts.

NOTE: This is based on a recipe by Lynne Johnson of Darrel & Oliver's Café Maxx in Pompano Beach, Florida

raspberry brûleé with vanilla and black pepper tuiles

SERVES 2

150 ml (¼ pint) double cream
½ vanilla pod, split and seeds reserved
3 egg yolks
25 g (1 oz) sugar
20 raspberries

TUILES

90 g (3¼ oz) plain flour
100 g (3½ oz) unsalted butter
120 g (4 oz) icing sugar, plus extra for dusting
3 egg whites
½ tsp vanilla essence
15 ml (1 tbsp) crushed and ground black pepper
10 ml (2 tsp) demerara sugar

1 Place the double cream, ½ vanilla pod and seeds in a pan over a gentle heat.

Whisk the egg yolks and sugar in a bowl until pale and creamy. When the cream is near boiling point, remove from the heat, remove the pod and add to the yolks. Whisk, then return the mixture to the pan. Stir continuously over a gentle heat for 2 minutes, but do not allow the mixture to boil.

2 Place 10 raspberries in the bottom of 2 ramekins. Then pour the custard into the 2 ramekins. Place the ramekins in a bain-marie or a roasting tin half-filled with hot water, placing a piece of newspaper underneath the ramekins to prevent disruption from air bubbles. Place on the top shelf of a preheated oven at 165°C (325°F) mark 3 for about 40 minutes, until set.

3 Meanwhile, make the tuiles. You will need a template cut from an ice-cream tub lid, measuring 5 cm (2 in) x 10 cm (4 in). Place the flour, butter, icing sugar and egg whites in a food processor and mix well. Transfer to a bowl and refrigerate for at least 5 minutes. Stir in the vanilla essence.

4 Cover a baking sheet with foil. Using the template and a spatula, spread 2 rectangles of the mixture on the foil. Use the depth of the template as the thickness level. Sprinkle the pastry rectangles with the black pepper. Place in a preheated oven at 180°C (350°F) mark 4 for 5–6 minutes. Remove from the oven and allow to cool. Once cool, remove from foil and return to the oven for 1 minute. Remove each one individually and shape while warm. Either roll it into a cigar shape, or simply twist around a rolling pin.

5 Remove the ramekins from the oven. Place 5 ml (1 tsp) of Demerara sugar on each one and then use a blowtorch to caramelize the top. Alternatively, place under a hot grill for 3–4 minutes. Allow to cool for 1 minute, by which time a hard layer should have formed. Dust with a little icing sugar, if liked, and serve with the tuiles.

raspberry-passion fruit swirls with lemon tuiles

SERVES 2
350 g (12 oz) raspberries
250 ml (8 fl oz) double cream
2 passion fruit
15 ml (1 tbsp) caster sugar
2 sprigs of fresh mint

TUILES
1 egg white
60 g (2½ oz) caster sugar
25 g (1 oz) plain flour
grated zest of ½ lemon
25 g (1 oz) butter

1 Reserve 2 raspberries for decoration and mash the remainder in a small bowl with a fork. Whip the double cream until stiff.

2 Scoop out the passion fruit seeds and pulp into a separate bowl and mix with the double cream and sugar.

3 Spoon alternate spoonfuls of the raspberry pulp and whipped cream mixture into 2 stemmed glasses to create a swirled effect.

4 To make the tuiles, place the egg white in a bowl and beat in the sugar. Add the remaining ingredients and mix well. Place teaspoonfuls of the mixture well apart on greased baking sheets and spread out thinly with a palette knife. Bake in a preheated oven at 180°C (350°F) mark 4 for 6–8 minutes. Remove with a palette knife and mould round a rolling pin to curl. Leave until cool and set.

5 To serve, decorate each glass with a raspberry and a sprig of mint. Serve chilled, with the tuiles.

raspberry sorbet in spun sugar baskets

SERVES 2
100 g (3½ oz) caster sugar
250 ml (8 fl oz) water
400 g (14 oz) raspberries
the juice of ½ lemon

BASKETS
250 g (9 oz) caster sugar
90 ml (3 fl oz) water

1 Dissolve the sugar in the water in a small pan, then boil for 5–8 minutes until a light syrup is formed. Place the syrup in a food processor with the raspberries and lemon juice and purée. Place mixture in a suitable container and freeze, or churn in an ice-cream maker until frozen.

2 To make the baskets, heat the sugar and water in an aluminium pan until sugar is fully dissolved. Boil until a golden brown syrup is formed, brushing down the inside of the pan with cold water if necessary to stop crystals forming. Grease the backs of 2 ladles with lard or cover with nonstick baking parchment. Using the end of a whisk, trickle the caramel over the ladles to form a basket-like structure. Leave until completely cold and firm. Carefully remove the baskets from the ladles.

3 To serve, scoop the sorbet into the sugar baskets.

sickhen with maati

615 g (1¼ lb) curd cheese
200 ml (7 fl oz) double cream
200 g (7 oz) caster sugar
10 ml (2 tsp) cardamom seeds,
crushed
45 ml (3 tbsp) chopped almonds
2 heaped pinches of saffron
extra chopped almonds and
cardamom seeds, to sprinkle

MAATI (SAVOURY BISCUITS)
200 g (7 oz) plain flour
7.5 ml (1½ tsp) salt
5 ml (1 tsp) cumin seeds
2.5 ml (½ tsp) ahjmo (ajwain)
seeds
175 g (6 oz) butter
120 ml (4 fl oz) milk
120 ml (4 fl oz) water
vegetable oil for deep-frying

1 Place the curd cheese in a mixing bowl and whisk with the double cream and caster sugar. Whisk until the caster sugar has dissolved, 6–8 minutes. Add the crushed cardamom seeds, the almonds and the saffron and stir with a wooden spoon (do not whisk). Chill for 1–2 hours. The more chilled the mixture the better the taste.

2 To make the maati, place all the dry ingredients in a bowl and mix well. Rub in the butter until the mixture resembles breadcrumbs. Place the milk and water in a pan and heat until lukewarm. Mix the liquid into the flour mixture and stir until it forms a stiff dough. Leave the dough in the refrigerator overnight, covered with cling film.

3 Form the dough into small round balls. Roll each ball into a small circular shape and prick each one with a sharp knife. Heat the oil in a deep-fryer. Deep-fry the biscuits in batches until golden brown on both sides. Remove with a slotted spoon and drain on paper towels. Let the biscuits cool slightly and serve with sickhen.

4 To serve, spoon the sickhen into a bowl and sprinkle extra almonds and green cardamom seeds on top. Serve with warm maati.

tiramisu with cointreau in chocolate baskets

SERVES 2
150 g (5 oz) good quality milk
chocolate, broken up
150 g (5 oz) mascarpone
30 ml (2 tbsp) icing sugar
15 ml (1 tbsp) Cointreau
3 drops of vanilla essence
40 g (1½ oz) Madeira cake
10 ml (2 tsp) instant coffee
granules
15 ml (1 tbsp) boiling water
cocoa powder, for dusting
strawberries, to decorate (optional)

1 Line 2 ramekin dishes with cling film.

2 Melt 125 g (4 oz) of the chocolate in a bowl set over simmering water. Use the melted chocolate to coat thickly the inside of the ramekins, and to pipe 4 small 'handles' for the baskets onto nonstick baking parchment. Put the ramekins into the freezer to set.

3 Place the mascarpone, icing sugar, Cointreau and vanilla essence in a bowl and beat well. Finely chop the remaining chocolate and fold into the mixture.

4 Remove the ramekins from the freezer and spoon the mascarpone mixture into the bottom. Cut the Madeira cake into 4 thin slices. Mix the coffee with the boiling water in a dish. Soak a slice of cake in the coffee and lay on top of the mascarpone mixture. Repeat this layering once more and finish off with a layer of mascarpone mixture.

5 Carefully remove the chocolate 'baskets' from the ramekins. Add the 'handles' and dust with cocoa powder. Decorate with strawberries, if liked.

island dessert with heather cream

SERVES 2

25 g (1 oz) unsalted butter
15 ml (1 tbsp) heather honey
1 cm (½ in) piece of fresh root
ginger, peeled and grated
40 g (1½ oz) oat flakes
150 ml (¼ pint) double cream
5 ml (1 tsp) heather honey
15 ml (1 tbsp) Heather Cream
liqueur
100 g (3½ oz) fresh raspberries

TO SERVE
2–3 raspberries
2 small sprigs of heather

1 Melt the butter in a pan over a low heat. Add the honey and ginger and stir until the honey has melted. Slowly add the oats until all the butter has been absorbed and the mixture has a crumbly texture.

2 Turn up the heat slightly and fry until the mixture is slightly browned and crunchy (3–4 minutes). Spoon the mixture into 2 greased moulds about 8 cm (3½ in) in diameter and 1 cm (½ in) deep. Turn out onto 2 serving plates and chill.

3 Beat the cream with the honey until stiff, then mix in the liqueur. Cover the base of each mould with a layer of cream. Add half the raspberries then top with the remaining cream.

Decorate with fresh raspberries and sprigs of heather.

vanilla cream and fruit purée in brandy baskets

SERVES 2

50 ml (2 fl oz) cream
50 ml (2 fl oz) yogurt
seeds from ½ vanilla pod

PURÉE

a few raspberries
a few strawberries
a few redcurrants
a few blackberries
caster sugar, to taste

BRANDY BASKETS

60 g (2½ oz) butter
60 g (2½ oz) muscovado sugar
60 g (2½ oz) golden syrup
60 g (2½ oz) plain flour
pinch of ground ginger
5 ml (1 tsp) lemon juice
drop of vanilla essence

1 Mix together the cream and yogurt. Whisk until firm then add the vanilla seeds.

2 To make the purée, place the fruit in a bowl, add the sugar and whisk with an electric blender until soft.

3 To make the baskets, place the butter, sugar and golden syrup in a pan and heat gently until melted. Mix well, then add the flour and ginger and mix in. Stir in the lemon juice and vanilla essence. Line a baking sheet with nonstick baking parchment. Put 5ml (1 tsp) of mixture for each basket required on the baking parchment. Cook in a preheated oven at 150°C (300°F) mark 2 for about 8 minutes. Allow to cool slightly then turn out and shape over small foil pudding basins. Leave to set until cold.

4 To serve, spoon the vanilla cream into each basket and top with some fruit purée.

banoffee pie

SERVES 2

35 g (2½ oz) butter
130 g (4½ oz) ginger biscuits, crushed
60 g (2½ oz) sugar
200 g (7 oz) condensed milk
3 bananas
finely grated zest and juice of 1 lime
50 ml (2 fl oz) whipping cream
flake bar, to decorate

1 Melt 60 g (2½ oz) of the butter in a small pan then add the ginger biscuits. Mix well then press into 4 small flan tins and put into the refrigerator.

2 Mash 1 banana and add half the lime juice. Spread over the ginger biscuits and chill again.

3 Melt the remaining butter and the sugar together in a pan. Add the condensed milk and stir constantly until it reaches a simmer. Simmer on a low heat for exactly 5 minutes to make a light golden caramel. Be careful not to allow it to burn.

Pour the caramel into the flan tins and return to the refrigerator.

4 Slice the remaining bananas and soak in the remaining lime juice. Whip the cream. Remove the flan tins when set and unmould onto individual plates.

5 Top each tart with a layer of banana, a layer of cream and another layer of banana. Pipe cream rosettes on top. Decorate with lime zest and a few shreds of chocolate flake.

english rhubarb trifle

1 kg (2¼ lb) ripe rhubarb, chopped
200 g (7 oz) caster sugar

CUSTARD
4 tsp caster sugar
4 tsp cornflour
6 egg yolks
6 drops of vanilla essence
425 ml (¾ pint) double cream

SPONGE
50 g (2 oz) self-raising flour
½tsp baking powder
50 g (2 oz) butter
50 g (2 oz) caster sugar
1 large egg
1 drop of vanilla essence
15 ml (1 tbsp) sherry
15 ml (1 tbsp) brandy

TO DECORATE
425 ml (¾ pint) double cream
50 g (2 oz) chopped almonds, toasted

1 Sweat the rhubarb and caster sugar in a pan over gentle heat until soft. Remove from the heat and leave to cool.

2 To make the custard, mix together the caster sugar, cornflour, egg yolks and vanilla essence in a bowl. Heat the cream in a small pan until it almost comes to the boil, then pour onto the egg mixture, stirring continuously. Return the mixture to the pan over a low heat and stir until it is thick enough to coat the back of a wooden spoon. Allow to cool, then place in the refrigerator.

3 To make the sponge, line a 18 cm (7 in) sponge tin with nonstick baking parchment. Sift the flour and baking powder into a large mixing bowl, holding the sieve high. Add the butter, sugar, egg and vanilla essence and whisk with an electric hand whisk until well combined. Pour into the tin and level the surface. Bake in a preheated oven at 170°C (325°F) mark 3 for 30 minutes. Leave to cool in the tin for 30 minutes, then turn out onto a cooling rack. When cold, dice the sponge, place in a bowl and add the sherry and brandy.

4 To assemble, whip the cream. Place the diced sponge in the bottom of a glass serving dish and add the rhubarb compote, then the custard. Decorate with the whipped cream and toasted nuts.

light lemon cheesecake with orange and galliano ice cream

SERVES 2
ICE CREAM SERVES 6

15 g (½ oz) unsalted butter
125 g (4 oz) digestive biscuits, crushed
125 g (4 oz) quark cheese
125 g (4 oz) mascarpone
25 g (1 oz) caster sugar
juice and zest of ½ lemon
15 g (½ oz) cornflour
75 ml (2½ fl oz) sour cream
dark chocolate curls, to decorate

ORANGE AND GALLIANO ICE CREAM
8 egg yolks
150 g (5 oz) caster sugar
5 ml (1 tsp) Galliano
juice of 1 orange
250 ml (8 fl oz) double cream

1 Melt the butter in a bowl over a pan of simmering water. Mix with the crushed biscuits until well incorporated. Press down firmly into 2 greased and base-lined 9 cm (3½ in) tins. Chill in the refrigerator.

2 Blend the two cheeses together. Add the caster sugar and mix well again. Mix in the lemon juice, zest and cornflour, then fold in the sour cream.

3 Spoon the mixture into the tins and bake at 180°C (350°F) mark 4 for 40–45 minutes or until the top is firm and set.

4 To make the ice cream, beat the egg yolks in a bowl until very thick. Add the caster sugar and beat well again. Stir in the Galliano and orange juice .

5 In a separate bowl, whip the double cream until it forms soft peaks. Gently fold into the egg and sugar mixture. Transfer to an ice-cream maker and churn for about 30 minutes, until frozen.

6 To serve, decorate the cheesecake with dark chocolate curls. Serve with scoops of the ice cream.

meringue raspberry whisky and cream towers

3 egg whites
175 g (6 oz) caster sugar
2.5 ml (½ tsp) cornflour
2.5 ml (½ tsp) wine vinegar
75 g (3 oz) good quality plain chocolate, broken up
175 ml (6 fl oz) whipping cream
225 g (8 oz) mixed berries, including raspberries
15 ml (1 tbsp) whisky
10 ml (2 tsp) icing sugar
berries and mint leaves, to decorate

1 Line a Swiss roll sheet with nonstick baking parchment. Whisk the egg whites until firm but not dry. Add the sugar a little at a time, whisking for about 10 minutes. Whisk in the cornflour and vinegar. Spread on the baking sheet and bake in a preheated oven at 180°C (350°F) mark 4 for 25 minutes in the centre of the oven. Remove and allow to cool.

2 Melt the chocolate in a bowl set over a pan of simmering water. Whip the cream in a bowl and mix in 50 g (2 oz) of crushed raspberries and whisky. Cut 4 strips of baking parchment, 10 cm (4 in) high, to fit round a 6 cm (2½ in) pastry cutter. Cut 12 rounds with the 6 cm (2½ in) cutter from the cold meringue. Layer 3 discs at a time with the cream mixture to form towers. Spread the melted chocolate on the paper strips and leave until almost setting. Wrap the strips around the meringue towers and place in the refrigerator to chill. Reserve a few berries for decoration and push the remainder through a sieve. Add the icing sugar.

3 To serve, peel the paper from the meringue towers and pour the coulis around the plate. Decorate with berries and mint leaves.

peach pavlova with spun sugar nests and raspberry sauce

5 egg whites
225 g (8 oz) caster sugar
7.5 ml (1½ tsp) cornflour
284 ml (9½ oz) double cream
15 ml (1 tbsp) lemon juice
2 peaches
300 g (10 oz) raspberries
25 g (1 oz) icing sugar
lemon juice
4 sprigs of mint or lemon balm, to decorate

SPUN SUGAR NESTS
250 g (9 oz) sugar
90 ml (3 fl oz) water
65 ml (2¼ fl oz) liquid glucose

1 Using a hand-held electric whisk, whisk the egg whites in a bowl until they start to thicken. Whisk in the caster sugar a little at a time until fully incorporated. Slake the cornflour with the lemon juice, then pour onto the egg whites and whisk on full speed for 6–8 minutes.

2 Line a 25 cm (10 in) round cake tin with nonstick baking parchment. Spoon in the meringue and smooth with a palette knife. Bake in a pre-heated oven at 160°C (325°F) mark 3 for 45 minutes until slightly risen and browned on top. Leave to cool in the tin. Turn out onto baking parchment and cut out 4 circles using a 7.5 cm (3 in) cutter. Place each circle in the middle of a plate. Whip the cream to the soft peak stage and spread thickly on top of the meringues.

3 Bring a large pan of water to the boil and poach the peaches for 1 minute. Drain, refresh in cold water and drain again. Skin, halve and stone. Place one peach half on top of each Pavlova.

4 Reserve 12 raspberries for decoration and purée the remainder in a food processor. Sieve and add icing sugar and lemon juice to taste.

5 To make the nests, dissolve the sugar in the water, add the liquid glucose and boil to 152°C (305°F) using a sugar thermometer. Cool for 2 minutes. Place 2 rolling pins on a work surface side by side, about 20 cm (8 in) apart. Hold 2 forks back to back, dip them into the molten sugar and flick them back and forth over the rolling pins to make spun sugar. Lift the spun sugar carefully and form into 4 small nests. Place them on top of the Pavlovas.

6 To serve, drizzle the raspberry sauce around the plates, and decorate with the reserved raspberries and mint or lemon balm sprigs.

peaches poached in zinfandel served on mascarpone and meringue with raspberry and pineapple mint sorbet

6 peaches, halved and stoned
red Zinfandel wine
125 g (4 oz) sugar
750 ml (1½ pints) raspberry pulp
600 ml (1 pint) stock syrup, made
with 600 ml (1 pint) water and
450 g (1 lb) sugar
juice of 1 lemon, plus extra if
necessary
1 egg white
250 ml (8 fl oz) mascarpone
10 ml (2 tsp) rose water
crisp broken bits of meringue

TO SERVE
4 sprigs of redcurrants
4 sprigs of mint

1 Place the peaches in a wide-bottomed pan with a lid, and add enough Zinfandel to cover them. Add 75 g (3 oz) of the sugar. Simmer for 20 minutes, until tender, and leave to cool.

2 Reserve 175 ml (6 fl oz) of the raspberry purée and mix the remainder in a bowl with the stock syrup and the lemon juice. Put into an ice-cream maker with the egg white for a lighter sorbet, and churn until frozen. Place in the freezer until ready to serve.

3 Mix the mascarpone and rose water in a bowl and add the broken meringue.

4 Remove the peaches with a slotted spoon and skin them. Taste the poaching liquid and adjust the sweetness after adding the reserved raspberry purée, either with the remaining sugar or lemon juice.

5 To serve, place 1–2 spoonfuls of the mascarpone mixture on each plate and top with 3 halves of peaches. Top these with a scoop of the sorbet. Spoon some of the sauce over and around and decorate with sprigs of mint and redcurrants.

summer trifle with lemon syllabub

SERVES 2
90 ml (3 fl oz) sherry
50 g (2 oz) caster sugar
juice of ½ lemon
grated zest of 1 lemon
300 ml (½ pint) double cream
1 egg yolk
150 g (5 oz) raspberries
15 ml (1 tbsp) water
4 slices of brioche
2 drops of vanilla essence
candied lemon peel, to decorate

1 To make the syllabub place 20 ml (2 tbsp) sherry, 15 g (½ oz) caster sugar, the lemon juice and zest in a bowl and leave for 20–30 minutes. Strain and slowly add 120 ml (4 fl oz) of the cream. Whisk until it forms soft peaks.

2 To make the custard place the remaining cream in a pan and slowly bring to the boil. Whisk the egg yolk with 15 ml (1 tbsp) caster sugar and the vanilla essence until light and creamy, then pour on the hot cream. Beat over a simmering pan of water for about 10 minutes, whisking continuously until the custard is thick enough to coat the back of a wooden spoon.

3 To make the raspberry sauce put 75 g (3 oz) of the raspberries in a pan and soften for 3–4 minutes over a low heat. Add 1 tablespoon of water and 1 oz of caster sugar. Allow to cool, then purée in a blender until smooth. Push through a sieve to remove the seeds.

4 To assemble the trifle, place a slice of brioche in each glass dish and spoon on 15ml (1 tbsp) of sherry. Spoon one-quarter of the raspberry sauce on top with 5 or 6 raspberries, followed by one-quarter of the custard. Repeat the layers, finishing with 15 ml (1 tbsp) of the syllabub. Decorate with candied lemon peel.

almond biscuits filled with creamy rice and elderflower scented gooseberries

BISCUITS
75 g (3 oz) plain flour
40 g (1½ oz) caster sugar
20 g (¾ oz) ground almonds
50 g (2 oz) unsalted butter, diced, plus extra for greasing
1 egg yolk
a pinch of salt

CREAMY RICE
50 g (2 oz) pudding rice
15 g (½ oz) unsalted butter
300 ml (½ pint) full cream milk
2 egg yolks
25 g (1 oz) caster sugar
60 ml (2 fl oz) double cream

GOOSEBERRIES
225 g (8 oz) gooseberries, topped and tailed
25 g (1 oz) caster sugar
15 ml (1 tbsp) elderflower cordial
icing sugar, to serve

1 To make the biscuits, place all the ingredients except the egg yolk in a food processor until combined. Add egg yolk and a little water if necessary, combine until a dough is formed. Wrap the dough in cling film and refrigerate for at least 30 minutes.

2 Roll out the dough very thinly and using a 10 cm (4 in) cutter cut out the biscuits. Place on greased baking sheets. Bake in a preheated oven at 180°C (350°F) mark 4 for about 10 minutes, until golden brown. Cool on a wire rack.

3 To make the creamy rice, put the rice in a pan and cover with water. Bring to the boil. Drain and refresh with cold water. Place the rice, all except 15 ml (1 tbsp) of the milk and the butter in a clean pan. Bring to the boil and cook for 20 minutes, until the rice is tender. Mix the egg yolks with the sugar and mix in the cream and reserved milk. Add this egg mixture to the rice and cook until thick. Transfer to a bowl and allow to cool.

4 To cook the gooseberries, place in a pan with the sugar and elderflower cordial and cook until tender, about 10 minutes. Drain and reserve the juice. Boil the juice briskly until only 15–30 ml (1–2 tbsp) remain. Pour over the gooseberries and allow to cool.

5 To serve, spread 2 biscuits per serving with the creamy rice mix and sandwich together with a quarter of the gooseberries. Arrange on individual plates and dredge with icing sugar.

almond biscuits, fresh fruits, mascarpone cream and raspberry sauce

SERVES 2

BISCUITS

20 g (¾ oz) ground almonds
50 g (2 oz) soft unsalted butter
25 g (1 oz) caster sugar, plus extra
for sprinkling
50 g (2 oz) self-raising flour

MASCARPONE CREAM

75 g (3 oz) mascarpone
15 g (½ oz) caster sugar
25 ml (1 fl oz) double cream

RASPBERRY SAUCE

125 g (4 oz) raspberries
15 g (½ oz) icing sugar, sifted

FILLING

125 g (4 oz) mixed summer fruits
such as strawberries, raspberries
and blackberries

TO DECORATE

fresh berries
2 mint leaves

1 To make the biscuits, place the almonds, butter, sugar and flour in a food processor and process to a soft dough. Shape into a log 6 cm (2½ in) in diameter, wrap in cling film and chill for 10 minutes in the freezer. Remove from freezer, remove cling film and cut into four 5mm (¼ in) slices with a sharp knife. Place on a greased baking sheet. Bake in a preheated oven at 180°C (350°F) mark 4 for 8 minutes until pale golden. Cool for 1–2 minutes then place on wire rack. Sprinkle 2 biscuits with caster sugar when cool.

2 To make the mascarpone cream, beat the mascarpone and caster sugar until smooth, then whisk in the double cream.

3 To make the raspberry sauce, place raspberries in a food processor and process until smooth. Sieve the purée and stir in the icing sugar.

4 Wash the fruit for the filling and slice the strawberries, if using.

5 To assemble, for each serving place an unsugared biscuit on a plate, top with mascarpone cream and fruit, place a sugared biscuit on top then a small dollop of cream. Decorate with a berry and a mint leaf. Spoon some raspberry sauce onto the plate.

apple and spice slices with forest fruit coulis and cream

SERVES 2

175 g (6 oz) puff pastry
1 apple, peeled, cored, sliced thinly and sprinkled with lemon juice
20 ml (4 tsp) brown sugar
5 ml (1 tsp) mixed spice
1 egg, beaten
10 ml (2 tsp) caster sugar

COULIS

50 g (2 oz) blueberries
30 ml (2 tbsp) water
30 ml (2 tbsp) sugar

TO SERVE

50 ml (2 fl oz) double cream
5 ml (1 tsp) caster sugar
5 ml (1 tsp) vanilla extract

1 Roll out the pastry thinly into 2 pieces, about 12 cm (5 in) square. Place apple slices down the centre of each square and sprinkle with the sugar and mixed spice. Cut 2 facing sides of the pastry into strips, then fold alternate strips over the apple to make a plait. Fold over the other 2 ends to seal. Brush the pastry with the beaten egg and sprinkle with caster sugar. Bake in a preheated oven at 200°C (400°F) mark 6 until golden brown, about 10–15 minutes.

2 To make the coulis, place the blueberries, water and sugar in a pan and bring to the boil. Cook until the fruit is soft, then remove from the heat and push through a sieve. Return the coulis to the pan and heat until syrupy. Remove from the heat and allow to cool.

3 To serve, whip the cream with the sugar and vanilla. Place an apple slice on each plate and serve with some coulis. Decorate with the whipped cream.

caramelized apple cake and cinnamon ice cream

200 ml (7 fl oz) milk
1 cinnamon stick
2 egg yolks
30 ml (2 tbsp) honey
200 ml (7 fl oz) cream
200 ml (7 fl oz) crème fraîche
125 g (4 oz) butter, plus extra for greasing
2 eating apples
125 g (4 oz) sugar
15 ml (1 tbsp) Calvados
75 g (3 oz) plain flour
25 g (1 oz) ground almonds
2 eggs
45 ml (3 tbsp) milk
melted butter for brushing
a little brown sugar
icing sugar, for dusting
ground cinnamon, for dusting

1 Warm the milk in a pan with the cinnamon stick for 15 minutes, then remove from the heat and leave to cool. Remove the cinnamon. Beat the egg yolks and honey in a bowl. Add the milk slowly and return to the pan. Warm gently and stir continuously until the custard thickens. Add the cream and crème fraîche. Leave to cool, then place in an ice-cream maker and churn for 30 minutes.

2 Melt 25 g (1 oz) of butter in a pan. Peel, core and finely dice 1 apple. Add to the pan and cook until soft. Increase the heat, add 25 g (1 oz) sugar and caramelize. Flambée with the Calvados. Place this mixture into the bottom of 4 buttered ramekins.

3 Put the flour, remaining butter and sugar, the ground almonds and eggs into a food processor. Process and drizzle in the milk until a very thick batter is achieved. Spoon the batter onto the apple mixture in the ramekins. Finely slice the other apple and arrange slices on top of the batter. Brush with melted butter and sprinkle on brown sugar. Bake in a preheated oven at 180°C (350°F) mark 4 for about 20 minutes until puffed up and apple slices browned. Dust with icing sugar.

4 To serve, dust 4 plates with powdered cinnamon and place a ramekin on each with a spoonful of ice cream.

apricot ice cream, almond biscuits and toffee and almond sauce

APRICOT ICE CREAM
225 g (8 oz) no-soak dried apricots, plus 12 dried apricots
180 ml (6 fl oz) milk
45 g (1¾ oz) granulated sugar
3 egg yolks
few drops of vanilla essence
150 ml (¼ pint) double cream
15 ml (1 tbsp) Amaretto
15 ml (1 tbsp) caster sugar

ALMOND BISCUITS
80 g (3¼ oz)unsalted butter
80 g (3¼ oz) caster sugar
50 g (2 oz) plain flour
pinch of salt
80 g (3¼ oz) flaked almonds

TOFFEE AND ALMOND SAUCE
125 g (4 oz) granulated sugar
50 g (2 oz) unsalted butter
150 ml (¼ pint) double cream
30 ml (2 tbsp) toasted flaked almonds
15–30 ml (1–2 tbsp) Amaretto

1 Place the 225 g (8 oz) apricots in a pan, just cover with water and bring to the boil. Simmer until the fruit is soft. Purée the fruit with its cooking juices in a food processor and sieve. Chill.

2 Combine the milk and half the sugar in a pan and bring to boiling point. Whisk the egg yolks with the remaining sugar. Pour the milk onto the egg, whisking all the time. Return the mixture to the pan, add the vanilla and cook over a very low heat, stirring continuously, until the mixture is thick enough to coat the back of a wooden spoon. Pour into a cold bowl and chill.

3 Whisk the custard, cream and apricot purée together. Pour into an ice-cream maker and churn until frozen.

4 Poach the remaining apricots in a little water with the Amaretto until they are soft and plump. Add 1 tbsp sugar towards the end of the cooking time. Leave to cool in the liquid. Drain well when cold and use to decorate the ice cream.

5 To make the biscuits, process the butter and sugar in a food processor until light and fluffy. Sift in the flour and salt and stir in the almonds. Put teaspoonfuls of the mixture on to a baking sheet lined with nonstick baking parchment, spacing them well apart as they spread. Bake in a preheated oven at 200°C (400°F) mark 6 for 6–8 minutes. Allow to cool on the tin, before removing with a sharp knife.

6 To make the sauce, melt the sugar and butter in a pan. Bring the mixture to a gentle boil and cook for 5 minutes. Remove from the heat and stir in the cream. Stir in the almonds and Amaretto to taste. Leave to cool.

7 To serve, place a biscuit on a plate, top with a tablespoon of apricot ice cream, then another biscuit, more ice cream and a final biscuit. Place the reserved apricots on top and pour some toffee sauce around.

NOTE: The almond biscuits come from a Cordon Bleu Book called *Baking 1*

lemon curd millefeuilles with lime confit and lemon sauce

225 g (8 oz) puff pastry
butter, for greasing
300 ml (½ pint) double cream
1 egg white, beaten
15 ml (1 tbsp) caster sugar
icing sugar, for dusting

1 To make the lemon curd, place the lemon juice and zest, the beaten eggs, butter and sugar in a pan over a low heat. Mix well, and cook for 20 minutes, stirring continuously. Remove when thick and leave to cool, then chill.

2 Roll out the pastry to a thickness of 3 mm (⅛ in). Cut into 6 circles 7.5 cm (3 in) in diameter. Prick all over and place on a greased baking sheet.

150 ml (5 fl oz) single cream
4 sprigs of mint
LEMON CURD
juice and zest of 2 lemons
2 eggs, beaten
50 g (2 oz) butter
125–175 g (4–6 oz) caster sugar
CONFIT
grated zest of 1 lemon
grated zest of 1 lime
300 ml (½ pint) water
50 g (2 oz) sugar

Chill for 15 minutes. Remove from the refrigerator and bake in a preheated oven at 230°C (425°F) mark 8 for 10–15 minutes until brown and risen. Cool on the sheet. Split each circle in half and remove any uncooked pastry.

3 Whip the double cream until thick, then fold in the egg white and sugar. Assemble the millefeuilles, reserving 90 ml (6 tbsp) of the lemon curd for the sauce. For each serving, layer 3 pastry circles with the cream and curd, finishing with a pastry circle. Dust with icing sugar. Heat a skewer and press onto the icing sugar 3–4 times to make a crisscross pattern.

4 To make the confit, place the zest of lemon and lime in a pan with the water and sugar. Cook slowly over a low heat until thick and syrupy, then remove from the heat and chill. Remove the zest.

5 To make the sauce, thin the reserved lemon curd with the single cream and mix well.

6 To serve, place a millefeuille in the centre of each plate and pour the sauce around. Decorate with pieces of confit and mint sprigs.

millefeuille of summer berries

SERVES 2
150 g (5 oz) puff pastry
125 g (4 oz) icing sugar, plus extra for sprinkling
300 ml (½ pint) double cream
60 ml (4 tbsp) Amaretto liqueur
2.5 ml (½ tsp) ground cinnamon
60 g (2½ oz) raspberries
15 g (½ oz) caster sugar
225 g (8 oz) summer berries
mint leaves, to decorate

1 Roll out the puff pastry in half the icing sugar to a thickness of 3 mm (⅛ in). Then roll up the puff pastry in a sausage very tightly. Wrap in cling film tightly and twist the ends in opposite directions. Leave to refrigerate for 30–40 minutes.

2 Meanwhile, place the double cream, Amaretto and cinnamon in a bowl and whisk until thick. Refrigerate.

3 Place the raspberries in a pan with the sugar and heat until the raspberries have separated. Remove from the heat and strain through a sieve, then leave to cool.

4 Take the puff pastry out of the cling film and cut into 2.5 cm (1 in) pieces. Roll out in the remaining icing sugar and cut into equal-sized rounds using a cutter. Place the rounds on a piece of greased foil and then lay another piece of foil on top. Bake in a preheated oven at 180°C (350°F) mark 4 for 15 minutes. Remove from the foil and leave to cool.

5 Zigzag some coulis on each plate as a decoration.

6 To assemble the millefeuille, place a small blob of cream in the centre of the plate, then place the first pastry disc on top. This will help it not to slide around. Place 15 ml (1 tbsp) of cream on the disc and spread it over. Place some of the berries on the cream. Then place another small blob of cream on top and another disc. Repeat with the cream and fruit so you have 3 discs and 2 layers of cream and fruit on each plate, finishing with a pastry disc.

7 Sprinkle icing sugar all over the millefeuille and place 3 small raspberries on top. Decorate with mint leaves and serve immediately.

star–shaped fruit explosion

SERVES 2

350 g (12 oz) puff pastry
1 egg, beaten
30 ml (2 tbsp) crème fraîche
4 strawberries, diced
4 raspberries, diced
6 blueberries, diced
50 g (2 oz) caster sugar

CRÈME PATISSIÈRE

2 egg yolks
50 g (2 oz) caster sugar
15 ml (1 tbsp) plain flour
15 ml (1 tbsp) cornflour
150 ml (¼ pint) milk
1 egg white
2–3 drops of vanilla essence

1 Roll out the puff pastry to 5 mm (¼ in) thickness and cut out 4 big star shapes. Then use a small star cutter inside 2 of the big star shapes. Lay the small ones on top of the big ones, matching the points. Place on a baking sheet, brush with beaten egg and bake in a preheated oven at 220°C (425°F) mark 7 for 10–12 minutes. Remove from the heat and allow to cool.

2 To make the crème patissière, cream the egg yolks and caster sugar in a bowl until thick and pale in colour. Beat in the flour and cornflour and enough milk to make a smooth paste. Heat the remaining milk until almost boiling, then pour onto the egg mixture, stirring all the time. Return the mixture to the pan, stirring over high heat until the mixture boils. Whisk one egg white and fold into the custard off the heat. Return to the heat and add vanilla essence to taste. Cook for 2–3 minutes then remove from the heat and allow to cool, then refrigerate.

3 Mix the the crème pâtissière with the crème fraîche and use to fill the pastry cases. Top with half the summer fruits Put the pastry cases on plates.

4 In a pan melt the caster sugar until runny. Dip a wooden porridge mixer into it and flick from side to side or pull to make spun sugar. Place this on top of the pastry and arrange the remaining diced fruits around the pastry.

chocolate and crème fraîche torte with vanilla and raspberry sauce

SERVES 2

4 digestive biscuits, crushed
25 g (1 oz) butter, melted
¼ of 150g (5 oz) bar of dark chocolate, broken up
½ of 150 (5 oz) bar of milk chocolate, broken up
1 egg yolk
25 g (1 oz) sugar
125 g (4 oz) crème fraîche

VANILLA AND RASPBERRY SAUCE

130 ml (4½ fl oz) milk
130 ml (4½ fl oz) cream
¼ vanilla pod
3 egg yolks
40 g (1½ oz) sugar
50 g (2 oz) raspberries
25 g (1 oz) icing sugar

1 Mix the digestive biscuits with the melted butter and press into 2 individual tins. Melt the chocolate in a bowl set over a pan of simmering water. Mix the egg yolk and sugar together and add the crème fraîche. Mix in half the chocolate, then mix in the remainder. Pour into the tins and refrigerate.

2 To make the sauce, gently warm the milk and cream in a pan with the vanilla and allow to infuse for a few minutes, then remove the pod. Mix the 3 egg yolks with the sugar, then slowly pour in the milk. Return to the heat and stir continuously over gentle heat until the sauce has thickened. Cool and sieve. Purée the raspberries and sugar, push through a sieve, then stir into the sauce.

3 Serve the tarts with the sauce poured around.

feuillantine of fresh fruits with kirsch, sabayon and raspberry coulis

SERVES 2

PASTRY DISCS
100 g (3½ oz) puff pastry
icing sugar, for dusting and sprinkling

RASPBERRY COULIS
60 g (2½ oz) caster sugar
150 g (5 oz) raspberries

SABAYON
1 egg
1 egg yolk
35 g (1¼ oz) caster sugar
200 ml (7 fl oz) whipping cream
1 gelatine leaf, melted in a microwave after being soaked in water
30 ml (2 tbsp) Kirsch

FILLING
100 g (3½ oz) strawberries
75 g (3 oz) blueberries
50 g (2 oz) raspberries

1 To make the pastry discs, roll out the puff pastry on a board dusted with icing sugar. Cut into 4 10 cm (4 in) circles and place in the refrigerator for 30 minutes. Sprinkle thinly with icing sugar, place on a baking sheet and bake in a preheated oven at 220°C (425°F) mark 7 for about 8 minutes until crisp and golden brown. Remove and leave to cool.

2 To make the coulis, blend the sugar and raspberries together in a food processor. Push through a sieve to remove the seeds. Stir in a little water if necessary if the consistency is too thick.

3 To make the sabayon, mix the egg and egg yolk with the sugar over a bain-marie and whisk over a gentle heat until warm. Whip the cream and fold in with the melted gelatine. Mix in the Kirsch then remove from the heat and allow to cool, then chill until ready to serve.

4 To serve, place a pastry disc in the centre of each plate and place on top of this some fruit, some coulis and a spoonful of sabayon. Place another pastry disc on top and dust with icing sugar. Decorate with a few pieces of fruit. To finish, spoon a ring of coulis around the pudding.

NOTE: adapted from a recipe by Marco Pierre White

JUNIOR MENUS

MAIN COURSE Fillet of Pork with Apricot & Madeira Glaze, Stir-fried Vegetables, Cream Potatoes with Parmesan & Parsley (p. 100)
DESSERT Apple & Spice Slices with Forest Fruit Coulis & Whipped Cream (p. 235)

JENNIE ELLIOTT-BOYD'S MENU

MAIN COURSE Lightly Grilled Salmon Tails with Gazpacho Dressing & Glazed Vegetables (p. 118)
DESSERT Petal Basket Filled with Summer Fruits & Rose Water Cream on a Summer Berry Coulis (p. 207)

DOMINIQUE FRASER'S MENU

MAIN COURSE Punjabi Tikka with Pilau Rice & Bhindi Masala, Dhai Bala, Popadom & Salad (pp. 56-7)
DESSERT Kheer (p. 215)

KOMAL KHAN'S MENU

MAIN COURSE Posh Fish & Chips with Tomato Sauce, White Wine Vinegar & Sea Salt (p. 110)
DESSERT Rhubarb & Ginger Clootie Dumplings with Lemon Custard (p. 204)

JOSEPH ANDERSON'S MENU

MAIN COURSE Pan-fried Breast of Duck in Honey & Balsamic Vinegar, Puréed Parmesan Potatoes with Nutmeg & Stir-fried Summer Vegetables (p. 65)
DESSERT Biscotti with Chocolate Cream on Raspberry Coulis (p. 210)

NATALIE WAGSTAFF'S MENU

MAIN COURSE Couscous Crusted Salmon with Asparagus (p. 120)
DESSERT Star-shaped Fruit Explosion (p. 238)

SEBASTIAN HOPKINSON'S MENU

MAIN COURSE Crusted Cod Steaks on Sweated Leeks, Roast Cherry Tomatoes & Kholrabi (p. 134)
DESSERT Dark Fruit Fool with Biscuits & Chocolate Leaves (p. 214)

EMMA STANFORD'S MENU

MAIN COURSE Paupiette of Dover Sole stuffed with Tomato & Dill Mousse, Lemon & Lime Beurre Blanc, Creamed Potatoes with Soured Cream & Asparagus (p. 137)
DESSERT Soufflé Omelette with Compote of Ginger & Basil-scented Berries, with Greek Yoghurt (p. 205)

SEBASTIAN VON TEICHMEISTER'S MENU

MAIN COURSE Seared Tuna Steak with a Lemon Grass, Lime & Coriander Marinade, Stir-fried Sesame Vegetables with Coconut Milk Risotto, Shiitake Mushrooms & Fresh Coriander (p. 113)
DESSERT Raspberry Clafoutis with Forest Fruit Coulis (p. 201)

PHILLIP HYMAN'S MENU

MAIN COURSE Pan-fried Welsh Lamb with Mushroom, Bacon & Spinach Rosti & Caramelized Shallots (p. 90)
DESSERT Chocolate & Banana Crème Brûlée & Shortbread (p. 208)

TOM GUTHRIE'S MENU

MAIN COURSE Venison Steaks in a Red Wine Sauce, Game Chips, Glazed Baby Carrots & Brussels Sprouts (p. 73)
DESSERT Light Lemon Cheesecake, Dark Chocolate Curls with Orange & Galliano Ice Cream (p. 230)

THOMAS WALKER'S MENU

MAIN COURSE Roasted Rosemary Pork with Red Wine Sauce & Orange Vegetables (p. 102)
DESSERT Chocolate Pudding with Fudge Sauce (p. 173)

HARRIET TREWIN'S MENU

MAIN COURSE Mushroom & Brie Tartlets with Potato & Leek Patties, Medley of Garden Vegetables with a Port & Cranberry Sauce (p. 142)
DESSERT Tiramisu with Cointreau in Chocolate Baskets (p. 225)

SARAH HILTON'S MENU

MAIN COURSE Pan-fried Sea Bass on a Bed of Baby Spinach with Scallops, a Green Herb Sauce & a Lemon Saffron Oil & Parisian Potatoes (p. 133)
DESSERT Bread & Butter Pudding with Vanilla Custard & Forest Fruits (p. 169)

PRIYA SHANKAR'S MENU

MAIN COURSE Grilled Lemon Chicken with Herbed Duchess Potatoes, Broccoli Florets, & Honey Glazed Carrots (p. 56)
DESSERT Vanilla Cream & Fruit Purée in Brandy Baskets (p. 228)

KATHRYN KANE'S MENU

MAIN COURSE Grilled Duck Breast on Red Wine Onions with Layered Stilton Potatoes & Leeks & Three Colour Steamed Cabbage with Walnuts (p. 68)
DESSERT Lemon & Lime Soufflé Custard with Lemon Syllabub in Almond Tuiles (p. 220)

GEORGE HAMLYN WILLIAMS'S MENU

MAIN COURSE Grilled Fillet of Orange Roughy on a Potato Rosti, with Asparagus, Battoned Carrots & Mange Tout, with a Light Orange Sauce (p. 125)
DESSERT Raspberry Sorbet in a Spun Sugar Basket with Dainty Shortbread Pieces & a Tangy Raspberry Coulis (p. 224)

ROBERT KNIGHT'S MENU

MAIN COURSE Mataar Paneer with Jeeru Chawal & Rathu, Papaad & Garlic & Coriander Naan Bread (p. 148)
DESSERT Sickhen with Maati (p. 225)

VIRESH PATEL'S MENU

MAIN COURSE Tarragon Chicken in a Lime & Crème Fraîche Sauce with Butter Nut Squash & Parmesan Mash Potatoes (p. 60)
DESSERT Traditional Bread & Butter Pudding with Seville Orange Marmalade (p. 183)

GUY FALKSON'S MENU

MAIN COURSE Crab Cakes with Tomato & Mango Salsa & Sweet Potato & Celeriac Purée (p. 108)
DESSERT Coconut Ice Cream with Tangy Lime Syrup (p. 213)

CHLOE NAHUM'S MENU

MAIN COURSE Air-dried Ham & Chicken Rolls with Pork Stuffing & Cider Sauce, New Potatoes, Carrot Gratin, & Rocket & Apple Salad (p. 97)
DESSERT Chocolate Honeycomb Mousse with Redcurrant & Orange Sauce (p. 212)

MARY LEWIS-CROSBY'S MENU

MAIN COURSE Sesame Glazed Duck Breast with Plum & Yellow Pepper Confit (p. 62)
DESSERT Banoffee Pie (p. 228)

EMMA CRESSWELL-MAYNARD'S MENU

MAIN COURSE Roast Herb-stuffed Chicken with Pomme Fondant, Confit of Garlic & Vegetable Bundles (p. 61)
DESSERT Feuillantine of Fresh Fruits with Kirsch Sabayon & Raspberry Coulis (p. 240)

TIM CASTLE'S MENU

MAIN COURSE Eastern Spiced Lamb with Spiced Apricot & Nut Pilau with Roasted Vegetables & Cucumber Raita (p. 92)
DESSERT Tarte Tatin (p. 194)

ALEX LUKE'S MENU

MAIN COURSE Marinated Tuna Steak with Parmesan Potato Cakes & Avocado Cream with Fresh Herbs, Spring Onion & Basil Oil (p. 114)
DESSERT Almond Biscuits with Fresh Fruits, Mascarpone Cream & Raspberry Sauce (p. 234)

KATY REID'S MENU

MAIN COURSE Pan-fried Lamb's Liver with Cream Potatoes & Caramelized Aubergine (pp. 84-5)
DESSERT Tarte Tatin with Plums (p. 194)

DANIEL RICHARDSON'S MENU

MAIN COURSE Chicken Fajitas with Roasted Peppers & Coriander, with Guacamole, Salsa, Sour Cream & Flour Tortillas (pp. 50-1)
DESSERT Island Dessert with Heather Cream with Raspberries on Crunchy Honey & Oat Base (p. 226)

HEATHER WHYTOCK'S MENU

MAIN COURSE Duck stuffed with Langoustines & Parma Ham, with Fondant Potato & Spinach (p. 64)
DESSERT Millefeuille of Summer Berries (p. 242)

SEMI-FINAL MENU

MAIN COURSE Stuffed Sole Rolls, Broccoli & New Potatoes (p. 134)
DESSERT Raspberry & Passion Fruit Swirls (p. 224)

SEMI-FINAL MENU

MAIN COURSE Fillet of Lamb with a Mushroom & Olive Stuffing, Goats' Cheese Mash & Chargrilled Mediterranean Vegetables (p. 88)
DESSERT Summer Pudding with Greek Yogurt & Honey (p. 177)

SEMI-FINAL MENU

MAIN COURSE Fillet of Lamb with Port & Redcurrant Sauce, on a bed of Camargue Rice with Seasonal Green Vegetables (p. 89)
DESSERT Chocolate & Crème Fraîche Torte, Vanilla & Raspberry Sauce (p. 238)

SEMI-FINAL MENU

menus

MAIN COURSE Mozzarella & Sun-dried Tomatoes wrapped in Prosciutto, Stir-fried Pak-choy & Yellow Peppers, Olive Oil & Garlic Mash (p. 96)
DESSERT Summer Trifle with Lemon Syllabub (p. 232)

SEMI-FINAL MENU

MAIN COURSE Ravaya (Stuffed Aubergines with Potato & Onion), Bhaji (Spinach Curry) Pilau Rice & Karri (Yellow Sauce) & Salad & Chapati (p. 144-5)
DESSERT Gulab Jambo (Exotic Delight Kebabs) (p. 197)

SEMI-FINAL MENU

MAIN COURSE Smoked Haddock in a Cream Sauce with Pasta, Sliced Green Beans & Smoked Bacon, Carrots with Sesame Seeds & Honey (p. 128)
DESSERT Flambéd Bananas with Honey Ice Cream (p. 197)

SEMI-FINAL MENU

MAIN COURSE Tiger Prawns, Monkfish & Scallops with Leek Risotto & Deep-fried Parma Ham, Lemon & Tarragon Vinaigrette (p. 109)
DESSERT Warm Chocolate Puddings with White & Dark Chocolate Sauce & Crème Fraîche (p. 181)

SEMI-FINAL MENU

MAIN COURSE Spinach Gnocchi with Roast Capsicum & Blue Cheese Sauces, with a wedge of Stottie Cake (p. 146)
DESSERT Sautéed Peppered Pears with China Tea Sorbet (p. 204)

SEMI-FINAL MENU

MAIN COURSE Scottish Salmon Fillets with an Asparagus & Baby Leek Topping garnished with Herby Orange Crème Fraîche, Spring Onion Mash (p. 119)
DESSERT Baked Cheesecake served with Mixed Fruits & Blackberry Sauce (p. 186)

FINAL MENU

MAIN COURSE Hake with Red Wine Sweet & Sour Fish Jus on Roasted Braised Leeks with Mussels & Warm Salad (pp. 128-9)
DESSERT Raspberry Brûlée with Vanilla Black Pepper Tuile Biscuits (p. 222)

FINAL MENU

MAIN COURSE Monkfish & Scallops on a bed of Thai Noodles, with a Coconut, Lime Leaf & Chilli Sauce, with an Asparagus Salad (p. 126)
DESSERT Peach Marsala Crème Brûlée (p. 216)

FINAL MENU

ADULT MENUS

STARTER Pan-fried Foie Gras & Leeks with Orange Muscat & Shallots with Watercress Salad & Hazelnut Oil Dressing (p. 40)
MAIN COURSE Fricassée of Langoustine & Monkfish with Tarragon & Baby Vegetables (p. 122)
DESSERT Lemon Tart with Pistachio Ice Cream & Raspberry Coulis (p. 192)

ANNABEL ANDERSON'S MENU

STARTER Gorgonzola & Mascarpone Cheesecake with Onion Compote (p. 46)
MAIN COURSE Loin of Lamb on Fragrant Fruity Couscous with Spicy Apricot Sauce & Balsamic Reduction (p. 83)
DESSERT Fresh Walnut Tart with Armagnac Glaze & Clove Ice Cream (p. 191)

JANICE PRICE'S MENU

STARTER Crispy Chicken Boudin on Buttered Leeks (p. 33)
MAIN COURSE Pan-fried Wild Sea Bass with Samphire, Girolles in a Cream Sauce, Pea Purée (p. 130)
DESSERT English Rhubarb Trifle (p. 229)

SAM REDFERN'S MENU

STARTER Salmon Mousse with Cucumber & Dill Sauce (p. 28)
MAIN COURSE Roast Strip Loin of Lincoln Red Beef with Basil & Mustard Gravy, Horseradish Mashed Potatoes, Broad Beans with Herb Butter, & Spinach (p. 76)
DESSERT Almond Biscuits filled with Creamy Rice & Elderflower-scented Gooseberries (p. 233)

CHRISTINE LLOYD-KNIGHT'S MENU

STARTER Chicken Livers in Madeira Sauce with Balsamic Vinaigrette Salad (p. 32)
MAIN COURSE Marinated Wild Boar with Port Wine Sauce, Poached Pears & Onion Spätzel (p. 72)
DESSERT Brioche Bread & Butter Pudding with Orange & Almond (p. 170)

REBEKAH JONES-WHITE'S MENU

STARTER Wild Mushroom Risotto with Parmesan Tuiles (p. 45)
MAIN COURSE Soufflé of Dover Sole, Crab & Scallops with Lemon Grass & Ginger Sauce, Pomme Fondant & Mediterranean Vegetables (p. 136)
DESSERT Caramelized Lemon Tart, Passion Fruit Sorbet, Wild Berries & Meringue Mushrooms (p. 184)

ALI STEVENSON'S MENU

STARTER Clear Gazpacho (p. 16)
MAIN COURSE Smoked Loin of Venison with Liquorice & Game Jus, Grilled Polenta, Morel Mushrooms, Runner Beans & Pears (p. 70)
DESSERT Almond Sourdough Cake with Plum Compote & Orange Curd Ice Cream (p. 168)

LLOYD BURGESS' MENU

menus

STARTER Rosemary-scented Roast Sea Bass with Lime & Coriander Vinaigrette (p. 24)
MAIN COURSE Stuffed Welsh Organic Chicken Breast, on Puy Lentils, Timbale of Coarse Purée Carrots & Spinach, Julienne of Roasted Red Pepper & Tarragon Scented Sauce (p. 53)
DESSERT Poached Pear with Mascarpone & Amaretto Ice Cream & Port Jus (p. 200)

MARK HATENBOER'S MENU

STARTER 'Railway Breakfast' Hot Crab Soufflé on leaves with Coriander Relish (p. 21)
MAIN COURSE Madurai Pork on Spiced Rice & Lentils, with Orange, Honey & Spiced Sauce & Charred Peppers with Mustard Seed (p. 100)
DESSERT Carrot Halva Sponge with Cinnamon, Cardamom & Rose Water, Nutmeg Cream & Fruit Garnish (p. 174)

SHEKHAR VARMA'S MENU

STARTER Aubergine 'Pitta' & Rocket Salad (p. 40)
MAIN COURSE Calves Liver in Cassis Sauce, Garlic Mashed Potato & Savoy Cabbage Parcels (p. 82)
DESSERT Caramelized Apple Cake with Cinnamon Ice Cream (p. 235)

JAMES BEASLEY'S MENU

STARTER Crevettes in Roast Red Pepper Sauce (p. 22)
MAIN COURSE Rabbit marinated in Cider, Pan-fried with Lemon Grass, Roast Baby Vegetables & Parsnip Purée (p. 69)
DESSERT Ginger Pudding with Whisky Ice Cream (p. 175)

PAUL MARTIN'S MENU

STARTER Red Pepper & Soft Cheese Flower on a Yellow Pepper Coulis, with Green Salad (p. 17)
MAIN COURSE Herb Lamb Cutlets with Speck & Saffron Gnocchi, Spinach Cake (p. 93)
DESSERT Layered Coffee & Vanilla Set Cream, Apricot & Brandy Sauce, Raspberry Purée (p. 216)

SAM LAMPUGNANIA'S MENU

STARTER Goats Cheese Tower with Griddled Aubergine, Roast Cherry Tomatoes & Pesto (p. 37)
MAIN COURSE Grilled Chicken Breast & King Prawns with Ginger Glazed Scallions, Cardamom Scented Spicy Butter Sauce & Garam Masala Pommes Parisienne (p. 52)
DESSERT Thick Lemon Tart with Raspberry Compote (p. 196)

BRIAN HODGSON'S MENU

STARTER Roast Red Pepper Gazpacho with Pesto Croûtes (p. 14)
MAIN COURSE Seared Tuna on Celeriac Mash, with Spinach, Coriander & Lime Salsa in a Red Wine Reduction (p. 112)
DESSERT Summer Berries in a Tuile Basket with Lemon Balm Ice Cream (p. 206)

MARGO KEATING'S MENU

STARTER Roasted Mediterranean Vegetable Tart (p. 43)
MAIN COURSE Grilled Fillets of American Sea Bass with Squat Lobster Sauce, Lemon & Garlic New Potatoes, Braised Fennel & Wilted Spinach (p. 132)
DESSERT Steamed Lemon Sponge Pudding with Caramelized Orange & Vanilla Ice Cream (p. 182)

PAUL MOWER'S MENU

STARTER Savoury Summer Pudding with Yellow Pepper Sauce (p. 42)
MAIN COURSE Quartet of Salmon, Salmon Caviar Sauce, Fresh Seasonal Vegetables (p. 121)
DESSERT Passion Fruit Mousse, Caramel Crack, Mango Sauce (p. 217)

DAVID EVERITT'S MENU

STARTER Smoked Haddock Consommé (p. 9)
MAIN COURSE Fillet Steak with Elderberry Sauce, Celeriac Purée, Spinach Creams, Chips (p. 82)
DESSERT Baked Lemon Custards with Orange Sauce & Caramel Abstracts (p. 209)

JOHN CRITCHLEY'S MENU

STARTER Broccoli Soup, Goats Cheese & Truffle Oil Tortellini (p. 8)
MAIN COURSE Fillet Beef, Sherry Sauce, Creamed Parsley Quenelles, Carrot Cakes, Green Mash & Deep-fried Garlic Cloves (p. 80)
DESSERT Mango & Cardamom Gratins, Coconut Sauce & Biscotti (p. 198)

BEE WILSON'S MENU

STARTER Bruschetta with Spiced Onion Marmalade, Toasted Goats' Cheese, & Green Salad (p. 42)
MAIN COURSE Roast Cod, Tapenade, Tomato Sauce, Potato Mayonnaise & French Bean Vinaigrette (p. 138)
DESSERT Warm Chocolate & Pecan Tart with Vanilla Ice Cream (p. 180)

JANINE LISHMAN-PEAT'S MENU

STARTER Herbed Savoury Custards with Tomato Sauce & Aubergine Crisps (p. 41)
MAIN COURSE Fillet of Beef wrapped in Parma Ham, with Red Wine Sauce & Mustard Jacket Soufflé (p.77)
DESSERT Amaretti, Pear & Almond Tart, with Poire Williams Sauce (p. 189)

STEPHEN THOMPSON'S MENU

STARTER Tomato & Freshwater Crayfish Soup (p. 13)
MAIN COURSE Fricassée of Chicken with Morels & Vin Jaune D'Arbois with Steamed Spinach, Vichy Carrots (p. 50)
DESSERT Chocolate Tart with Apricot Sorbet & Peach Coulis (p. 188)

AMANDA ROBIN'S MENU

STARTER Pea & Mint Pots with Herb & Mint Sauces (p. 37)
MAIN COURSE Fillet of Aberdeenshire Lamb with Red Wine & Port Gravy, Rosemary Potatoes, Red Onions & an Anchovy Sauce (p. 89)
DESSERT Lemon Curd Millefeuilles with a Lime Confit (p. 241)

DEBORAH RATCLIFFE'S MENU

STARTER Spicy Salmon on Green Leaves with Sherry & Walnut Oil Dressing (p. 28)
MAIN COURSE Sirloin of Highland Beef with Pepper Cheese & Pastry, Bramble Sauce, Creamed Celeriac & Glazed Shallots (p. 78)
DESSERT Meringue & Raspberry Cream Towers with Chocolate Collar & Mixed Berry Sauce (p. 230)

IRENE ROSS' MENU

menus

STARTER Grilled Irish Goats' Cheese on Olive Bread with Red Pepper & Chilli Oil Dressing (p. 44)
MAIN COURSE Chargrilled Lamb in Warm Basil & Pepper Salad with Crispy Buttered Potatoes & Plum & Ginger Drizzle (p. 94)
DESSERT Strawberry & Mascarpone Torte with Mango on Light Butter Shortbread (p. 193)

LAWRENCE MCGARRY'S MENU

STARTER Cream of Lettuce & Spring Onion Soup with Herby Croutons (p. 12)
MAIN COURSE Roasted Fillet of Organic Pork with Dijon Mashed Potato, Braised Red Cabbage & Timbale of Summer Vegetables (p. 106)
DESSERT Warm Chocolate Pudding with Belgian Chocolate Sauce & Orange Cream Swirl (p. 178)

HELEN DICKENS' MENU

STARTER Tomato Tartlet with a Parmesan Crust with Crème Fraîche & Tapenade (p. 34)
MAIN COURSE Lamb with Mint Pesto, Roasted Herb Potatoes & Summer Vegetables (p. 94)
DESSERT Ice Coffee & Amaretto Soufflé with Strawberry Salsa (p. 214)

SUSANNA JARRETT'S MENU

STARTER Bermuda Salt Cod Fishcakes with Banana Relish (p. 18)
MAIN COURSE Saturday Roast Beef with Fricassée of Mushrooms & Pommes Savoyarde (p. 81)
DESSERT Brioche & Butter Pudding with Mascarpone Ice Cream (p. 172)

VANESSA GUIVER'S MENU

STARTER Thai Spiced Mussels (p. 26)
MAIN COURSE Braised Lamb Shank with Cardamon, Garlic & Rosemary on White Bean Purée with Mini Fondant Potato, Confit of Garlic & Lamb Jus (p. 84)
DESSERT Poached Peaches in Zinfandel on Mascarpone & Meringue with Raspberry & Pineapple-Mint Sorbet (p. 232)

SEMI-FINAL MENU

STARTER Roasted Beetroot with Goats' Cheese Fondant & Potato Wafers (p. 48)
MAIN COURSE Anchovy-larded Blue Fin Tuna with Garlic Mash, Green Beans & Wasabi Vinaigrette (p. 116)
DESSERT Orange-scented Manjari Chocolate Mousse wrapped in a Striped Sponge with Citrus Fruit Salad & Chocolate Orange Sorbets (p. 176)

SEMI-FINAL MENU

STARTER Ravioli of Rock Lobster with Sauce Vierge on Buttered Cabbage (p. 20)
MAIN COURSE Roast Loin of Roe Deer wrapped in Prosciutto on Leek Julienne with Fennel Mash (p. 74)
DESSERT Champagne Rhubarb Cheesecake with a Compote of Strawberries & Rhubarb (p. 185)

SEMI-FINAL MENU

STARTER Garlic Tiger Prawns with Squid (p. 22)
MAIN COURSE Crispy Duck Confit on a Bed of Cucumber Ribbons with Honey & Hoisin, Steamed Samphire & Lentil Dhal (p. 66)
DESSERT Kiwi Soup with Passion Fruit Ice Cream (p. 215)

SEMI-FINAL MENU

STARTER Asparagus & Shiitake Mushroom Salad with Walnut Crostini (p. 30)
MAIN COURSE Chargrilled Fennel Tuna with Red Wine Sauce & Radicchio & Confit Tomato & Carnaroli Rice, (p. 117)
DESSERT Chocolate Flans with Strawberry Sorbet, Ginger Cream & Candied Orange Peel (p. 190)

SEMI-FINAL MENU

STARTER Asparagus Risotto with Shropshire Blue Cheese (p. 33)
MAIN COURSE Pork with Herefordshire Cider Sauce & Cidered Apple Sauce, New Potatoes, Runner Beans & Baby Sweetcorn (p. 105)
DESSERT Chocolate Terrine with White Chocolate Ice Cream (p. 213)

SEMI-FINAL MENU

STARTER Smoked Salmon Fillets on Pear Salsa with Sweet Chilli Sauce (p. 29)
MAIN COURSE Duck Breast stuffed with Figs wrapped in Speck, Cider & Honey Sauce, Carrot & Fennel Purée, Dauphinoise Potatoes, Buttered Courgettes (p. 68)
DESSERT Chilled Hazlenut Soufflé Bitter Chocolate Sauce (p. 211)

SEMI-FINAL MENU

STARTER Roasted Red Pepper Gazpacho with Herb Soda Bread (p. 15)
MAIN COURSE Pan-fried Fillet of Lamb, Aubergine & Tomato Salad, Potato & Carrot Dauphinoise (p. 95)
DESSERT Chocolate & Walnut Tart with Praline Ice Cream (p. 187)

SEMI-FINAL MENU

STARTER Trout with Bacon & Mustard & Dill Sauce (p. 25)
MAIN COURSE Roast Fillet of Pork with Lemon & Parsley, Himmel und Erde with Sage, White Wine & Cream Sauce, Seasonal Vegetables (p. 97)
DESSERT Apricot Ice Cream, Almond Biscuits & Toffee & Almond Sauce (p. 236)

SEMI-FINAL MENU

STARTER French Brie in Filo Parcels deep-fried with a Summer Fruit Coulis (p. 44)
MAIN COURSE Honey-glazed Monkfish with a Creamy Pepper & Caviar Sauce, with Enoki Mushrooms, Buttered Asparagus & Sauteed Potatoes (p. 124)
DESSERT Pear & Almond Upside Down Cake, with Amaretto Crème Anglaise (p. 199)

FINAL MENU

STARTER Salmon with Pesto, Tomato & Pesto Vinaigrette, Parmesan Crisps (p. 26)
MAIN COURSE Roast Rack of Lamb, Mediterranean Vegetable Gâteaux, Griddled Potatoes, Red Wine Sauce (p. 90)
DESSERT Peach Pavlova with a Spun Sugar Nest, Raspberry Sauce (p. 231)

FINAL MENU

STARTER Olive Oil-poached Tomatoes with Peas & Meat Jus (p. 36)
MAIN COURSE Fillet of Pork with Fennel & Apple Salad, Fennel Puree, Apple Chips & Mustard Vinaigrette (p. 104)
DESSERT Peanut Butter Mousse wrapped in Chocolate with Raspberry Jelly & Chocolate Sauce (p. 220)

FINAL MENU

INDEX

18.05 FRI —
24.05 THUR Bank Hol